TREASURY OPERATIONS AND THE FOREIGN EXCHANGE CHALLENGE

WILEY FINANCE EDITIONS

FINANCIAL STATEMENT ANALYSIS
Martin S. Fridson

DYNAMIC ASSET ALLOCATION
David A. Hammer

INTERMARKET TECHNICAL ANALYSIS
John J. Murphy

INVESTING IN INTANGIBLE ASSETS
Russell L. Parr

FORECASTING FINANCIAL MARKETS
Tony Plummer

PORTFOLIO MANAGEMENT FORMULAS
Ralph Vince

TRADING AND INVESTING IN BOND OPTIONS
M. Anthony Wong

THE COMPLETE GUIDE TO CONVERTIBLE SECURITIES WORLDWIDE
Laura A. Zubulake

MANAGED FUTURES IN THE INSTITUTIONAL PORTFOLIO
Charles B. Epstein, Editor

ANALYZING AND FORECASTING FUTURES PRICES
Anthony F. Herbst

CHAOS AND ORDER IN THE CAPITAL MARKETS
Edgar E. Peters

INSIDE THE FINANCIAL FUTURES MARKETS, THIRD EDITION
Mark J. Powers and Mark G. Castelino

RELATIVE DIVIDEND YIELD
Anthony E. Spare

SELLING SHORT
Joseph A. Walker

THE FOREIGN EXCHANGE AND MONEY MARKETS GUIDE
Julian Walmsley

TREASURY OPERATIONS AND THE FOREIGN EXCHANGE
CHALLENGE: A GUIDE TO RISK MANAGEMENT STRATEGIES
FOR THE NEW WORLD MARKETS
Dimitris N. Chorafas

CORPORATE FINANCIAL RISK MANAGEMENT
Diane B. Wunnicke, David R. Wilson, Brooke Wunnicke

TREASURY OPERATIONS AND THE FOREIGN EXCHANGE CHALLENGE

A Guide to Risk Management Strategies for the New World Markets

Dimitris N. Chorafas

John Wiley & Sons, Inc.

New York • Chichester • Brisbane • Toronto • Singapore

Copyright © 1992 by Dimitris N. Chorafas

Published by John Wiley & Sons, Inc.

Library of Congress Cataloging-in-Publication Data

Chorafas, Dimitris N.
    Treasury operations and the foreign exchange challenge: a guide to risk
  management strategies for the new world markets / Dimitris N. Chorafas.
      p.   cm.
    Includes index.
    ISBN 0-471-54393-4 (cloth)
    1. Foreign exchange.   2. Financial services industry.
  3. International finance.   I. Title.
  HG3651.0473   1992
  332.4'5—dc20   91-35940

Printed and bound by Malloy Lithographing, Inc.

10 9 8 7 6 5 4 3 2 1

"No man owns a fortune. It owns him."

Amadeo Giannini

Foreword

Although many people agree that money is the second most important thing in life, few would spontaneously put prices in a third place.

Those who do not, however, should do so, since their money obviously makes only as much sense as do the prices they have to pay. A typical story in this context is about the farmer's young wife, who proudly told her husband upon her return from the market that she was able to sell their goat for $3,000, whereupon the good farmer of course complimented his wife for her previously unknown charms as an outstanding saleswoman. Questioned on where she had the money, the young lady announced no less proudly that she had bought three superb chickens at $1,000 each.

This little story is not meant to serve as an example of how the perception of money and prices can diverge between the sexes; it should, rather, illustrate the need to differentiate between those people who merely consider a price as a rate of exchange and those for whom prices have become things of their own, things that can be good or bad, tempting or repelling, big or small.

If the reader allows me further to sustain this intellectual arabesque, I would even venture to draft a life cycle for the most excellent product of the financial economy, the "price." At its beginning, the product is rough and is offered by a few pioneers and specialists in pricing; then, as more and more offer the product, prices tend to become "just fine." Later on, quality diminishes, prices become bad, and price makers are left with rotten prices on stock before it gets phased out.

This rather peculiar model is only a desperate attempt to explain a much more peculiar reality in the financial world: the fact that the population of that world is split into two species—a minority that buys at low prices and sells thereafter at high prices, and a majority that buys at high prices and sells at low prices.

Since price fixing in the financial economy obeys the good old law of offer and demand, it is most amazing to acknowledge that the perception of scarcity and abundance is subject to swings comparable to the moods of a psychologically unstable person who sees a half-empty bottle where minutes before he saw a half-full one. Obviously, in this model, as well as in reality, the stable minority makes the money and the unstable majority loses its money.

Another reality is that this sort of money making easily raises all sorts of expectations and, with entrance costs into the industry of price making being fairly low, the minority never lacks a majority.

Even if the attentive reader of this book does not discover the secret of making money in the financial economy, it is the great merit of the book that the same reader ought to find all necessary ways and means to at least avoid losing money.

I wish to beg one more time the reader's indulgence for this terribly basic, if not trivial, approach to things of this life. If the reader agrees that things are this way, I would like to make my point by saying that nothing in this world, and especially in the financial world, exists without a purpose. The impressive size of the financial economy, the volumes traded, the equipment put into place, and the level of salaries paid stand on their own, to certify the utility of the financial economy to the rest of the world.

Throughout the seventies and eighties, a large part of the banking and brokering industry was drawn into a fairly new business, at least as far as its magnitude was concerned: the distribution and absorption of price fluctuation risks in financial markets. With hindsight, we can say with authority that never before have there been such tremendous fluctuations imposed on such an interdependent world. The size of the turbulences in the financial markets generated by inconsistencies in economic policies and macro management could only be matched by the inventiveness of market participants to metabolize the risks related to these turbulences.

The know-how, methods, instruments, and equipment to anticipate possible developments, to deal with risks, and to manage exposure to change have reached a remarkably high level of sophistication. Speculation, as this type of business was called in the past with a rather negative connotation, has turned out to be a true value-adding industry and become the major pillar for the preservation and functioning of the so-called "free" financial markets in an environment where trend-setting decisions by relevant authorities, either individually or collectively, were treated as *secrets d'état*. As frustrating as these secrets might appear to market participants, comfort can be taken from the fact that this secrecy and delicacy above all witnesses the due respect everybody has toward the market mechanics created for dealing with risks.

This book is an extraordinarily valuable tool in understanding the market mechanics and provides in the clearest possible manner the know-how of ways and means to deal with market risks, for which I respectfully congratulate Professor Chorafas.

GILBERT LICHTER
Secretary General and Chief of Staff
CEDEL, Luxembourg
Former Secretary General of the
    ECU Association, Paris

Preface

Since the 1980s, the major industrial corporations have financed themselves directly in the money market and in the capital market, leaving banks neither much time nor much space in which to make their key decisions on alternative business roles. Yet innovative roles, new markets, and advanced products are necessary for the banks to make up for profits lost by being no more the classical financial intermediary—a situation that is in the process of intensifying in the 1990s.

Two of the growing new roles—the global trading activity in foreign exchange and the revitalized domain of treasury operations—are the subjects of this book. Both underpin the focal interest of banks as well as manufacturing and merchandising firms when it comes to financial matters. This is particularly true of companies with multinational expansion or commercial interests. By presenting an integrated picture of several fields, this book addresses itself to professionals in treasuries, foreign exchange, and securities, as well as to management decision makers who wish to:

- Gain a comprehensive view on the evolution of the financial markets

- Know more about key issues that affect globalization

Today the financial industry finds itself at strategic crossroads with securities, foreign exchange, and treasury operations, thus opening up new business horizons. New business opportunity is crucial because the future of classical banking is rather bleak, its profits marginal and declining.

But whether in banking or in the manufacturing and merchandising industries, financial opportunities must be developed. As the 14 chapters of this book explain in a factual and well-documented manner, opportunities will not come by themselves. Chapter 1 describes the new world of treasury functions and the reasons behind their restructuring. It does so from both a strategic planning viewpoint and that of the mounting flow of international capital. The organization of modern treasury operations is presented in Chapter 2, including the description of treasury duties concerning risk management.

All financial operations involve risk, and the treasurer has a direct responsibility in this regard. This is shown in Chapter 3, which includes a case study on how the Japanese face the challenge of global risk.

Chapter 4 deals with ways and means for transacting foreign exchange deals, including the issues involved in taxation. The mechanics of foreign exchange operations are the focal points of Chapter 5, which starts with the players in the foreign exchange (forex) market, and covers the assistance expert systems can give in forex trading. Swaps, hedging, and currency management are treated in Chapter 6, which also takes a glimpse at bond dealing. The rise and fall of currency values, including capital flows, trading decisions, and investment perspectives, are handled in Chapter 7. Also included are innovation in financial products and the aftermath of panics.

The European Currency Unit (ECU) and its most likely future are addressed in Chapters 8 and 9, which include the concept of a single common currency for the European Community (EC), ECU-denominated instruments, and ECU clearing. The perspectives of the European Monetary Union (EMU) are explained and presented, as are the mechanics of the European Monetary System (EMS) and the Exchange Rate Mechanism (ERM).

Chapter 9 compares the ECU to the German mark (DM or Deutsche mark) and the dollar, and Chapter 10 considers the impact of economic planning. This chapter subsequently handles the controversial subject of the economy in Eastern Europe and the Soviet Union. Communism is on its way out, but will this truly benefit the West in economic and financial terms?

The next two chapters talk of the tools of the trade. Chapter 11 covers commodities and futures trading and Chapter 12 the mechanics of dealing in options—from the general perspective down to the level of basic definitions, including precious metals trading.

Chapter 13 demystifies arbitrage, spread management, and gap analysis in financial operations. There is an overview of the role of computer-based models, widening the reader's horizon without using any mathematical equations.

Analytics today rest on two pillars: simulation and knowledge engineering. Again in a comprehensive way, without involving algorithmic expressions, Chapter 14 presents concrete suggestions for implementation and a scenario of tailoring financial advisory constructs to the specific needs of treasury operations.

The requirements for the 1990s are presented in the conclusion. It is estimated that by the year 2000 some 70 percent of all jobs in the industrialized world will require *cerebral skills* rather than manual skills. People as well as organizations will be out of business if they cannot adapt to this knowledge-oriented landscape.

Many examples are being provided throughout this book; they are derived from the foremost financial institutions in America, Japan, and Europe, as well as from the author's personal experience. The leading banks' response to the market challenge, the way they design new financial products, and the technology they use may not be representative of the whole industry, but they are a good indication of the strategic directions being taken and the key management decisions the 1990s necessarily involve.

ACKNOWLEDGMENTS

The writer feels indebted to a great number of senior bankers, corporate treasurers, forex operators, securities brokers, and technologists who have contributed ideas as well as reviewed and commented on many parts of this book. Thanks also go to Karl Weber of Wiley for his help in shaping this volume. To Eva-Maria Binder goes the credit for the artwork, typing, and index.

DIMITRIS N. CHORAFAS

Valmer, France and Vitznau, Switzerland
February 1992

Contents

1   **The New World of Treasury Functions**   1

International Capital Transfers   2
The Role of the Financial Services Organization   6
The Aftermath of Deregulation and Tax Reform   9
Economies of Scale, Mergers, and Consolidations   12
Balanced Liquidity and the Cash Flow Challenge   14
Looking After the Free Cash Flow   17

2   **The Treasurer's Responsibility for Risk Management**   20

The Concept of Risk and Exposure   21
Avoiding the Deception of Off–Balance-Sheet Finance   25
Establishing and Following Behavioral Patterns   27
Can We Optimize the Level of Risk?   29
Risk-Adjusted Return on Capital   33

3   **Problems in Risk Control: How the Japanese
    Face the Challenge**   37

The FISC Report on Global Risk   39
How Japanese Banks Focus on Risk Control   41
Capitalizing on Global Investment Advice   43
Accounting for Market Volatility   46
Risk Control and Hedging Against Volatility   49
Dealing with International Bankers   51
Networks and "Rocket Scientists"   53

4   Transacting Foreign Exchange Deals   **55**

Spot, Forward, and the Transnational Company   56
Keeping Abreast of Forex Rates   60
Tracking the Transnational Economy   61
Can the Transnational Corporation Act as Its Own
    Money Center Bank?   63
Discounting Foreseeable Market Trends   65
Solutions to Global Custody   67
Advising on Taxation for the Transnational Corporation   70
Global Custody and Taxation   72

5   Foreign Exchange Operations   **75**

The Forex Market   76
Using Technology to Improve Performance   79
Technological Assistance to the Forex Trader   82
Currency Forecasting and Portfolio Management   85
An Environment for Profit   88

**6   Swaps, Hedging, Bond Dealing, and
      Currency Management**   **92**

The Essence of Swaps Transactions   93
The Use of Swaps Instruments   96
How Secure Is Foreign Exchange Hedging?   99
The Hedging Plan and the Risk Premium   101
Maneuvering Through Variable Currency Rates
    and Bond Instruments   103
The Bond Market, the Forex Market,
    and Netting   105
Searching for New Opportunities in
    Currency Management   107

7   Dealing in Currencies   **110**

Rise and Fall of a Currency's Value   111
The Market Is the Arbiter   114
Capital Flows and Trading Decisions   116
Is There Protection Against Currency Fluctuations?   118
Integrating Forex and Investment Perspectives   120
Innovation in Financial Products   123
Dealing with Panics   125

8   West European Currency, Political Union, and the
     Financial Infrastructure   128

     The Single European Act and the European
        Monetary Union   129
     The European Monetary System and Exchange
        Rate Mechanism   132
     Pros and Cons of the European Exchange
        Rate Mechanism   134
     The Need for a Market-Driven EMU   136
     Workings of the ERM   138
     Weighting the ECU   141
     Economic Growth, Technological Leadership,
        and Currency Values   144

9   The ECU, the German Mark, and the Dollar   148

     Using the ECU   149
     ECU-Denominated Instruments   151
     Advantages of a Single Common Currency   153
     ECU Clearing   155
     International Investments in Strong Currencies   157
     Competition from the German Mark   161
     Eurodollars and the Acid Test   164
     The European Economic Area   166

10   Economic Planning and the East European
     Transformation   170

     The Four Components of a Long-Range Plan   171
     Planning for Competitive Advantage   174
     From Karl Marx to Adam Smith   178
     The Role of Policies and Regulations   180
     Eastern Europe, the Common Market,
        and the United States   183
     "The Only Cure Is to Go Cold Turkey"   186
     The Difficulty of Cultural Change   189

11   Commodities and Futures Trading   191

     The Commodity Futures Trading Commission (CFTC)   192
     Monitoring Volatility in the Commodity Exchanges   194
     The Concept of Futures Contracts   195

Currency Futures and Interest Rate Futures   198
Treasury and Money Market Instruments   201
Trading in Securities and Commodity Funds   204
Trading in Commodity Futures   206

12 Dealing in Options   211

Long and Short Contracts   212
Currency Options and Interest Rate Options   214
Spots and Forwards from an Options Viewpoint   218
Options on Precious Metals   221
Developing an Options Trading System   224
A Contribution by Knowledge Engineering Technology   226
The Options Trading Training System   228

13 Arbitrage, Spread Management, and Gap Analysis   233

The Essence of Technology-Assisted Arbitrage   234
Using Simple Rule-Based Models   236
Models for Sophisticated Trading   239
Liability Management and Spread Management   242
Noninterest Revenues and Policy Planning   245
Solutions to Gap Analysis   248

14 A Financial Advisor System Project   251

Prototyping the Expert System Solution   252
Capitalizing on the Parallelization of Data   256
The Contribution of a Semantic Network   258
Utilizing the Power of New Generation Computers   260
Virtual Processors and Teraops Power   263

Looking Forward: Treasury Operations in the Year 2000 266

Index   269

TREASURY OPERATIONS AND THE FOREIGN EXCHANGE CHALLENGE

1
The New World of Treasury Functions

There are two ways of evaluating treasury functions: one based on a narrower and the other on a broader perspective. The former tends to look at a treasury as the division that raises funds and manages the cash of an industrial company or financial institution. The latter, which will concern us in this book, focuses on treasury operations as a whole, with a full range of services beyond cash management, including:

- Foreign exchange

- Money market deposits and loans

- Interest rate swaps

- Forward rate agreements

- Options

- Financial futures

- Commercial paper

Treasury operations are often done in a wide variety of currencies and are increasingly characterized by 24-hour service. This is the way treasury functions will be defined in the 1990s, requiring an appropriate organization and job description.

The broader interpretation of treasury functions sees to it that a bank offers a comprehensive range of services, being able to enrich the customer relationship at any time. If the financial institution is to act as the *assistant treasurer* to a corporate client, then it must be ready to closely supervise:

- Financial planning
- Credit management
- Cash management
- Collections
- Securities' flotation
- Custody of funds and securities
- Trustee functions

These activities are the necessary counterparts to the other, more advanced functions listed after the opening paragraph. As we will see in this book, old and new treasury operations cover much common ground, and nothing serves better as an integrator than *risk management*.

Furthermore, whether we look at it from the bank's viewpoint or the corporation's, the ability to handle operation at an international level is crucial to any major organization. The same is true about the need for automating the production and delivery of treasury services.

Put at the disposal of the treasury, computers, communications, and artificial intelligence must provide gateways to planning, execution, and control. This is a statement valid for every subject that has financial implications, which essentially means every issue that has undergone substantial evolution in response to changes in financial techniques, technological impact, and market demand.

In this chapter, as well as in Chapters 2 and 3, we will take a bird's eye view of the treasury's duties and the factors underpinning its revival, including international capital transfers. We will also look into exogenous factors such as deregulation, globalization, and financial engineering, which made mandatory the formalization of financial management.

INTERNATIONAL CAPITAL TRANSFERS

The financial industry, and the treasury function within any other branch of business and industry, have been going through evolutionary change since the end of World War II. One of the ingredients of this evolution was a unified currency for world trade, the U.S. dollar, which came of age under:

- The Marshall Plan and its aftereffects
- The building of American-owned plants in Europe and Asia

- The denomination of key commodities such as oil and gold in U.S. dollars

- The expansion of European and Japanese businesses in America

The dollar currently is the leading but not the only *reserve currency*, the term used to describe central banks' holdings of foreign reserves. The Special Drawing Rights (SDR) was introduced in 1970 as a reserve currency to partly replace national currencies and gold in settling international transactions, but the currency of SDR is also dollars.

Although in late 1988 came a Japanese proposal to expand the reserve use of the International Monetary Fund's (IMF's) special drawing rights with the yen and possibly other currencies complementing the dollar's key role, the dollar still remains the international reserve currency. This should not be confused with the *reference currency*, which is a currency of the user's choice.

The true globalization of the flow of funds has required not only a reserve currency and a reference currency, but also the breaking down of barriers among the various agents involved in the *money flow*. This concept took shape as American, European, and Japanese consumers—in short, the First World—became affluent, as its countries assumed more control over their own assets and liabilities, and as the dollar acted as a pole of attraction for the internationalization of manufacturing, commercial, and financial organizations.

At the same time, a major role in the promotion of internal capital transfers has been played by advanced technology: communications, computers, software, and their influence in the recognition of the importance of integration between the dealing, front office; confirmations and settlements ("middle office"); and accounting, or back-office, functions. Reliance on technology brought workstations, databases, and networks to put together a true multiuser environment within the organization and an environment for the organization, its clients, suppliers, and bankers.

The integration goes well beyond electronic funds transfer (EFT).* Part of the progress is due to the supply of treasury workstation software interlinking electronic banking services. Balance update, transactions download (including zero balance transfers, netting, lockbox, controlled disbursement reporting), and automated bank reconciliation are examples of value-added applications. At the treasurer's site, electronic banking software—often offered free of charge by the prime bank with which the treasurer deals—can generate on-line payment instructions to be passed, under the appropriate controls, through the bank's EFT or wire transfer system.

---

*See D. N. Chorafas, *Electronic Funds Transfer*, London: Butterworths, 1988.

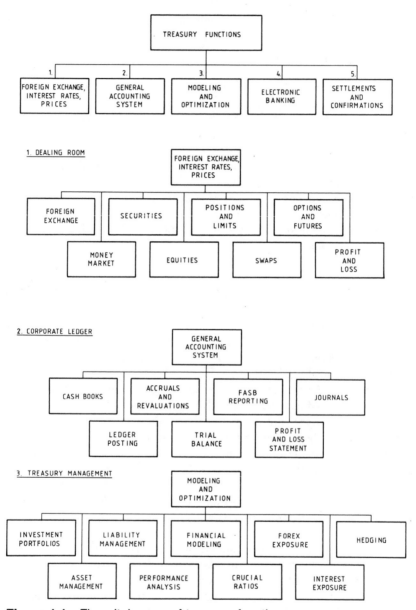

Figure 1.1 Five vital areas of treasury functions.

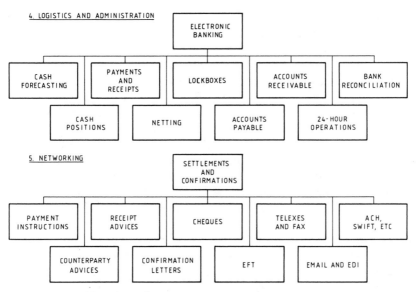

Figure 1.1 (*Continued*)

A full range of treasury services is shown in Figure 1.1. They can be divided into five interconnecting groups linked to other computer-based subsystems:

1. Foreign exchange, interest rates, and prices

2. General accounting system

3. Modeling and optimization

4. Electronic banking

5. Settlements and confirmations

Networking plays a leading role in these applications both in terms of incoming streams—information providers, clients, and corresponding banks—and in terms of the outgoing text and data flows.

In a treasury environment, on-line activities range from external rate and price feeds integrated with realtime market information sources to the generation of confirmation and settlement instructions for direct transmission by telex, fax, or electronic mail. Internal facilities include the end-users' ability to define their own output (through report writers), as well as user-definable interfaces complete with windowing, color selection, and pop-up menus.

Propelled by technology, factors such as interactive planning, optimization, on-line execution, and feedback control have recast treasury functions. Another key factor that has helped create the new environment is the intensification of *international capital transfers*. There has been significant evolution in the means by which a payment is made in the money of one country and received in the money of another.

International trade has been instrumental in bringing about these results, and the same is true of the multinationalization of manufacturing and banking operations. If we exclude the agricultural sector, 25 percent of world production is today controlled by multinational companies. That has both *financial* results in terms of money flow and *economic* aftermaths in real payments: The *real payment* is the development of an export surplus of goods and services on the part of the payer and of an import surplus for the payee.

The real payment contrasts to the capital flow from a lendor country to the borrower: In *pure* capital flows, the export surplus typically develops from the excess savings of the lending country and the import needs for consumption or investment of the borrower.

Although these are classical relations and nothing has changed in terms of basic definitions, many economists believe that lower interest rates and the taming of inflation have undoubtedly been important catalysts of the capital flow changes we have experienced during the last decade.

THE ROLE OF THE FINANCIAL SERVICES ORGANIZATION

The disinflationary environment has made financial assets the holdings of choice, relegating fixed assets to a less desirable status. Hence it is not surprising that banks and other financial institutions became a center of attention and will continue as such in the 1990s even if the financial environment changes.

As we will subsequently see, there are a number of reasons why the role of a financial institution has dramatically changed. Although during the 1980s the emphasis on restructuring and reorienting was placed with the smaller and more agile investment bank, the focal point of the 1990s may well be on commercial banking, particularly the larger organizations, if and when they are able to overcome the crisis of growth in their development.

Figure 1.2 identifies the five principal crises through which an organization goes, from birth to maturity to eventual decline.

- In phase 1 of its existence, the crucial criterion is market acceptance, and the leading edge is based on creativity.

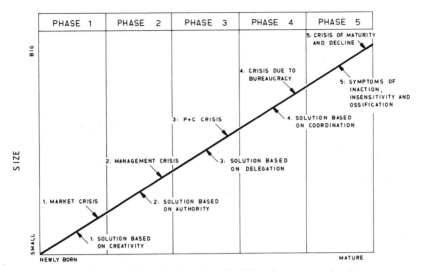

Figure 1.2 Five principal crises in the life of an organization.

- Phase 2 is characterized by a management crisis in which sufficient authority is the answer.

- With phase 3 the company grows, and its survival greatly depends on planning and control (P + C).

The treasury function is formalized at this phase but will undergo changes in the subsequent development steps toward maturity. There is a strong relationship, during this transformation, between able money management and the ability to survive.

- The crisis of bureaucracy characterizes phase 4.

Solutions are based on better coordination, with flexible automation having the upper hand, because too much structuring leads into a crisis of growth characterized by the final phase.

- The fatal flows of phase 5, where maturity may be followed by decline rather than a new departure.

Other pitfalls left aside and in spite of its great size, the company may run out of cash unless the treasury is instrumental in managing the cash flow, balancing receipts versus expenditures, and experimenting with and projecting on cash requirements. In phase 5, many organizations also run out of products. New product planning is not a treasury function, but new financial products usually require a great amount of financial engineering in order to establish themselves in the market.

Financial engineering is the domain where the treasurer can be of much value. It is an expanding field in which limited change is often outpaced by events that are leading to broader, structural, and functional reforms. In that regard, many treasurers have found that once they attach their personality to a proposition, other executives start reacting to the personality and stop reacting to the proposition.

In the 1990s phase 5 will be the most challenging for large commercial banks. Almost everything about a retail bank will need to be turned inside out in this decade, with the integration and handling of different moneys being a focal point. The business of the commercial bank will be well beyond accepting deposits and making loans. It will focus on financial services: selling new products, issuing insurance, or developing credit instruments in more than one currency—at least in the First World. The change will not come passively; it will require not only plans but also a new culture.

Instead of waiting for customers to come to them, banks will have to go aggressively after the client base, as do other sales organizations. This marketing-led approach will make retail bankers highly concerned about lost sales, with emphasis placed on turning a branch into a sales office for capital transfers and investments:

- Financial services are intangible, expansive, and often complex; hence, not only are clear definitions mandatory, but the definitions should also be dynamic, adjustable to changing requirements.

- The market expands; therefore, the range of products that banks offer through their branches will have to be revamped and integrated.

- Sales attitudes have to be developed and sales principles distilled, because the staff at the branches have traditionally not been salespeople.

Since some of their clients, like the multinational corporations, are becoming their competitors, banks have to make their money from selling services—with receipts that appear on their profit statements as increased *fee income*. To face this service challenge, in the 1990s banks will be using technology less to cut costs than to *enhance revenues*, and treasury functions are a prime domain to apply that approach.

The new solution should not diminish the attention to be paid to cost control; even for technologically advanced banks, labor is still the biggest component in costs, accounting for 60 to 70 percent of noninterest expenses. Even today most people are employed in routine jobs, such as cashing checks or opening letters of credit and getting those transactions logged on the bank's records. Relatively few sell to customers or design new products, and that is where change is coming.

In the 1990s the aim will be that of using staff to sell rather than process, and the profit possibilities look impressive. Commercial banks will increasingly resemble polyvalent businesses ranking themselves by *cash flow* and *return on equity* (ROE) rather than simply by size. Instrumental in this new orientation will be the capital requirements agreed to in 1987, under the auspices of the Bank for International Settlements (BIS), and scheduled to be implemented by 1992.

Although designed to encourage banks to be prudent, the BIS rules will also compel them to use their capital more effectively, and here again the treasury has a prime role to play. Bank management must be steadily:

- Analyzing the profitability of the businesses of the financial institution

- Innovating to hold and increase market share

- Pulling out of activities that do not provide a proper return

The developing market perspectives will also prompt banks to specialize, as the manufacturing industries have done. Research and development, marketing, polyvalent products, but also channels, switching centers, gateways, intelligent networks, and supercomputers—along with a continually retrained human capital—will make up their force.

THE AFTERMATH OF DEREGULATION AND TAX REFORM

When, during the 1980s, reference was made to the new banking environment, invariably deregulation came up as the primary reason. Even though it is quite true that deregulation has been instrumental in a number of changes, it is just as true that it is one factor out of many—it is by no means the only one. And there are consequences to address.

One of the less recognized effects of banking deregulation is that it brought much closer the bank products and services to the tools that the treasurer of a large corporation needs in order to function in an able manner. Although the evolution of both the treasury functions and the bank's product line proceeded with their own priorities, there is no denying that there has been a convergence.

Deregulation

Deregulation broke down old product boundaries as well as customer boundaries and lines of business segregation. As a result, more players are offering more products to more customers than ever before. That has led to a financial marketplace that has become increasingly complex and competitive and that has created great business opportunities with their own dynamic characteristics.

Deregulation has made possible *globalization*, that is, the process of ensuring a presence in those world markets where good earnings can be achieved. Open-eyed banks have understood that they must gradually endeavor to get out of the habit of stressing their past strengths market by market. They must focus on the *future strengths* and do so with a multinational perspective.

At the same time that deregulation and the new technologies have been shaking the structure of banking, leveraged buyouts (LBOs) have introduced one more crucial factor into the financial equation. Management started realizing that those institutions failing to please the stock market run the risk of being taken over.

Industry is subject to a wave of takeovers only when it is dynamic—as contrasted to single incidents. Deregulation, globalization, and technology had this effect on the banking industry: They made top performers out of some financial institutions while others fell by the wayside—this is true in general, not only of savings and loan associations. As one of the top performers, Security Pacific's senior management seems to have done its homework on establishing objectives for a 1991–1995 timeframe. The foremost goals are:

- *Cost control*, aiming both at decreasing expenditures and driving up the stock price. All costs are charged to product level. Each *product* is a profit center with a responsible manager in charge. Internal billing is at cost level. External billing includes profit margin.

- *Acquisitions*. Security Pacific has already gone through some large acquisitions in interstate banking and is presently operating in six states: California, Alaska, Washington, Oregon, Nevada, and Arizona. The company's interstate banking includes 100 percent of Security Pacific Bank Washington (Rainier), Security Pacific Bank Oregon (ORBANCO), The Arizona Bank, Nevada National Bank, and a financial services system that appeals to consumers but also includes venture capital.

- *Product range*, which is greater and is leveraged in California, the rest of the United States, and internationally—however, the latter on a selective basis. An active R + D operation aims not only to develop new products but also to enrich existing products with technological content. That permits a better market appeal but also a significant reduction in costs, thus serving the first purpose.

- *Common systems.* One organization, the Security Pacific Automation Company, provides technology for all financial companies in the Group and does so through a nearly standard software. Not only the banks and other financial institutions in the holding are operating under common computers and communication systems but also the information systems of newly acquired entities.

All this is done within a new operating perspective established at top-management level and focused both at the market *and* at the regulatory authorities, because, in essence, deregulation means *new regulation.* The Federal Reserve and other central banks know that they must ensure financial stability at all times, particularly if they see an ebbing of confidence—a constant worry in all financial markets.

While the reserve banks decide on monetary policy, the governments of the First World are busy overhauling their fiscal policies. This, too, influences the financial industry through regulatory aspects that should be accommodated.

Tax Reform

Tax reform shifted the boundaries among service sectors in the economy and most particularly within the financial services industry. It did so both for the products that banks offer and for the returns they can achieve from their services. Financial institutions are beneficiaries of the overall ascendancy of the service sector in the First World. Although the manufacturing industries have seen their competitive position eroded, the importance of financial products continues to grow. The service sector already makes up about 65 percent of the domestic economy in First World countries.

Most observers expect that this two-thirds ratio of people working in the ternary sector* will rise further in the foreseeable future. It is also likely that government policy will become increasingly favorable to the service industries at the expense of the manufacturing industries—and a number of different tax reform packages (actual and proposed) are among the first manifestations of that shift in political thinking.

*Labeled according to the historical basis of their evolution, agriculture is the primary sector of the economy; manufacturing is the secondary sector; and the service industry is the ternary.

The new tax laws narrow the gap between *real* and *nominal* earnings growth, but do not reduce the level of real earnings from which that growth comes. The real price/earnings (P/E) ratio is unaffected by the mid-1980s change in American tax law. And the same is true about the tax-deductibility of debt in the United States and in other First World countries.

Tax reform has a significant impact on treasury functions. As the providers of financial services try to differentiate themselves and their products in the marketplace, treasurers are keen to capitalize on new provisions as they are made.

The optimization of tax structures in a multinational sense, and keeping abreast of diverse legislation, is a monumental task for multinational corporations, as well as for global banks, which address different issues in each country of operation and do so in realtime. Expert systems can be of significant assistance in that job.*

ECONOMIES OF SCALE, MERGERS, AND CONSOLIDATIONS

The range of the treasury functions is widening and the necessary financial services are getting more complex; but that does not mean that the associated services could or should be offered at any cost. The preservation of corporate resources is only one of the treasurer's basic responsibilities; it is also the treasurer's duty to capitalize on the best tools and techniques that technology has to offer. No company can afford big talk and small deeds.

The thrust for bigger size and *economies of scale*, and the bias that exists in the tax laws against equity and in favor of debt, have given rise to *a merger wave*, which must be planned and financed. At the same time, bankers push for cost control as a way to improve profitability.

The existence of economies of scale provides the one rational reason behind the fact that through the 1980s the pace of acquisitions and mergers had been accelerating. The other reason had been greed. What may be in store for the 1990s? Wall Street says that at least 20 percent of the 10,000 independent U.S. banks will be subject to mergers and acquisitions by 1996. Savings and loans are also in for major reform; many will shut their doors or sell out to banks since they are unable to meet the tougher capital standards imposed by the 1989 thrift bailout law.

Consolidation is expected to be the most important event in banking over the next five to seven years; and consolidation will bring

---

*See also D. N. Chorafas, *Using Technology in Treasury and Forex Operations*, John Wiley, New York, in press; and D. N. Chorafas and H. Steinmann, *Expert Systems in Banking*, London: Macmillan, 1991; and New York: New York University Press, 1991.

downsizing—which in a way contradicts the hypothesis of economies of scale. Like most industries emerging from overregulation, banking suffers from overcapacity. The financial industries are no different from airlines or steel firms. In America, Europe, and Japan there are simply too many banks. Consolidation is one of deregulation's immediate consequences.

The first successful hostile takeover of a bank came in 1988 when, after a year-long struggle, the Bank of New York acquired Irving Trust. Appeals by Irving to the Federal Reserve drew a cool response and the hostile takeover went through. Another big-name merger in America has been the acquisition of Republic Bank of Texas by North Carolina National Bank (NCNB), though this took place not as a hostile takeover but in a way similar to the 1983 acquisition of Seafirst by Bank of America. It was a salvaging operation.

If the treasury function had performed its duties in a capable manner with the Republic Bank of Texas, such salvaging operations would not have been necessary. However, the fact is that, in the majority of cases, treasury functions as described from Chapter 2 onward, are neither properly planned nor capably executed. An ingenious treasurer would ensure that:

- Commitments are steadily balanced against financial assets

- Available resources, both financial and human, are raised to meet not only current but also projected commitments

A good example of imbalances that are developing because treasury management is not careful enough, is that of *loans*. Senior credit examiners assigned to clean up problem loans often find that, under pressure to build up a portfolio, bank officers begin dispersing money before all the financial analyses and documentation are complete. This is a classic violation of good banking practice; it happens surprisingly often and has very costly results.

There is a counterargument to the violation just described, and it says that under the downward pressure on loan demand the quality of the bank's portfolio has to erode. Such an argument is erroneous, though there is no denying that the percentage of bad and questionable loans has increased significantly in the last five years. The message here is also quite clear: Lending is no longer as safe an activity as it used to be, further underlining the wisdom of conducting an adroit balancing act between the lenders and the treasury.

At the receiving end of loan operations—the corporate treasurer's functions—it can be observed that whereas bank loans tend to increase rather slowly with an expanding economy, other forms of credit are increasing two to three times faster. Corporate customers are bypassing (disintermediating) the banks by going to investors with instruments such as *commercial paper* and *corporate bonds*.

Contrary to a rather widespread opinion, those forms of fund raising cannot be carried out without intermediaries. The intermediaries are still useful and needed, but now they are the *investment banks*. With lucrative business shifting from commercial to investment banks, it is not a surprise that through the decade of the 1980s the financial performance of the latter has been superior to that of commercial banks.

But income of all sorts, and therefore income from loans, is one part of the delicate balance to be kept at all times. As we have seen, many bankers today believe that the other key to profitability is stringent cost control. Banks historically overhire in good times. Now mergers provide a good excuse to cut some of the fat.

Acquisitions, properly studied from an efficiency viewpoint, make sense in the 1990s because big banks are technologically sophisticated enough to achieve economies of scale if they truly try to get results. As banking moves further from manual paper shuffling to compound electronic documents, through the use of *photonics,** the savings from blending size with technology will become increasingly attractive to every one who can comprehend the transformation taking place in the financial industry.

Being bigger does not automatically produce profitability. There is much more to the fact that the largest 35 American banks have increased their profitability with the average return on assets rising during the past five years.

Through economies of scale and better management, it is possible to handle more business and shrink the unit costs. And at the same time, big banks have enough muscle to increase their noninterest (fee) income. But smaller financial institutions are more flexible, easier to adapt to changing financial conditions, and can therefore be very profitable.

BALANCED LIQUIDITY AND THE CASH FLOW CHALLENGE

Liquidity is the ability to pay off quickly, either by having available cash, raising money somewhere, selling short-term investments, or liquefying longer-term ones without undue losses. Watching after liquidity is one of the treasury's most important functions. As every financial officer knows, if the liquidity of a particular financial instrument worsens, the bid-ask spread widens. As a result, losses materialize when selling the security even if all other market conditions are unaltered.

*Optical disks, optical fibers, eventually optical switching—and the huge cost-effectiveness that they make feasible.

Illiquidity can happen at the corporate or at the national level. In the latter case, when a liquidity crunch starts, the complex international interaction that characterizes today's markets can spread extreme tightness in market liquidity, driving down world commodity prices. The resulting recession or depression can be communicated from country to country by rapidly shifting capital movements and through the prices of internationally traded goods.

In addition, there are snowballing effects. When credit becomes tight, it obliges dealers to dump stocks of commodities. The aftermaths are felt on corporate liquidity with the treasury function getting that much more complicated.

With any kind of debt that is carried by the treasury, the key term is *anticipated liquidity*. Money will be made or lost not only by virtue of sound pricing and lending policies, but also in relation to the *cost of liquidity*.

If the cost of liquidity increases, then the cost of capital will also increase, making it more difficult to pay the interest, repay the principal, or restructure the loan. A basic law in business is that for *every security* there is an *option*, and this is *liquidity*. Other things equal, the more business expands, the more valuable liquidity becomes and, in certain cases, the less available. That fact alone can upset many treasury calculations because it runs contrary to the thinking of people who have come to take liquidity for granted.

The treasurer should know the facts: A financial institution, industrial company, or investor may get into a trade, but it may not be able to get out of the trade so easily. As with Third World debt, it is the cumulative size of demand for liquidity, as dramatized for example by leveraged buyouts (LBOs), which is disturbing. That being said, the crunch that the treasurer may face can conceivably be his or hers alone—depending on the liquidity.

An illiquidity in the market does not hit all parties with the same intensity. Sound management will always see to it that extra funds will be available to face the following contingencies:

- Potential credit demand

- Budgetary expenses

- Possible volatility

These are situations that require additional funds, and *our* bank (or *our* industrial firm) may be called to meet this demand for funds by a controlled conversion of assets to cash. We must ensure a *balanced* liquidity position.

Liquidity, however, costs money. Therefore, another issue demanding the right focus is the equilibration of *liquidity* versus *profitability*.

- What effect does a good liquidity position have upon profitability?

- Are we aware of the cost involved in failing to maintain a balanced liquidity?

- Have we calculated the risk inherent in being caught short of cash?

A time-honored method of looking after potential liquidity, and therefore solvency, is an acid test—the ratio of current assets to current debt. Current assets are the sum of cash, notes and accounts receivable (less reserves for bad debt), advances on merchandise, merchandise inventories, and listed securities not in excess of market value. Current debt is the total of all liabilities falling due within one year.

Not only the treasury operations as such, but also any fund-management planning must show a sense of balance, as suggested in Figure 1.3. Investment goals may, and sometimes do, conflict with liquidity goals and risk guidelines—hence the wisdom of *equilibration*.

One of the basic principles involved with liquidity is that too much of it leads toward more expensive deals in more cyclical industries, and it produces more *risky* results. Furthermore, some moves are done for the wrong reason. Liquidity has to be balanced, and the best way to balance it is to "tune" disbursement obligations with the cash flow. Throughout industry today more emphasis is being placed on cash flow than on profits. Some securities analysts think that it took the leveraged-buyout and takeover wave of the 1980s to teach the importance of cash flow; investors

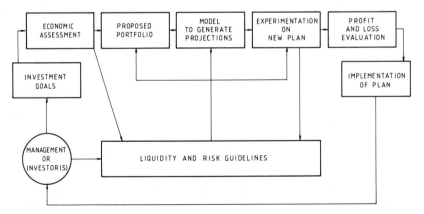

Figure 1.3   Balance in the funds-management planning process.

must also learn another lesson that treasurers already know—the need for patience in examining financial statements in order to derive meaningful information.

Companies with rich cash flows can be expected to demonstrate the best financial staying power. Cash flow tells another, more fundamental story than the one recounted by earnings: It is a measure of how much spendable cash a company's operations generate.

LOOKING AFTER THE FREE CASH FLOW

One difficulty of using cash flow is that many financial analysts have their own definition of what it is and is not. Each one of the cash flow definitions begins with the same data, but does not use the same algorithms. Most of their differences revolve around the best way to estimate *free cash flow*.

Free cash flow is a measure of how much cash flow is left over after subtracting what must be spent to keep the company running, namely capital expenditures, the cost of doing business, and the cost of staying in business. Free cash flow will increase whenever capital spending declines and depreciation increases—as well as when management exercises tough cost control.

This means that if a thorough cost accounting system based on standard costs was a proof of good management in the 1970s and 1980s, then in the 1990s it is an *absolute necessity*. Not only must it be implemented without delay and with attention to detail, but it should also be fully computer-based, operating on-line, enriched with expert systems, and providing fast feedback capabilities.

No treasurer can afford to forget about the company's cost control, even if it is not a function under the treasurer's direct dependence. Eventually the treasury will feel the squeeze on free cash flow and then on liquidity. We must constantly try to find new ways of ensuring that *our* company's costs do not get out of control, and that means:

- Implementing new monitoring systems
- Trimming manpower budgets
- Establishing efficient means of measurement
- Watching cash balances

We need a good standard cost study, and we must run its metrics on a realtime basis. Every operation must be cost accounted to produce costing information for senior management and for the treasury. In the foremost financial institutions, for example, such realtime implementation focuses both on the client and on the service. It provides management with the needed tools to watch profitability, to make adjustments, and to ensure that there is enough liquidity to meet cash obligations without rush and costly measures.

Spain's BankInter enriches such a watchdog system with artificial intelligence. Together with one of its computer vendors, it has developed an expert system to interpret costing information and give advice according to obtained results. The expert system focuses on the balance sheet but also elaborates on a detailed evaluation basis by:

- Analyzing costs versus benefits

- Spotting and identifying out-of-control items

- Preparing graphics presentations for management

- Explaining *why* an organizational unit of the bank made or lost money

Another expert system module examines alternatives through a "what if" approach. The *validations* to be done are linked on the bank's already established cost-accounting procedures, further underlining the fact that the banking business is a system of interrelated, interlocking parts. In that case, as in many others, the interpretation of financial ratios, statements, and results—done from different points of view—requires a considerable amount of know-how and technological support. It is not enough that the analyst has obtained complete, essential information, the analyst must also be qualified to make a judgment that is basic and thorough. Expert systems can greatly help.

Whether the required analysis is performed by the treasurer, another business executive, a commercial or investment banker, a credit manager, an investor, a speculator, or a business counselor, it makes no material difference. After the basic analysis is made, then individuals in different positions will act upon the conclusions of that analysis in different ways. Therefore, the *analytical results* must be sound and objective; the *interpretations* are personal and subjective.

An analysis might indicate that a particular enterprise is carrying too many loans or an excessive inventory. On the basis of that conclusion, top management must decide if the risk is worthwhile. It must act upon the recommendation of the treasurer to accelerate or increase the cash flow—for instance, through an intensive sales campaign.

From where will the cash come that we will need to operate our company? Relative to a manufacturing firm, the answer to this query is from the sale of products and services. But the calculation of cash flow in a financial industry is more complex, falling into the following three classes:

1. Pure cash liquidity
   - Demand deposits (lower-cost cash)
   - Other financial instruments (money market, savings, time accounts)
   - Bought money (higher-cost cash)

2. Productization
   - Securitization (for instance, mortgage-backed, financing)
   - Sales of funds minus redemptions

3. Industrial-type cash flow
   - Depreciation
   - Retained earnings (whether from interest, commissions, or fees)
   - Sales of assets

Notice that the three items under pure cash liquidity are at the same time debt toward depositors or corresponding banks. Securitization is the sale of debt obligations into which have been packetized loans advanced, for instance, for residential housing. However, acting as the intermediary between its debtors and its creditors, the bank guarantees such debt.

Debt is easier to trade on a global scale than equity, and taxation favors corporate debt. Those facts were discovered and utilized in the 1980s. The reality, however, is that nobody can control the worldwide debt market—this explains why the watchword in the 1990s is *anticipated liquidity*, which has become a basic treasury function.

2

The Treasurer's Responsibility for Risk Management

With the continuing expansion of the treasurer's business activities, the need to adequately manage the associated exposure—and do so both on a detailed and on a global basis—becomes increasingly important. The operational aspects of new business segments have to be technically studied and the accompanying problems solved one by one—always bringing the aspect of risk into perspective.

Some treasury functions today have introduced, and others are planning to introduce, an overall exposure monitoring and management system, able to integrate balance-sheet and off–balance-sheet business activities. This is done by consolidating all information elements relevant to risk and exposure, offering a comprehensive view that facilitates control. At the technical side, the consolidation requires steady access to distributed databases, which should be homogeneous and compatible in terms of data structures. It also calls for the development and implementation of mathematical models to calculate and consolidate risks.

Since this is a fairly demanding job particularly in the starting phase, approaches are necessary to reduce complexity and get the first results within a short timetable. And even though the mechanics are not easy, by far more challenging is the establishment of the right concept for financial risk management as well as of the associated methodology.

There is no point in taking sweeping, high-stakes initiatives in risk management without the proper planning. The following should therefore *be included:*

- Policies to properly define risk elements according to specific treasury operations

- Fail-safe limits and measures to control the damage if risk exceeds set values

- A vision about how to bring into line deviations and where to end risk taking

The bottom line is hedging, which is one of the components of risk management. To be successful in this function, the treasurer must be able to determine and evaluate the prospects for profit or loss in the current and prospective positions—a process that requires both brains and technology.

Among the treasurer's key decisions is that of determining exposure, inferring future events, and mapping a course of action accordingly. The information requirements for these duties include investment portfolio and trading limits, consolidated trading positions and single trades, economic and market analyses, evaluation of current conditions, and steady reevaluation of the investment strategy as well as overall performance. Both goals and results must be part of the picture.

THE CONCEPT OF RISK AND EXPOSURE

Heisenberg's *uncertainty principle* states that the act of studying a problem, let alone attempting to correct it, can fundamentally alter the nature of the problem itself. This is true throughout science and it is just as valid in finance—where there exists no better documentation than the calculation of *exposure* and *risk*. Risk events are uncertain in the sense that they do *not* have a *well-defined* or *sure* outcome. In everyday usage, and in the business life as a whole, risk refers to a situation, position, or choice involving possible loss or danger. With risk events, loss or danger is apt to be substantial. Hence, investments as well as loans should not be calculated on face value but on the basis of risk-adjusted return on capital (RAROC), as discussed later in this chapter.

The concept of risk—and therefore that of exposure—is closely related to the idea of an outcome, which may be probable, *but not* certain. Risk is the cost of this uncertainty. When the outcome is either gain or a neutral value, then we talk not of risk but of *opportunity*. Generally, however, risk and opportunity are related. There is no significant gain without our ability to *overcome adversity* and therefore to take controllable risks.

High technology can be instrumental for gathering intelligence in the evaluation of risk for global operations, for dealer support systems, securities or foreign exchange trading, portfolio management, and financial planning. Risk evaluation for global operations is wide-ranging:

- Liquidity risk

- Currency risk

- Country risk

- Interest rate risk

- Credit risk

- Investment risk

- Sales conditions risk

- Position risk (precious metals versus bonds, versus stocks, versus cash)

- Funds transfer risk

- Transaction processing risk (errors in the back office)

Many of these risks reflect as much upon the client as upon the bank. From investments to forex and lending, nothing is proven and nothing is guaranteed. Business is a game of risk. What really counts is:

1. Knowing ourselves, our markets, and our opponents

2. Having the necessary financial staying power

3. Possessing superior know-how

In making financial decisions, we have to distinguish between the forest and the trees. Is the staying power really there? Can our institution survive the storm and cover its present cost of doing business? Are we able to calculate and cover *our* future cost of doing business?*

Risks can be said to be under control if there is a system that alerts us every time they exceed set values either individually or in a consolidated

---

*See also D. N. Chorafas, *Risk Management in Financial Institutions*, London: Butterworths, 1990.

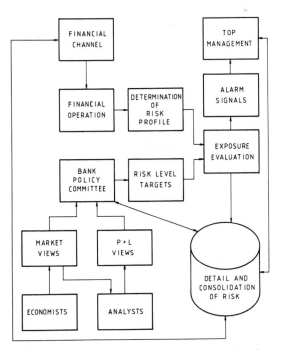

Figure 2.1 Structure of a risk management organization.

manner. Such values cannot be set once and for all; they have to be kept dynamic—which means that we need both:

1. A policy instrument able to set and adjust risk levels as a function of the economy and the market

2. A system able to track risk on a realtime basis worldwide, therefore in a *realspace* manner.*

Figure 2.1 presents one approach toward the establishment of such a system; more precisely, it outlines the structure of a risk management organization.

Acceptable risk values are set by the bank policy committee. Risks are accumulated through financial operations. The exposure evaluation system focuses on *patterns*; top management receives alarm signals while

---

Realspace solutions operate in realtime but also use intelligent networks for interconnecting the global marketplace, support experimentation to discover trading opportunities, and use supercomputers for number crunching—one of the goals being in control of risk.

both risk values and risk patterns are stored in a dedicated database explored through expert systems and accessible by all authorized executives.

A multinational financial institution will see to it that the distributed risk databases are exploited as a network. The knowledge engineering constructs running these databases should provide for *one* consistent image with transparent passthrough. Both alarms and trend calculations should be based on pattern analysis, and graphics must be steadily employed to ensure effective utilization.

The tracking of financial risks will be that much more effective if all executives and professionals have it explained to them that risks are inherent not only in business but also in every walk of life. The duration of our life itself—and its quality—depends on probabilities. Such probabilities reflect risks that we and others take. Therefore, it is important to explain to ourselves the risks to which we are exposed both in *qualitative* and in *quantitative* terms. That is what the treasurer and staff should do, and they can do it successfully if they truly have *risk consciousness*.

The treasury business today is faced with risks due to currencies, interest rates, credit lines, investments, takeover events, positions, sales conditions, funds transfers, and transaction processing. Other risks are due to liquidity, volatility, market choice, cash flow, placing, partner, and fraud. All must be watched very carefully, a job that must be done on-line through networks, databases, and AI constructs.

Is the banking industry today confronting this job in an able manner? Although exceptions do exist—and they essentially are the most successful financial institutions—the general answer is *no*! In the majority of cases, the systems are obsolete and follow paleolithic concepts. Table 2.1 gives the reason. Realspace solutions are vital as banks and multina-

Table 2.1 Technology for Controlling International Risk

	Currently Is	Should Be
1. Currency risk	RT[a]	RS[a]
2. Interest rate risk	—	RS
3. Exchange rate risk	batch/RT	RS
4. Credit risk	batch/RT	RT
5. Investment risk	batch/RT	RT
6. Event risk	—	RT
7. Position risk	batch/RT	RS
8. Sales conditions risk	batch/RT	RS
9. Funds transfer risk	batch/RT	RT
10. Transaction processing risk	batch/RT	RT

[a] RS stands for realspace; RT for realtime.

tional industrial companies with an international network must monitor and control these risks on a global basis: looking at the client relationship, constantly evaluating assets and liabilities, and always assessing the underlying business risk.

AVOIDING THE DECEPTION OF OFF–BALANCE-SHEET FINANCE

Amadeo P. Giannini, the man who built Bank of America, Transamerica Corporation, and the network of smaller financial institutions that became the First Interstate Bancorporation, advised his friends and employees not to gamble on leveraged deals: "Pay off your debts and sit tight. If you own your stock, you have nothing to fear no matter how deep a crisis may be."

By contrast, banks, manufacturing companies, and governments today gamble with the dual deception of off–balance-sheet and off-budget financing. By doing so, they cheat their own citizenry in the case of governments, and their stockholders in the case of manufacturing companies and banks. Coming from a study by Prudential-Bache, Figure 2.2 dramatizes the political aspect of this off-budget reference. The U.S. off-budget accounts during the 1980–1989 period moved from a slight surplus in fiscal 1982 to over a $50 billion deficit in fiscal 1989. In addition, borrowing from Social Security and other trust funds increased to $71

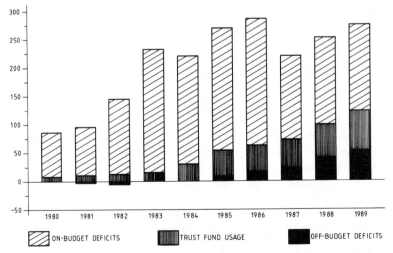

Figure 2.2 The Reagan-Bush trust fund and off-budget loopholes (in billions of dollars).

billion from just under $10 billion. This is a good example on how fast a loophole is exploited to death.

In my book *Risk Management in Financial Institutions,** I have elaborated why such practices are unwise and unwarranted. Here are the reasons in a nutshell.

Off–balance-sheet finance and accounting started in order to disclose additional information for special transactions: for instance, leasing and the assets that such operations involve, as well as the resulting future obligations. This accounting was extended to include controlled nonsubsidiaries and securitized receivables. Generally the distinction is that

- Money transactions are balance sheet
- Off–balance-sheet items are those not regulated by legislation.

Here is precisely where the risk starts. Although off–balance-sheet items theoretically do not directly involve money, liability can be contracted. With this gimmick, the *risk* side does not appear on the balance sheet, yet it may be substantial: crippling the corporation and altering the results of even the most solid balance-sheet analysis.

In January 1986 the Federal Reserve Board advanced some guidelines for calculating *bank capital ratios based on risk*, both on– and off–balance sheet. This proposal is consistent with the fact that regulators have been raising capital ratios for several years. Their concern is that banks expanded their assets too rapidly in the inflationary period of the 1970s, took on excessive risk in doing so, and further magnified such risk through off–balance-sheet practices.

As anybody who took finance courses and got a better than "C" grade would understand, in order to keep the financial house in order, the treasury must have records based on *standard* rules and procedures. The more that ad hoc accounting is introduced and practiced, the less we are in control and the greater the unpleasant surprises that we will face.

Off-budget practices by the government and off–balance sheet by corporations have this in common: They are both bypasses of established accounting principles, opening Pandora's box. Both are elusive and ill-defined concepts interpreted in a subjective manner according to current needs and aimed at avoiding control.

Off–balance sheet essentially means *contingent liabilities*, a concept that may seem confusing at first glance:

- A bank loan is counted as an asset on a bank's balance sheet; *a promise to make a loan* is a liability, or obligation.

---

*London: Butterworths, 1990.

- A contingent liability does not represent actual money lent by the bank; it does represent firm commitment and therefore potential risk.

Bankers differ in their *appreciation of risk* in such areas as commitments. A number of financial experts, however, concede that keeping better tabs on contingent liabilities is a useful step. And let's not forget that it is a fast-growing segment of the banking business that demands much greater control by management and, therefore, *disclosure*.

A bank may provide, for a fee, a standby letter of credit guaranteeing that a corporation will pay off a bond when it matures. If the company pays off the bond, the bank simply keeps its fee. But if it defaults, the bank must pay the bondholders who are suffering a loss.

In 1984 Salomon Brothers estimated that if the government required banks to maintain capital against standby letters of credit alone, the 35 banks it studied could be forced to raise $2.7 billion to $3.5 billion in new capital. Some other estimates put the figures far higher.

Another example of the risk taken through contingent liabilities is provided by the National Mortgage Equity Corporation scandal, which attached the name of Bank of America to more than $133 million of mortgage-backed securities. The story began at the bank's branch in Inglewood, California, which agreed to place the Bank of America name as trustee and escrow agent to a certain issue; it ended by costing the bank $95 million when the insurance company that backed the paper went bankrupt.

ESTABLISHING AND FOLLOWING BEHAVIORAL PATTERNS

Decentralization of responsibility is only a valid process when *accountability* is steadily watched and controlled on-line. New financial instruments are welcome, but their combined effect with that of untested accounting and management control practices can be deadly—hence the need for vigilance.

If novel accounting approaches are to be admitted, then we would need to develop realtime

- *Heuristic solutions* able to operate at all times as trusted auditors

- *Behavioral patterns* for investigating and defining the way normal business is done—as well as the exceptional

Appropriate legislation should also be on hand, something like the Racketeer-Influenced and Corrupt Organizations Act (RICO), which has become almighty in controlling fraud in the United States. RICO gives law enforcers extraordinary latitude because it focuses on *patterns* of criminal behavior rather than on individual crimes. It can target anyone involved in a business that engages at least twice a decade in any of a broad range of unlawful activities, from murder and extortion to mail and wire fraud. It authorizes heavy prison sentences and carries a powerful economic punch. Convicted defendents must forfeit all their ill-gotten gains, including all proceeds from their business.

In a similar manner in finance, there are cases where extraordinary measures are warranted, and others where management control action would suffice, provided that the proper checks and balances are in place to make such control effective. Precisely the lack of such control is the reason that off–balance sheet and off-budget present great risk.

What is more, because of multinational, 24-hour financial business, the laws regulating accounting procedures should be universal in their letter as well as in their interpretation. That is hardly the case today with off–balance sheet and other practices.

Among reserve banks of the First World, different laws and bylaws guarantee that approaches differ on how to handle the more risky parts of the financial business. An example is *selling securities* for repurchasing. There are also risk elements that fall *outside* both the balance sheet and off–balance sheet, for instance:

- Market-to-market revaluations
- Repricing of services
- Transfer risk
- Country risk

Confronted with the problems that novel practices may bring, by mid-1983 federal regulators in America began requesting regular reports from banks regarding their off–balance sheet items. They feared that, as they began to press for banks to increase their capital in proportion to their loans, the banks might try to shift some direct loans into categories that did not show up on their balance sheets, thus circumventing the demands for increased capital.

Some banks, however, are more prudent than others. For instance, Bankers Trust treats loan commitments as risks for its internal capital accounting. It includes one-eighth of the amount of its loan commitments among its assets for capital-assigning purposes. Nevertheless, the discovery of the existence of large amounts of money in contingent liabilities throughout the American financial system was enough to alarm regulators and to a certain measure the banks themselves.

For years the banking system also has debated whether certain activities, including the esoteric but increasingly used *interest rate swaps*, should be included in the reports to the regulators. Through swaps, a bank enables its clients to switch from fixed-rate to adjustable-rate interest payments, and in doing so in effect guarantees the payment of interest. Morgan Guaranty Trust, for example, considers such activities to involve risk, and it reports that risk to the Federal Reserve. But other banks assert that little if any risk is involved and therefore have not included swaps in their reports to regulators.

The debate over the off–balance-sheet liabilities is not abating, and bankers still try to take some items off their balance sheet. They are backing a move being studied by the American Institute of Certified Public Accountants to remove *bankers' acceptances* from a bank balance sheet. Acceptances are bank gurantees in IOUs issued by private concerns.

The increase in floating rate liabilities has also caused a dangerous mismatch at many commercial banks. Not enough new *floating rate assets* are being created to offset *new floating rate liabilities*. If interest rates go up and the mismatch is large, then a major earnings squeeze develops. That is what has happened to the savings and loans associations in America.

These are the results of taking freedom with accounting approaches and of *substituting debt for equity*. New entities are established, and people who should know better avoid treating them within the balance sheet; in other words, they *avoid regulation*. The hidden objective is the elimination of risk; the net result is its magnification.

CAN WE OPTIMIZE THE LEVEL OF RISK?

Quite often management wants to optimize the assets to liabilities ratio but also to mitigate risk. That raises a number of questions whose answers will determine the success with which a financial operation will be performed: the opportunities that are involved, the risks that are taken, and the most likely profitability that will result.

To see how risk factors must be evaluated relative to *trade, investments,* and *loans*, let's take foreign exchange risk as an example. It involves three exposures:

1. The transaction itself

2. The conversion of currencies

3. The operational factors, in an execution sense

The risk resulting from the transaction itself will be present in every currency, but if all currencies are taken together and one of them is chosen as the *reference currency*, that will add an extra dimension because of the risk caused by exchange rate fluctuations.

Treasurers who manage portfolios in foreign currencies will lose when other exchange rates depreciate as compared to their base currency; they will gain when they appreciate. Another type of risk in international currency holding is political—essentially, country risk. Governments may change tax policy, trade policy, or even devalue currencies at unexpected times. Similar factors may affect interest rate risk.

Prior to optimization, an analysis into basic components must be made of credit risk. For instance, in terms of the treasurer's portfolio it will involve default risk, maturity risk, and sovereign risk. The latter is again a function of political risk, and though the treasurer may be hedging in securities in the overall, he or she may also be as exposed as in the case of currency risk.

A consolidated investment perspective, shown in Figure 2.3, is divided into three main parts: total investment concerning the portfolio under examination, new transactions involving this portfolio, and optimization. In both cases, a crucial input is that of *opportunity* and *risk* to

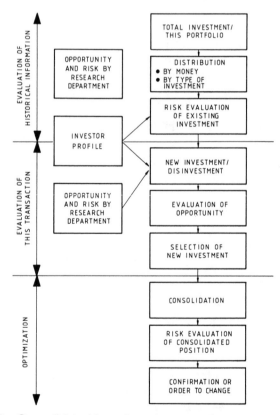

Figure 2.3 Consolidated investment perspective.

be given by the bank's research department. The same reference is valid regarding the input by an expert system, acting as an investor profile analyzer.

Optimization is being done *not* in the abstract, but in accordance with set objectives. In this example the objectives are given by the investor profile, which often may present conflicting signals, such as maximum profit with minimum risk. An effort to optimize is often an attempt to compromise between conflicting goals. This is true of any financial operation, from investment to loans and other channels of business activity.

In fact, as seen by its creditors, a company's own operations are themselves subject to *credit risk*. This covers risks due to downgrading of a borrower's credit worthiness, due to changing prospects — or, in the case of issuing securities — on the issuer's ability to meet all future obligations. If a borrower is more likely to default on some or all future payments, the borrower's creditworthiness deteriorates. In turn, investors demand a higher premium for holding the debt, which implies a price drop, hence risk.

Although it is widely admitted that credit risk is important when considering corporate bonds, it should not be forgotten that it is also of major influence on corporate money market instruments. Bonds exposed to credit risk can be thought of as contingent claims, with credit risk related to volatility factors. Many variables relating to the quality of management and the industrial activities of the issuing firm contribute to credit risk: for instance, variation of earnings, debt/equity ratio, and so on. Ratings of debt are designed to indicate creditworthiness, helping to control portfolio composition. Therefore, ratings may be used as a means of partial credit risk protection. This statement is valid only when an analysis of the individual firm is done in a factual and documented manner, in order to establish if circumstances justify extending credit or, to the contrary, suggest the wisdom of doing a switch.

Although what has just been said is valid by country, the challenge becomes greater when we consider *global risk*, based on the company's multinational operations seen as a network. The treasurer must monitor exposure, feeding the findings into a risk matrix. Other contributions to this matrix will be cash flow projections and the calculation of liquidity risk, including these factors:

- Payables
- Financing
- Refinancing
- Maturing
- Calling exposure

One of the firms having taken this approach has found that it leads to a sizeable database. Experience from other applications also demonstrated that to keep risk under control, everything should be on-line and no financial work should continue being executed in a manual form. Figure 2.4 presents an overview of an integrated approach to risk management.

The foremost multinational corporations have already established the policy that all applications regarding risk and exposure evaluation should operate in an integrative way and in realtime. Some have added to their managerial control tools the possibility for experimentation not only in the evaluation of current risk, but also in hypothetical calculations regarding future risk positions.

At least one corporation instituted, in 1989, a new treasury system that is completely parametrized, including optimization procedures. It is also rich in graphics for effective visualization. This application started with the following premises concerning the status quo:

- There are no commodity tools available to fine-tune risk, no matter what may be said in the literature.

- The market changes instantaneously, thus deviating from a supposed equilibrium—even if one could be found.

- The hypothesis of an efficient market has been described in the literature, but it has still to be proved in everyday business life.

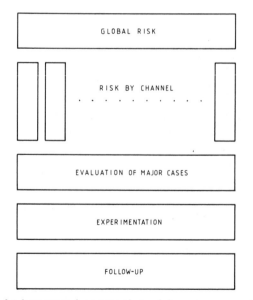

Figure 2.4   An integrated approach to risk management.

For these reasons, this particular treasury organization has developed its own mathematical models. It has also built expert systems that filter and analyze incoming financial information in order to:

1. Alert the treasurer and staff to changes

2. Locate opportunities in financial markets

3. Evaluate low-risk sectors and situations

For instance, one of the expert systems continuously evaluates which investment areas are overpriced and which are undervalued. The key decision to which this leads is the identification of financial products that are rich and those that are cheap—a conclusion reached after having considered security performance and valuation.

RISK-ADJUSTED RETURN ON CAPITAL

The risks considered earlier in this chapter suggest that when we evaluate the return on our investment we should give due consideration to exposure factors, adjusting—which essentially means downsizing—the benefits we are projecting. The treasurer should be very sensitive to this need, and much can be learned by what leading banks and industrial firms have done in this domain.

In the late 1970s, Bankers Trust developed a complex system for judging the profitability, in terms of return on equity (ROE), of every activity in which it becomes engaged. That is critical because the bank's overall goal has been to obtain an annual return of $20 on each $100 of stockholders' equity, a goal of 20 percent ROE.

That system is known as risk-adjusted return on capital (RAROC) and is being applied bankwide. Under RAROC every loan or other financial transaction is assigned a portion of the bank's capital, depending on the level of the activity's risk. Each officer is judged by the earnings produced in relation to the capital attributed to his or her activity, although adjustment is made for officers in charge of new and developing businesses that are not expected to produce high returns immediately.

Whereas some of these components exhibit no difference from the way other banks operate, the novelty lies in the fact that risk is an integral part of financial calculation and is being tracked in a constant manner. The computer-based mathematical model sees to it that what happens in other institutions where the digging is slow, but the spending is fast, does not take place at Bankers Trust. RAROC is also an example of the extraordinary degree of integration necessary in the financial business. In most cases, when a borrower (say, a company) goes to a bank for a loan, a binary decision is made: "Qualified/Not qualified." RAROC is not black or white but has tonalities of gray in its response: It *stratifies* and sets a premium based on the risk ceiling.

Risk assessment quantifies dangers so that responsible officers can decide if a particular risk is worth taking. Every time the customer's risk level changes (more precisely, worsens) the system calculates the insurance necessary to cover such risk and raises the premium. Covered by premiums, such calculated risks:

- Permit the expansion of money and securities trading activities, while keeping a tap on risk.

- Make it feasible to further build up market share in terms of financial services.

The idea is excellent but, as in the example seen in Figure 2.1, it makes mandatory both a firm policy and a system. A focused policy requires:

- Maintaining and selectively enhancing the risk factors associated with financial services

- Accessing on-line private and public distributed databases

- Developing new algorithms and heuristics to enhance *interactive computational finance*

- Ensuring the existence of a system solution that has no geographic limitations and no time-zone constraints

The benefit of RAROC and similar approaches is helping management decide where to draw the line in terms of committed positions, credit risk, liquidity and maturity, exposure, and profitability evaluations.

Along the same lines of reasoning, another financial institution has designed a risk evaluator enriched through artificial intelligence constructs. As shown in Figure 2.5, each database is explored on-line through an expert system module, with the evaluator responding to interactive queries. Following its first successful implementation, this solution has been enriched by other modules, specifically:

1. *Environment assessor*, focusing on market forecasts, industry trends, and the external business climate.

2. *Strategy analyst*, whose task is to investigate the fit between a group of transactions to be performed and the strategic objectives of the bank.

3. *Financial analyst*, able to investigate the financial strengths and weaknesses of a business partner.

4. *Borrower assessor*, able to analyze the nonfinancial strengths and weaknesses of the corporate client.

5. *Profit analyst*, whose mission is to determine the actual profit of the projected transaction.

The message is that this type of experimentation is in no way limited to risk management, though a dependable estimation of exposure is a focal point.

Let's also take notice of the fact that the risk and profit evaluation system that we just considered, as well as its modules, is not necessarily limited within the confines of a financial institution. The treasury function of a corporation acts a great deal like an investment bank— and vice versa.

In the leveraged buyout of Avis Europe by Avis USA, General Motors, and a Belgian holding company, the investment bank involved has been Lazard Brothers. Analysts at Lazard Brothers took notice of the fact that each of the 12 countries where Avis Europe operates has a different set of laws governing how much debt can be assumed by a local subsidiary and how much interest they will allow to be deducted from corporate

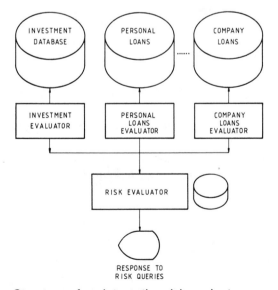

Figure 2.5 Structure of an interactive risk evaluator.

taxes. To facilitate the Avis transaction, Lazard Brothers designed a computer model able to:

- Figure out the optimal placement of the debt to minimize taxes

- Experiment with and maximize the effect of lower interest rates

- Avoid running afoul of corporate laws on currency and dividend outflows

From Bankers Trust to Lazard Brothers, this is the landscape in which corporate treasurers and investment bankers work together. They develop computer models for automated analysis to optimize transactions, measure performance of equity and debt products, evaluate various market conditions, and reach decisions that are properly documented.

Algorithms and heuristics help determine the payment stream and/or interest of a given financial product as well as the anticipated performance under different market conditions: Risk, product characteristics, pricing, cash flow, and projected performance have to be thoroughly investigated. Voluminous, quantitative economic and market analysis focuses on the need for a security sinking fund, the characteristics of a security call feature, and a number of other critical factors.

Because they realize the contribution analytical techniques can have on their function, corporate treasurers are attracted to working with financial institutions who *lead* in that domain. A result of this trend is that the number of banks that a major corporation works with is shrinking, while the business it is doing with each one of them is growing.

- In 1980 AAA American companies had an average of 36 banks to deal with.

- Today, the number has been reduced to 9 and is still decreasing.

One result of high technology in finance is that the bank becomes the corporation's *assistant treasurer*. It will remain in this position as long as it is inventive in the types of products which it offers to its clients, and is able to keep ahead in technological know-how, so that its clients will continue to need its services.

3
Problems in Risk Control: How the Japanese Face the Challenge

Are there failures in the control of risk at the treasurer's level? The answer to this query can be only "yes!" and there is a horde of reasons behind it. Among the foremost are the lack of a global risk concept, nonexistent or deficient management directives, and substandard technological support.

A careful analysis of underlying reasons, which I performed in America, Japan, and Western Europe, has unearthed other issues, such as:

- Obsolete, incompatible, or even contradictory rules for risk control

- Failure to account for the synergy of risks, particularly in a global sense

- Lack of dynamic cut-off limits for exposure

- The fact that on-line knowledge engineering assistance has not been developed to automate part of risk control

What this means in simple terms is that the proper structure is not in place. The lack of a structure could have negligence or even intentionally avoided in the hope that the worst would never happen. But there are financial organizations that take positive action in risk control, with Japan offering some of the better examples.

In 1989 Japan's Ministry of Finance established a blue-ribbon committee under the president of the Financial Information Systems Center

(FISC),* which in 1990 published Report no. 13, on global risk management. We will examine its recommendations in the next section of this chapter.

Today, FISC is working on four major projects, with a common interest and infrastructure on risk control:

1. Cross-vendor environment, with particular focus on database integration

2. Risk management to be implemented in a cross-database sense

3. Security of personal information, following the tighter rules made in Europe

4. The coming "big bang" in Japanese banking and the effects that its aftermaths have on risk

At the same time, the reserve Bank of Japan, specifically its Institute for Financial and Monetary Affairs, is looking into the prerequisites of a global system for forex transactions. It is being studied in a cross-database sense including currency, country, and credit risks.

Since classical approaches have been judged insufficient to ensure global risk control, the Bank of Japan has begun a study to implement fuzzy engineering[†] and neural networks. Related to that project is another one emphasizing integrative electronic funds transfer (EFT) with bank-to-bank connection. Work is also progressing on financial database modeling for balance sheet as well as profit and loss.

As we will see in this chapter, the use of fuzzy engineering in treasury and forex is taking hold in the financial industry. "Registering what has happened in the market is not enough," suggested Sam Gibb, the chief technology officer of County NatWest. "We have to filter the data, and integrate the news items. This calls for different approaches than those we practiced in the past."

The Japanese are doing precisely that through fuzzy logic. The Laboratory of International Fuzzy Engineering (LIFE), in Yokohama, uses fuzzy sets to interpret news items. Then it integrates their sense with the results of a neural network that predicts yen/dollar exchange rates.

---

*FISC's founding members were the leading Japanese banks, computer manufacturers, and the government.

[†]In a nutshell, fuzzy engineering is a branch of science that accounts for vagueness and uncertainty existing in management decisions as well as in forex, securities, and treasury dealings. Since this book is addressed to management, the mathematics of fuzzy engineering will not be discussed. This is done in *Using High Technology in Treasury and Forex Operations* and D. N. Chorafas, *Knowledge Engineering*, New York: Van Nostrand Reinhold, 1990.

Such tools can be of tremendous help to the treasurer, who has to closely watch a group of ten or twelve currencies for hedging as well as for profit reasons. The theory behind fuzzy engineering has been developed in America by Dr. Richard Bellman and Dr. Lotfi Zadeh, formerly of Stanford University, and is now applied in Japan.

THE FISC REPORT ON GLOBAL RISK

The FISC Report no. 13, "Global Risk Management," has focused on markets and their volatility, the credit system as a whole, exchanges, the soundness of company management, systems and procedures, and new product risk. Because of the complexity of risk calculation facing modern financial institutions, the Japanese Ministry of Finance advises both *analytical* solutions and a *global* approach. Emphasis is placed on properly defined risk classes and on starting with the fundamentals and doing a thorough, analytical job. FISC has included in the risk factors:

1. *New financial products* and their associated procedures (LBO, project financing, floating interest bonds, and so on)

2. *Risk Hedging* in a cross-product manner, including futures, options, swaps, off–balance sheet and offshore financial services

3. *Mathematics*, that is, algorithmic and heuristic approaches to asset/liability management, with risk analysis covering differences in maturities and the duration gap

The FISC/Ministry of Finance study strongly advises banks to experiment on risk through computer-based simulation models and to forecast on asset/liability management by extrapolating trends and targeting on:

- International and domestic economic indicators

- Global and national interest rates

- Exchange rate fluctuation in major currencies

The FISC study makes specific reference to practical examples including practices by American financial institutions, such as Citibank. The Japanese researchers have appreciated the fact that Citibank has prepared a number of models applicable to international banking operations, including exchange, country, and global trading risk.

Report no. 13 also stresses attention to an issue that is often overlooked, yet it can make the difference between profit and loss. *Funding methods* can provide additional risks, such as interest rate risk and market volatility risk. The study underlines the fact that the complexity of credit allocation and subsequent global control augments these risks, and dealing in government bonds and municipals involves additional issues such as marketing risk.

To emphasize the possible mismatch risk, Report no. 13 refers to the case of the Long Term Credit Bank of Japan, with 70 percent of its commitments in long–term lending while over 50 percent of its money is coming from big corporations. This, it is stated, requires both wholesale banking concepts and focused risk management practices. It is also underlined that some industries, such as aircraft, have greater risks than others—hence the need for tighter credit control. In addition, as the financed projects themselves get bigger, so does the associated risk—hence the wisdom of using analytical approaches (algorithms, heuristics) on-line to enrich databases.

Part of the FISC/Ministry of Finance study reflected in Report no. 13 focuses on Trust Banks, with the statement being made that many of the risks are the same as those of City Banks (Japanese commercial banks); however there is an exclusive trust side concerning:

- Mutual fund asset management

- Pension fund management

- Big corporation funding

Finally, Report no. 13 discusses risk management at corporations including their expansion and acquisitions (and LBOs) as well as their scale-down through disinvestments. The classes being considered are:

- Investment risk

- Inventory risk

- Funding risk

- Fund management risk

- Risks related to international activities

Practical examples are taken on risk management by industry class, country of origin, currency, and exchange rate. The need to control positions is emphasized—-and the advice is given that it must be done by credit portfolio, using simulation and experimentation on credit allocation.

In all, this is a well–crafted risk control concept. It includes many issues of practical importance to every commercial and investment bank, particularly within the perspectives of:

- Assets/liabilities management

- Global risk administration

- Cost control

The emphasis on cross-database access shows the need for working interactively on-line, not only because that is the current trend but also— if not primarily—because that is the only valid way of controlling risk. This statement is applicable to risk management in general and most particularly to the competent computation and analysis of global risk.

HOW JAPANESE BANKS FOCUS ON RISK CONTROL

Within less than a year after the Ministry of Finance issued its directives, Japanese financial institutions were working hard on their implementation. The scope and pace of their work goes well beyond compliance, implying that top management considers such guidelines to be in their interest. At the Sumitomo Bank, for instance, the three top–priority projects at this time are: global risk management, interest risk, and global cost control. Sanwa Bank, too, works on similar issues as well as on a new-generation, on-line system (network) that uses knowledge engineering. Among the key goals are:

- Closing of gap between fourth–generation networks and second–generation database management systems (offered by vendors).

- The interfacing and integration of heterogeneous databases, including extensive usage of optical disks

Both projects are greatly related to risk management, as its implementation requires not only seamless cross-database access but also *database mining* operations. The Fuji Bank offers a good example in this regard, including database restructuring solutions owing to its success in the exploitation of management information systems (MIS). On-line the bank has 750 gigabytes for MIS and 750 gigabytes for transactional operations. Major projects in database mining are client profiles, pricing models for bonds and options, asset/liability management, and risk control.

Fuji places great emphasis on the transition taking place in information technology. Their project involves 40 of the best information technology specialists of the bank and is done in cooperation with Hitachi.

Ad hoc analytical queries in a cross-database sense have been a management priority at Dai-Ichi. It is promoted by:

- Globalization

- Deregulation

- Risk control

- New financial products treated as commodities

End-user computing is emphasized in order to cut the huge backlog in applications programming and accelerate software development. "The only way out is to train the end user in developing his own applications," said the responsible executive. "But you can't do successful end-user computing without database restructuring and virtual homogeneity."

That is precisely what able risk management approaches require: a virtual homogeneity of the distributed databases. Not only in Japan, but also in America and Europe, many treasurers have asked their company's data processing (DP) department for this type of solution; but in the typical case, the classical DP department is too slow in its response—and often uncertain on how to go about it. By and large, the old generation of DP managers fails to appreciate the services rendered by knowledge engineering. Here again Japanese banks are ahead of others.* Although the leading American banks *are at par,* that cannot be said in general, and European banks *have fallen way behind* in knowledge engineering implementation.

Quite often, financial institutions do not appreciate that the use of knowledge engineering is a *political*—not a technical problem. As a result, DP departments fail to get top–management understanding and support in acquiring a good grasp of what knowledge engineering is and what it can do.

To break the impasse it is advisable to study what the Japanese have done: Be well organized and train a small team; select team members on performance, not age or grade; choose a couple of projects and work on a fast timetable.

There are other policies the Japanese are following that make sense: seeing to it that risk control models work on–line reaching distributed databases, and ensuring that the technologists as a whole show results through end–user acceptance and utilization of the software being made.

---

*See also D. N. Chorafas and H. Steinmann, *Expert Systems in Banking*, London: Macmillan 1991, and New York: New York University Press, 1991.

CAPITALIZING ON GLOBAL INVESTMENT ADVICE

Competition in the financial markets has been instrumental in developing an increasing sophistication among treasurers as well as the recognition of the fact that the more demanding clients are the bank's income earners. That dual effect led the management of leading financial institutions to appreciate the importance of providing their customer base with advanced technological support and skillful advice in making rational investment decisions.

The most solid infrastructures that are now being put in place feature a consistent application of analytical tools in financial reporting. That permits treasurers to make factual comparisons among alternative possibilities prior to reaching cash management and investment decisions.

Based on analytical approaches, capital commitments can be made in a more fundamental manner as cognizant executives are able to determine market exposure by instrument, currency, country, and as a whole. In the 1990s treasuries must decide in a realspace sense when the firm's capital should be commited; decisions that do not use up-to-date knowledge and information in a worldwide sense will be exposed to major errors.

By knowing in a realspace mode the economic and financial conditions in the First World's markets, the treasurer can sharpen his or her strategy and carefully analyze common and individual risk units, doing so by investment domain prior to making commitment decisions. Figure 3.1 outlines the components of a system tuned to a multi-instrument hedging strategy, thus reinforcing the need for both information and know-how.

Solutions based on simulators and heuristics help in attacking one of the more thorny problems in investment banking: the standardizing of how investment advice is given.

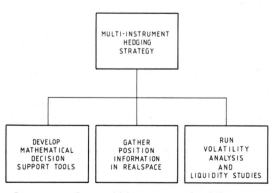

Figure 3.1   Structure of a multi-instrument hedging strategy system.

- What are the basic rules to be observed?

- What facts must be considered prior to giving an advice?

- What evaluation procedures are to be followed?

- What is best way of including both return on investment and exposure?

When investment evaluations are made, cash flow and the rate of return on equity (ROE), rather than profitability and assets, are becoming the more explicit objectives. As a result, there is a greater tendency to test each component of the business against the criterion of its contribution to ROE.

Management orientation shifts toward explicit allocation of capital to different parts of the business, and the requirement arises that each component is tested against its contribution to the rate of return on the capital absorbed by it. This is an approach embedded in RAROC (see Chapter 2), which incorporates risk-weighted returns and rests on a precise risk analysis.

The treasurer must, however, be aware that loopholes do exist. For instance, RAROC and ROE approaches may provide encouragement of the off–balance sheet business, with a view to raise the rate of return on equity by increasing income relative to assets. For instance, a traditional role of financial intermediation concerns the transformation of liabilities into assets with different characteristics—such as maturity transformation.

Since the treasurer cannot be on the lookout 24 hours every day given the way the global bank today operates, tools are necessary to complement the treasurer's skills. Like an expert financial analyst examining a collection of ratios for a given firm and judging them individually as being "too high," "too low," or "about right," a networked expert system can mount a 24-hour global watch; the judgments can then be used to draw qualitative conclusions such as investment worthiness. As an example, a collection of criteria and ratios applied in an automated decision network is shown in Figure 3.2. Equipped with *fuzzy sets*, the nodes react with shades of gray rather than black-or-white, with the performance of the system evaluated by means of imprecise qualitative assessments of the output nodes.

Fuzziness defines the following state of mind: We may not know exactly what we want, but we can describe the process of a weighted decision. The fuzzy sets are qualifiers; they have in the background a fuzzy logic, that is, a logic working with uncertainty and accepting vagueness when characterizing a certain decision environment. In the final analysis, that is the way a manager's mind often works.

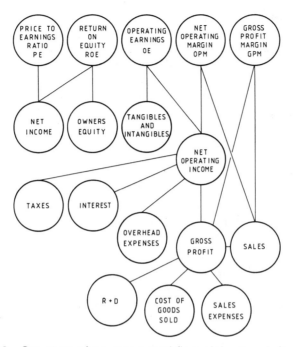

Figure 3.2 Structure of an automated financial network for decision support.

A decision process is *crisp* when it is amenable to sharp alternatives with answers clearly pointing to one clear direction. Something is black or white. Such situations very rarely, if ever at all, exist in financial markets—particularly in forex and options—and to a significant measure in securities.

A decision process is *fuzzy* when instead of only black and white as alternatives we are dealing with many tonalities of gray. The dividing lines are blurred and may even change as a function of time or market conditions—and, furthermore, *both* a yes and a no answer are not only possible on one and the same subject but also equally likely.

In a system designed by an investment bank, the classical financial ratios provide a quantitative input. Rules based on fuzzy logic, which often characterize the thinking of financial analysts, constitute the qualitative component—the two together have led to fairly accurate and well-documented opinions by the expert system.

This second generation of expert systems, which incorporates fuzzy sets and neural networks, is beginning to be used by financial institutions because it presents a better fit to the newer financial instruments than rule-based expert system approaches. Models have, for instance, been developed for *collateralized mortgage obligations* (CMO), which in essence are constraints with a share of vagueness and uncertainty. The existence of such constraints underlines the role of experimentation and optimization in financial engineering.

Knowledge in underwriting, in securities packaging, and in the sale of financial instruments is no doubt crucial; and the same is true of tools to enhance such know-how. From the evaluation of investments to the management of risk, the tools that we develop should increase our ability to face complex situations, leading to their investigation and eventually their control.

ACCOUNTING FOR MARKET VOLATILITY

Part of the risk that is taken in financial transactions and in investments is due to volatility. By definition, *volatility* is the quality of being volatile, and volatile means capable of evaporating rapidly, changing, diffusing. This term is applicable to market behavior, and metrics have been designed to measure it:

- *Beta* reflects the amount of market risk.

As the risk management metric of volatility, beta is mathematically calculated as the *standard deviation* of price movements, for example, stock prices. This is done on the assumption that such movements form a normal distribution, which is not necessarily the general case. In a managerial sense, beta is a measure of *change* regarding relative risks. As compared to a global index, the relative risks of an individual market can be expressed by means of that market's beta coefficient.

- A beta value greater than one means that the market in question shows stronger fluctuations than the global market.

- A beta value smaller than one indicates weaker fluctuations.

Although a market with a smaller beta coefficient presents less risk with regard to global events, it also offers less potential. But there is nothing permanent in beta. From period to period, the beta values of financial markets change.

For instance, as Table 3.1 indicates, from the 1986–88 timeframe to the 1989–91, the beta values for America and Canada contracted, whereas the beta rose relatively steeply for Japan. Varying factors influenced economic and stock market developments in both periods.

Table 3.1 Beta Values for Relative Risk Exposure

	1986–88	1989–91
America	1.2	0.9
Canada	1.0	0.8
Netherlands	0.9	0.7
England	0.8	0.7
Japan	0.7	1.3
Germany	0.7	0.7
France	0.6	0.5
Switzerland	0.6	0.5
Italy	0.5	0.5

Source: *Union Bank of Switzerland International Finance*, Zurich, Spring 1991.

- Between 1986 and 1988, price movements were largely determined by internal market mechanisms.

- Between 1989 and 1991, the determinants were external factors, particularly oil price and inflation trends.

Since beta values depend on a number of factors, it would be erroneous to assume that Japanese equities would react as strongly in future cycles as they have recently. The only way to project on volatility is to properly analyze the factors influencing stock prices and exchange rates. Fuzzy engineering can provide significant assistance.

It is wise to pay attention to two other metrics projected and implemented by Yamaichi Securities and other investment houses.

- *Alpha* helps calculate the company–specific risk distribution.

- *Gamma* handles the six most vital factors determining market behavior, known as themes, and focuses on their possible variation.

In the Tokyo Stock Exchange, the *themes* reflect government directives. Yamaichi analyzed about 40 themes prior to defining the six major factors, which it makes available to its institutional customers through a radar chart shown in Figure 3.3. Some of the themes influence a specific industry or company within an industry more than others. For instance, in the case of Toyota, that is true of the consumption, export, and domestic demand themes. With a multidimensioned* gamma at zero, a portfolio

---

*Multidimesional means weighted in accord with the product lines from which the company derives its business. A comglomerate, for instance may be: 30 percent in autos, 45 percent in heavy mechanical engineering, 25 percent in electronics.

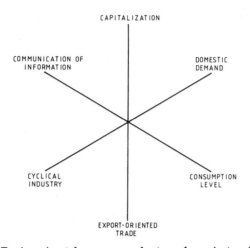

Figure 3.3 Radar chart for gamma factor of market volatility.

has the same sensitivity with regard to macroeconomic factors as the Tokyo Stock Exchange (TSE) index. In other words, for a specific company, gamma acts as a weighting factor.

The measure of volatility can be of significant assistance in focusing the treasurer's attention. However, a crucial issue with the alpha, beta, and gamma measures is having all applicable data on hand and being able to examine how closely their distribution approximates a bell curve. An associated requirement is that of using powerful mathematical models on supercomputers, to experiment in realtime on the *implied volatility.*

Operating on-line to databases, volatility models allow fund managers to experiment with and recompose the portfolio under their control. They also enable traders to do snapshot evaluations. Based on different scenarios regarding market trends, interest rates, monetary base factors, velocity of circulation of money, and variation in the exchange rate, financial institutions can experiment on coming events. That is important, since a key factor in successful securities handling—by treasurers, traders, portfolio managers, and investors—lies in understanding the market behavior and identifying patterns prior to reading the ups and downs in tomorrow's newspaper.

When forecasting is done in an able manner, we possess a risk management tool. That is the reason that the timely measure of volatility can greatly affect the treasurer's business. The treasurer is always vulnerable to sharp changes in interest rates and credit volatility adds to the need to hedge positions.

RISK CONTROL AND HEDGING AGAINST VOLATILITY

A project undertaken to hedge against market volatility will enhance risk management perspectives. Such a project should aim to provide accurate answers to focused questions, starting with the following:

- What are our options?

- Our hedging strategy?

- The risk associated with each position?

- The opportunities?

Focus should be by domain, with expert systems designed within a specific domain implementation to avoid repetitive (and often incompatible) evaluations of the same issue by human analysts, as new market data come in.

Constantly changing market drives as well as competition rules alter the weights and some of the rules being used. Hence, though operational and working 24 hours a day, the expert system should be under steady review and evaluation. Apart from keeping it in good shape, this helps steadily refine it.

The aim is to optimize, not to completely avoid, risk exposure; it is inseparable from the operation of the financial markets. Economic uncertainties typically lead to contrasts between opportunities and the possibility of failure. The key questions can be phrased in these terms:

- Is the treasury ready for informed trading activities based on experimental results?

- Or are its people waiting to take a beating before doing something?

Other questions concern the steadily developing activity in market transactions. How is the treasury going to face:

- The *risk* inherent in automated trading?

- The avalanche in dealing, which may increase market volatility?

Has the treasury measured the magnitude of possible developments over the next three to five years? How is *our* company going to face the challenge? With which weapons? What can we expect form the bow and arrows that Old DP can provide when our opponents use the atomic gun of artificial intelligence and supercomputers?

If we wish to be successful in risk management, we have to understand where the risks *really* are and how they can be managed. That requires market perspective, but because of market volatility such a perspective must extend along six axes of reference, which can profitably be mapped on a radar chart:

1. Global (worldwide) market and the principal market in which we operate

2. Transactions contracted in the different markets, such as interest on loans, conditions, tax laws

3. Currency in which our investments are or will be made

4. Specific equity or debt in which portfolio investment is or will be made

5. Prevailing risk within the different markets and currencies

6. *Carry*, the cost of leverage to hold a position*

The question about how to evaluate the different components of risk, in order to make reasonable hedges, has to be answered not only real-time but also realspace, as it has already been suggested. The volatility embedded in some of these components calls for a realspace approach. Hedging requires an instantaneous global market viewpoint as well as evaluation of trends in currencies and in industry sectors.

Through the use of AI and supercomputers the treasurer should aim at the clarification of complex situations and the industrialization of skills. With the exception of a few very talented individuals, most people find it difficult to mentally *map the whole market*. Therefore it is more efficient to map the market into the computer.

High-technology supports are that much more important as treasury requirements increase and market expectations focus on the best performers. To fare well against competition, we have to establish a dynamic methodology, able to minutely follow movement around an expected value. Able management wants instantaneous response regarding the risk in downside. The same is true when trading currencies, and when we are handling assets, such as securities. In the futures environment, currencies and assets are traded by the same market participants, and they both need increasingly powerful tools that enable players to navigate: alerting the existence of business opportunities in an environment of economic and financial uncertainty; providing experimentation

---

*As contrasted to deposit and loan bakers, traders are in the moving business. They cannot operate without holding positions, and that has a cost as well as a risk.

on possible outcomes prior to making a definite commitment; ensuring a way for developing new financial instruments that can help the bottom line of our bank.

DEALING WITH INTERNATIONAL BANKERS

During the late 1970s, American money center banks had 800 branches abroad, with roughly $300 billion, more or less half their financial base. It was a fast, almost revolutionary development as contrasted to the prevailing conditions of the early 1960s when only a small part of the financial race was outside the larger bank's country of origin.

In the decade of the 1980s, the trend toward multinationality of the financial sector became the credo of all large financial institutions in the First World. In one sense it led and in another sense it matched the needs of corporate treasurers who operated in many countries and had to worry about balances, currencies, interests, exchange rates, volatility by market, and political factors.

The international financial market was not monopolized by U.S. financial institutions, but they were the majority. By the late 1970s, other than American money center banks, the Japanese, British, German, Swiss, and French featured a thousand branch offices. Another important statistic is that all money center banks, independently of their country of origin, saw to it that an estimated 80 percent of their financial assets were in the First World.

How did the internationalization of banking materialize? Senior executives of financial institutions invariably suggest that their companies found it necessary to follow their large manufacturing and merchandizing customers, the multinational industrial firms. The second key factor is that, since the 1970s, an excess of deposit over loans in their country of origin pushed money center banks abroad.

For an increasing number of First World banks, there have been additional rewards with their expansion abroad. One was that the creation of operations in other countries made it feasible to *attract local capital* by providing a better image coupled with a dependability commensurate to or better than that of local banks.

Multinational diversification has had many merits. When the pace of increase of one national economy slows down, the money center bank finds in another country the expanding business horizon it had been accustomed to. And there is the added advantage of new opportunities in capital markets like the Eurodollar and the Petrodollar.

The recycling of Petrodollars has been, in fact, at the origin of the colossal debt the Third World has amassed toward the money center banks. Sovereign lending existed for many centuries, but never at the size and pace that it reached during the 1970s. It expended further in the 1980s particularly because of the interest and repayment of capital that had to be paid, could not be paid and continued being rescheduled.

Further, the internationalization of banking has been both a cause and an effect of the internationalization of the stock exchanges. Prior to World War II, the main stock exchanges treated local equity. Today, the same stock exchanges are interconnected with 24-hour trading networks. This trend has been assisted by communications, computers, and software, which accentuated the business drive, and in a way made the merger of the different markets unavoidable. By 1990 the after-hours network had become a reality and it slowly but surely is involving all principal financial markets in the world.

We have come a long way since the cash management service was first practiced in the early 1970s, starting with the Mars network of the Morgan Bank and soon followed by others. The developing concept is shown in Figure 3.4 and consists of:

- A global, intelligent network interconnecting client sites with the bank's international headquarters and multinational branches as well as a distributed but integrated database facility.

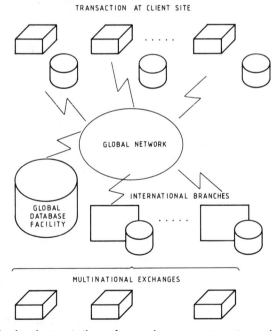

Figure 3.4 Implementation of a cash management service.

- Sophisticated use of computers and communications, enriched through simulators and expert systems for optimization and follow-up—available to the corporate treasurer on a 24-hour basis.

These advances go well beyond the old cash management perspectives that made it possible to consolidate and invest the treasury's balances, thus improving both the hedging possibilities and the profits, but fell short of many of the requirements currently present in the management of money.

NETWORKS AND "ROCKET SCIENTISTS"

Although good for the 1970s and part of the 1980s, the old model is now outdated. By 1986 Citibank had decided to withdraw gently from cash management, yet its Marty network was the second to come alive in the world. Was this an early indicator? Or a result of market saturation?

Today the answer is unambiguous: It was foresight. The market has shifted, and in order to stay in the game a bank has to provide for market differentiation which comes under other product names; an example is Quotron's Global Report.

Instrumental in the value differentiation arena are the analytical solutions, which are way ahead of the ancient data processing approaches still practiced by most banks—precisely the larger banks. They have the resource advantages of marketing, technical, financial, and human capital but also disadvantages. They can be awfully bureaucratic—particularly their DP infrastructure whose management knows of too many things that cannot be done. And there are also conflicts in departmental competence.

Nonetheless, avant-garde banks have gone beyond that stage. Thanks to the early adoption of advanced computer technology, the emphasis on telecommunications, and the use of expert systems, they have developed a strong technological edge that they intend to maintain with an impressive annual investment in systems research and development.

Just like the multinational companies that they serve and their treasury departments, such banks appreciate very well that in a dynamic financial industry new product development has become a prerequisite to profits; product research is therefore now part of their mainstream. Their "rocket scientists" are the number crunchers and logicians of financial services who are:

- *Inventing new generations of securities*, backed-up by almost any kind of debt

- *Developing instrumental forex schemes*, to benefit from currency differences in financial markets

- *Mapping-out computerized trading strategies*, that fuel wild girations in stock prices

- *Devising complex hedging formulas*, for pension funds and other institutional investors

Rocket scientists make up the banks', the securities firms', and the treasury's *R + D laboratories*. They project on exchange rates, simulate bond market movements, plot interest rate trends, calculate option against spread (OAS), and estimate the best market timing.

One example of this work is securitization. Another is the development of financial products such as Tactical Asset Allocation (TAA), which has become one of the hot concepts in the billion-dollar money-management business. The idea is to:

- Identify market opportunities on which the bank can capitalize

- Move money back and forth among stocks, bonds, and cash

- Do so very rapidly to profit from market anomalies

- Get the largest profit possible with the least amount of risk

Focus and speed are at a premium. Financial history teaches that at least 80 percent of the returns that investors earn do not come from choosing individual securities but rather from properly timing the move. The most critical decision is not whether to buy DEC, IBM, Ford, or General Motors, but whether to invest in stocks, bonds, or other instruments. That is the kind of decision that underpins successful asset management and that interests the treasurer the most.

From the concepts to the tools we need, there is plenty of such common ground between treasury, security and forex. The challenge is how to effectively benefit from the common ground.

4

Transacting Foreign Exchange Deals

Chapter 1 drew a distinction between the narrow view of treasury and the broader one that covers a full range of services beyond cash management. These include foreign exchange operations, both for day-to-day activities and for longer-term hedging reasons. A better way of looking at forex activities is to include:

- All claims payable abroad in any foreign currency, as well as balances at banks abroad, bills, and checks
- Buying and selling one foreign currency in exchange for another, which forms the basis for foreign exchange transactions

A foreign exchange business represents an agreement between a buyer and a seller that a fixed amount of foreign currency will be delivered at a fixed rate. There are two ways of contracting forex operations: *spot*, for immediate delivery and *forward*, at a later date.

A *spot transaction* regards the purchase or sale of foreign currency at a fixed price, with immediate delivery and payment. The term *immediate* is relative. Most of the payment takes place on the second business day after the day the transaction has been concluded. The delivery date is usually known as *value date* or maturity date.

Transactions with value dates up to and including seven business days from the date of trading are also considered spot. These, however, involve special agreements with regard to maturity, concluded at the time of dealing. The extended delivery and payment date is reflected in the exchange rate and does involve adjustments that resemble forward-type transactions.

A *forward transaction* consists of a commitment to buy or sell a specific amount of foreign currency (or currencies) at a later date, typically within a specific time period and at an exchange rate stipulated at the time the transaction is concluded. In contrast to spot transactions, the commitment of a forward transaction and its fulfillment are separated in terms of time. The commitment is made at the conclusion of an agreement; delivery and payment constitute the fulfillment. Delivery or receipt of the currency takes place on the agreed upon value date. Forward transactions are one of the most widespread hedging instruments for currency positions—both national and foreign.

Since the early 1970s forward forex transaction has become prominent because of the necessary hedging in currencies caused by fluctuating exchange rates. It is attributable to an appreciation that national borders are no longer defensible against the invasion of financial instruments—or for that matter of knowledge and ideas.

Walter Wriston (former chief executive officer of Citibank) once explained: "The Eurocurrency markets are a perfect example. No one designed them, no one authorized them, and no one controlled them. They were fathered by controls, raised by technology, and today they are refugees, if you will, from national attempts to allocate credit and capital for reasons which have little or nothing to do with finance and economics."

In Chapter 12 we will also discuss spot and forward but from an option trading perspective.

SPOT, FORWARD, AND THE TRANSNATIONAL COMPANY

The classical multinational company was invented in the nineteenth century, its concept being strengthened in the years between the two world wars. Particularly practiced by American and German firms in the 1920s and 1930s, the *multinational* concept consisted of a parent corporation with foreign affiliates.

- Design and manufacturing was done by the parent and focused on the domestic market.

- The foreign affiliates typically assembled knocked-down products for their local market.

These knocked-down products were typically exported by the parent company. But foreign affiliates sometimes made some minor components locally.

In the years after World War II this concept changed and today the *transnational* company operates in a totally different manner. Research is done not in one but in many countries, wherever there are talented scientists major markets to satisfy. As for production facilities, investments are made wherever the economics of manufacturing suggest that it is advisable in cost–effective terms.

In every country in which it operates, the transnational company requires both capital and an available stream of funds. Foreign exchange transactions are in the mainstream of operations given the company's network of manufacturing and marketing activities, which typically span many countries.

The task of cash management in a transnational sense and associated forex operations are the job of the treasurer. Most spot transactions are concluded by phone. Subsequent confirmation is not necessary if the transaction is conducted via foreign currency accounts at a given bank.

If a spot transaction is utilized to fix the rate for a currency payment to be made later in favor, for instance, of a third party, the term used to describe operation is *rate reservation.* In such a case, the payment order serves to a certain extent as confirmation of the transaction contracted over the phone. When a bank quotes a price: It will pay the bid price to buy foreign exchange and will sell at the offered price. Something similar applies to interest rates, in which case the bank pays the bid rate for deposits and lends at the offered rate.

From the viewpoint of the bank, buying means purchasing a certain amount of a traded currency at the bid of the buying price against the delivery of a second currency, also known as *counter-currency.* The corporation transacting the forex business sells when the bank buys the foreign currency and buys when the bank sells.

Again viewed from the bank's standpoint, *selling* means offering a certain foreign currency at the selling price against the receipt of another currency. Often foreign exchange transactions are understood to be *net.* The rate includes all costs, and no commission is charged. That, however, is not a universal practice, and whether or not a forex transaction is net should therefore be clarified in advance.

Equally important is to appreciate the concept of *cross rates.* In interbank operations, all currencies are normally traded against the U.S. dollar, in terms of which every exchange rate is calculated.

If a company or a firm sells British pounds for yen, the bank carries out the following transactions:

- U.S. dollars are bought with pounds at the $/£ offered price because the counterparty sells dollars and buys pounds.

- U.S. dollars obtained from this transaction are sold for yen at the $/¥ bid price, with the third party buying dollars and selling yen.

In this dual transaction, the offered and bid prices are used in cross-currency terms, hence the word *cross*.

As in the case of spot transactions, forward transactions in all of the major currencies may be concluded by telephone. Forex practice sees to it that the maximum period for most currencies is 12 months, but up to 5 years may be negotiated for the principal currencies. Little in terms of forex business is contracted at maximum range. The most common periods are 1, 3, and 6 months. However, broken dates, for instance, 10, 25, or 54 days are also possible.

A particularity of the forward transaction is that it cannot be cancelled. By contrast, it can be closed out at any time through repurchase or sale of the foreign currency amount, on the value date originally agreed upon. Possible losses or gains are realized on this date, as the forward price and the spot price of a currency typically differ. If the forward price is higher than the spot price, we speak of a *forward premium*; if lower, of a *forward discount*. Both reflect interest rate differentials between currencies.

If a foreign currency with higher interest rates is not sold on a spot basis but only forward, the seller enjoys an interest rate advantage during the period in reference. The buyer, however, is at a disadvantage because he or she must wait until it is possible invest his or her funds in the currency enjoying the higher interest rates. Therefore, such a transaction will make sense only if the interest rate disadvantage is offset by a price discount.

With this algorithm, it is not the level of the interest rates of the currencies involved but the difference in the interest rates that determines discounts and premiums that are in direct proportion to the term being contracted: The longer the term, the larger is the premium or discount.

Furthermore, since a forward transaction is settled in the future, the bank requires a *guarantee* or collateral. This is initially stipulated in a percentage of the contract amount but is adjusted to adverse market developments. Known as the *margin*, a collateral serves in the event of nonfulfillment to cover any losses that may occur by closing out. The client is often free to select the form of collateral to be provided.

In the case of private customers, such collateral usually takes the form of pledged assets: account balances, deposits, securities, or precious metals. Normally, the pledging of assets does not impair their earning power. In the case of corporate customers, a special credit line, or *margin limit*, may be opened to fulfill the guarantee requirements.

Both the mechanics of the forex business, which we are considering, and the underlying dynamics are very important. The treasurer of a transnational company appreciates that the world economy is shaped and driven by:

- Cash flows
- Credit availability
- Profit potential

The treasurer knows that in more than 90 percent of cases, financial transactions in transnational economies are not driven by economic factors as such, but by financial considerations. And he or she intends to have a share of the benefits derived through able exploitation of financial assets.

By observing the fluctuation in interest rates, foreign exchange rates, monetary and fiscal policies, government deficits, and political risks, the treasurer has been led to the need of managing the corporation's foreign exchange exposure. One of the instruments at his or her disposition are foreign transactions with variable maturities.

Forward transactions with variable maturities do not represent a new type of hedging but rather a variant of conventional foreign exchange forward operations. The requirements of the exporter and the importer relating to maturity date are given particular consideration, through their competent handling.

Another consideration is flexibility. There may be many reasons why the date when the payment is received or made cannot be exactly fixed. There are, for instance, delays in government approval procedures, delivery postponements because of strikes or late arrival of materials, and so on. For these cases, the banking system offers forward transactions with variable maturities:

- To initiate forward transactions as hedging instruments
- To carry them out in a relatively simple manner

These are sometimes erroneously called forward options, although they have little or nothing in common with an option, as we will see in the appropriate chapter.

The advantage derived from a variable maturity financial instrument is that its user is free to select a value date within the term stipulated at the time the transaction is concluded. Because of this, the hedging costs are known at the outset of the transaction and can be accounted for by the treasurer of the corporation.

KEEPING ABREAST OF FOREX RATES

Rare is the treasurer who does not assume that foreign exchange rates matter, even if his company's business seems to be mainly or even purely domestic. Wise executives also appreciate that to a large measure, foreign exchange rates have become an integral part of the *cost of doing business*—yet, unlike other such costs, they are politically determined and therefore inherently unstable.

This new twist in P + L evaluations means that treasurers must accept responsibility for protecting their company against foreign exchange risks. This has been something practically unknown prior to the early 1970s when, with the exception of devaluations, foreign exchange rates were to a considerable extent stable.

The change in concept regarding forex rates, their risks, and opportunities is significant. As such, it greatly impacts on a company's strategies as it competes every day for world market positions. At the background of this statement is the fact that increasingly the treasurer of the transnational corporation manages money for all operating companies in the group, rather than each one managing its financial resources in its own detached way:

A policy of global financial management greatly increases the treasurer's responsibilities. Not only the corporation's finances are transnational but also the business plans, management strategies, market perspectives, and key product decisions.

As the treasurer of the transnational corporation well knows, the dynamic economies of the world are shaped mainly by *money flows*—in contrast to flows created by goods and services. These money flows have their own *laws* and *rules* as, up to a point, the monetary and fiscal policies of governments:

- React to events in the transnational economy

- Account for the First World's capital markets and money markets

- Extend well beyond national economic events

This is a different way of telling the story of globalization, which has become the new reality in international affairs and whose more recent examples are in banking. The latter are overtaking the best examples of former times, which were in manufacturing. Financial services have already become as important as goods in terms of their impact on the world economy.

Commenting on the overseas expansion of Japanese financial institutions and manufacturing firms, London's *Economist* (December 8, 1990) has been critical of the fact that such expression has been financed in a risky way. Because Japanese banks do not have a large network of foreign branches, they have resorted to the practice of borrowing short to lend long with the chosen vehicle being the London-based offshore Euromarkets.*

As every treasurer should appreciate, such a practice raises the risk of a *liquidity panic* in the interbank market, triggered by some sort of financial accident:

- Japanese banks have to rotate their financial liabilities constantly, and the sums are not small.

- In total, the Japanese banks have borrowed some ¥200 trillion offshore, with nearly 40 percent of this sum lent out.

Quite often banks are not worried about these imbalances because of the comfort provided by hidden reserves. But because the Tokyo stockmarket has eroded the investors' capital gains, Japanese banks now have to pay a premium for their deposits, the so-called "Japan rate," just as some of the beleaguered New York money center banks are doing.

Since treasurers depend on the banking system for all sorts of intermediation in financial transactions, it is wise to take note of these facts. At the same time, regulators should appreciate that with the money they have borrowed abroad, banks have not always lent wisely—a fact which contributes to global risk.

TRACKING THE TRANSNATIONAL ECONOMY

Speculative bubbles can have significant impact both on the world's liquidity and, if they turn to panic, on exchange rates. The origin of bubbles can be quite diverse: tulips, South Seas investments, LBOs, gold, silver, yen, or real estate. Today, for instance,

- Japan's total stock of property is valued at a theoretical ¥2 quadrillion (two thousand trillion yen).

- That amount is about five times the size of Japan's gross national product, or four times the value of the total stock of property in America.

*See also the reference made about Japan's new rules regarding risk management in Chapter 3.

Any decline in that huge market, similar to what has befallen Japan's stock market, would mean a plunge in the value of the collateral held by financial institutions, which have lent against land. Since they also are the world's biggest commercial banks, accounting for nearly 40 percent of all cross-border lending, that would accelerate what the Tokyo stockmarket crash has already started: a contraction in the availability of Japanese credit worldwide.

This occurs at a time when America's banking system—the world's second largest—is in the midst of its own credit contraction. With Germany preoccupied with financing the huge and miscalculated costs of reunification, there is no obvious financial heavyweighter left to take up the slack.

That explains why it is wrong to consider, from the treasurer's viewpoint, developments in one country's finances solely in terms of their consequences inside that country. As the supplier of worldwide credit, issuer and purchaser of First World financial instruments, the banking system of any major country is an important player in world finances— and treasurers must consider that.

The First World's financial systems, and the components which make them up, are today the decisive factor in any business. In the transnational economy, land and labor, the traditional factors of production, have become secondary.

- Money, information, and knowledge are the moving gears.

- Finance, manufacturing, and trade companies increasingly follow the knowledge on how to make investments.

- Global strategies are instrumental in handling investments that determine the factors of production.

During the past 20 years, 24-hour banking and a wise investment policy by manufacturing and merchandizing firms have created a genuine and nearly *autonomous* world economy of money and credit. Such an environment has no national boundaries or impediments to money flows, knowledge flows, and information flows. Investment used to follow trade. Now trade follows investments. If these investments are not maintained, which essentially means upgraded, there will be a reduction in trade and surely no bettering in terms of market standing.

Just as important is the fact that the First World economy is becoming increasingly dependent on knowledge and information but less and less on materials. After the agricultural sector, the manufacturing sector shed its former labor-intensive characteristics. In the 1920s, 60 percent of the cost of the automobile represented raw materials and labor. In fact, back in the 1920s, direct labor stood at about one-third of the cost of a car—and that in spite of all the rationalization brought in by Henry Ford.

Today, well-managed auto companies have seen to it that direct labor in manufacturing has dropped well below 20 percent, and with robotics it is heading toward the 10 to 12 percent level. By the same token, well-managed companies in the auto industry consider the world to be their market and aim to export their produce well above the ratio of materials they are importing.

The automobile was the representative industrial product of the 1920s, but its dominance peaked in the 1950s and 1960s and started to decline in the 1970s. Correspondingly, the representative industrial product of the 1980s and 1990s is the microchip—and with microchips, materials represent only 2 percent of the finished product's cost.

All this change quite significantly identifies the dynamics of treasury functions and, quite importantly, where our primary interest should be. The currencies of the markets for *our* products should be hedged, and this is more important than hedging against the currencies of countries where we buy our raw materials—with the one major exception: oil.

CAN THE TRANSNATIONAL CORPORATION ACT AS ITS OWN MONEY CENTER BANK?

Managing growth is every bit as important as growth itself, or even more so. Therefore, some transnational companies have established their own finance business units to handle treasury-business related in a personalized way.

British Petroleum, for example, has an in-house investment bank: BP Finance, which handles its own foreign exchange trading. As of the end of 1990, BP Finance had issued $9 billion in commercial paper directly to investors and had also advised its parent company on two recent multibillion divestiture deals: BP's sale of its mineral operations to RTZ Corp. for $3.7 billion, and the sale of exploration licenses to Oryx Energy, for $1.3 billion. BP is not alone in the policy.

Big corporations that are direct users of the financial markets and their instruments are now highly sophisticated in tapping transnational resources: They have nearly the same kind of knowledge the investment banks have and are acting as their own money center banks.

What is it, in fact that a money center bank is doing? To answer this query let me start by pointing out that no patents are being granted for financial products. Hence whatever the wisest bank management is doing today, tomorrow it will be copied by other financial institutions.

The notion of a money center bank was developed by Citicorp, around twenty years ago. Unlike a traditional commercial bank, the money center does not loan money only on the basis of its clients' deposits or its shareholders' equity. Instead, it buys money from other banks, and in the Eurodollar or other markets. That way, it becomes like a financial broker—generally *not* dependent of its supply of depositors' funds but dependent on market liquidity and its own credit rating. Besides buying money in the worldwide financial market, the money center bank lends money not only to companies but also to governments and other banks. It is done on a transnational level, hence the notion of global risk.

Money is to a large measure a matter of belief. The word *credit* itself derives from the Latin *credere*, which means *to believe*. But money center banks do not just believe what they are told, they analyze the borrower's prospects using both algorithmic and heuristic tools.

In their drive to capture the world's financial market, however, many money center banks tend to forget about the analytics that should precede lending. Quality of the borrower is somehow pushed to the backburner. As a result in 1990:

- The major money center banks have had their credit rating downgraded.

- And as a result, they have begun to reduce their reliance on commercial paper.

By contrast, transnational companies with A-1 ratings from S&P and P-1 from Moody's (for instance, General Electric Capital, General Motors Acceptance, Ford Motor Credit, Sears Roebuck Acceptance, and American Express Credit) are very active in the transnational commercial paper market.

Despite the drop in demand for lower-rated issues, the growth of this market, overall, has not declined much because the appetite for top-rated paper remains strong. Companies with A-2 ratings from S&P and P-2 from Moody's account for only about 13 percent of the more than 1,000 firms that borrow in the commercial paper market. And companies in the lower investment grade levels, A-3 and P-3, account for only 2 percent of the market.

But the scare of speculative bubbles ensures the fact that well-managed financial business units and money center banks now look for longer-term guarantees. Apart from that, credit can be compared to a *single entry* bookkeeping that has only one way to go: down.

- If banks fail, sovereign countries default and businesses go bankrupt.

- The value of assets disintegrates and credits disappear.

Both manufacturing/merchandizing corporations and money center banks also tend to appreciate that, up to a point, financial markets can do anything they like. And they do so any time they choose, without particular constraint or great reservation. As a result of deregulation, risk can be compound. When a collapse comes, billions in capitalization disappear. For many banks these will be paper losses, often counterbalancing the paper profits they had done. For others, they will be real losses leading them to illiquidity or bankruptcy. Corporate treasurers who emulate money center bank behavior surely face similar risks. Therefore, those who are more careful limit the playing field to matters concerning the financial interests of the corporation. They do not venture into the wider market for speculative forays.

There is plenty of work to be done in-house. In the typical transnational corporation, only 30 percent of intercompany transactions relate to payments. Some 70 percent of transactions flowing around the cash manager regard:

- Ordering

- Invoicing

- Shipping and the like

Many corporations are now saying that they want to automate business data interchange, of which payments are a part. But the interchange is not going to come by revamping cash management. It requires a macro, top-down change. A business-wide electronic data interchange will involve *long transactions* and for that reason will most likely reshape the payment system. Treasury departments and banks are information conduits with multinational networks and on-line connection to both their suppliers and their customers.

DISCOUNTING FORESEEABLE MARKET TRENDS

Financial markets work on the margin, discounting policy changes by the different players—both at home and abroad. For instance, a change toward encouraging growth and employment disregarding inflation can translate into a significant alteration in the mood of financial markets:

- Higher yields will be required to prompt bond market investors to buy long-term financial assets because of their heightened concerns about inflation.

- Equity investors will tend to pay less for a future stream of earnings and dividends because they become less certain about its real value.

Concerns about inflation, economic uncertainty, and geopolitical instability tend to form a forex and investment mosaic, and the best that one can say, with certainty, is that the mosaic itself is highly unstable. For instance, after Iraq's invasion of Kuwait in August 1990, the foreign exchange trading volume rose significantly, mainly because of opportunities arising from more volatile exchange rates. The subsequent turmoil in forex, equities, and interest rate markets illustrates that market-makers cannot ignore politics any more than they can ignore economics. Such events help to remind prudent treasurers of the wisdom in:

- Considering longer–term market opportunities

- Extending risk management beyond foreign exchange to risk instruments and other derivatives

At the same time, as financial markets mature, investors require newer and more sophisticated products, including options and interest-rate swaps that are often used for hedging purposes.

Great attention must be paid to global liquidity conditions, where turmoil can be a clear warning that international equity markets are on the brink of another decline. Each successive wave of the liquidity squeeze triggers a crash on world equity markets. The first of the more recent crashes was October 1987. The second began in October 1989 and continued well into January 1990. Liquidity squeezes and volatility in the currency exchanges pose significant challenges for the treasurer who has to explore in a factual and documented manner whether currency-hedged foreign equities are better diversification vehicles than those unhedged.

Although it is impossible to predict beforehand whether currency hedging will increase or decrease the long-run return on a given portfolio, currency hedging has consistently reduced portfolio volatility—hence the wisdom of using currency-hedged securities as the base case in formulating an international investment strategy. Basic moves include the:

- Selection of multinational investments based on their intrinsic appeal, as a corrolary to the currency hedge.

- Decision on whether currency hedging is appropriate in view of trends and tendencies in financial markets.

- Evaluation of the wisdom of short-term currency deposits in the portfolio, in order to supplement capital investments in their current diversification.

Evidently, there are problems associated with currency hedging an equity portfolio, and the same is true of hedging business transactions. Hence, the treasurer must be always ready to evaluate the efficiency of hedges designed to solve problems.

It is wise also to extend risk management beyond foreign exchange and deposits to risk instruments and other derivatives. New opportunities almost constantly arise in the form of more sophisticated financial products: derivatives like options, futures, forward rate agreements, and interest rate swaps grow in importance.* Many treasurers, however, are not at home with such instruments. A study done in the Singapore foreign exchange market† in September 1990 indicated that exchange-traded foreign currency and interest rate options attracted very little attention at the treasurers' level. Only 10 percent of the respondents were involved in these products.

Hedging is, of course, no simple business. Whereas the diversification of currencies spreads risk, predicting their course is complex and often fruitless. There is very little if any correlation between a given currency and the real economy.

- The U.S. dollar started to appreciate in 1982 when the economy was in the tank.

- It peaked in 1985 when the economy was rising.

Political factors constitute the usual potent reason in foreign exchanges, whereas financial issues must be examined from a global perspective. Examine credit, also known as *credit inflation*, fuels stockmarket manias, spilling over into forex dealings and quite often extending into currency manipulation, which temporarily suppresses the impact of interest rates. The treasurer must also cope with the fact that sometimes complacency in market swings is widespread and against it he or she must be vigilant.

SOLUTIONS TO GLOBAL CUSTODY

Global custody is a combination of financial services designed to facilitate safekeeping, settlement, tax advising, and reporting for the investor. Such operations typically concern a fund's worldwide securities transactions.

---

*See also Chapter 6 on swaps, Chapter 11 on commodities and futures, and Chapter 12 on dealing in options.

†Singapore is today the fifth most important in the world; in 1990 the Asian time zone accounted for 37 percent of total forex turnover in a global sense.

Within the perspective of global custody come:

- Trade settlements, and therefore foreign exchange
- Cash management, including income collection
- Tax withholding and reclamation

Effective solutions facilitate corporate treasury actions through a multi-currency on-line reporting scheme, promoting proficient account management.

The task can be complex for housekeeping reasons, which demand first class information technology—and also on legal grounds. For instance, many foreign markets do not permit the transfer of ownership certificates beyond their borders, and there is always present the issue of taxation.

There exists no single correct or best process for evaluating and selecting a global custody procedure as well as a global custodian for the following reasons:

- Individual treasurers attribute differing levels of importance to varying product features.
- There is no general agreement on the most important service components and the custodial concept to each.*
- Different institutions offer diverse types of services, having defined in heterogeneous ways what the custodian procedure involves.

Many cognizant people, however, believe that the most important element is the way in which a global custodian balances all of the service components to provide a timely and accurate service. It should be consistent with predetermined client objectives; therefore, it should be handled in a dynamic sense.

Some banks believe that given the investments that have to be made in connection with global custody, as well as the level of competition, there is no reason to follow the global custody track as a different line of business. They choose to make it part of asset management. On the contrary, other financial institutions prefer to focus on global custody as a major thrust of their technological efforts:

- Doing database mining
- Extracting customers' data worldwide
- Handling and packaging the data

*The concept of financial responsibility is not the same in all countries.

- Sending data out via satellite or cable to the customers' own computers.

Realtime connection allows the client to do whatever is required (or desired) with the information being provided, for instance, feeding it directly into a person's accounting and portfolio management systems.

The competent execution of such activities suggests that clear goals have to be set. Management perspectives are not answered in the abstract. To plan global custody operations capably, it is necessary to:

- Gather information about the fund and its related investment objectives

- Engage in preliminary research and develop a list of requirements

- Obtain solid references to validate claims being made by banks

Written specifications of the goals to be reached establish the tone and focus of the search to be made for service providers. Therefore, they should be prepared with thought, offering an opportunity to clearly describe needed features.

A well-drawn list of specifications will elicit the finer technical points of providing a global custody service as well as identify the provider's organizational structure, custody experience, advanced technology, and philosophy of management. None of those issues should be overlooked, because they are representative of a bank's commitment to the custody business and of the support that could be provided for current and future client needs.

Small but significant details can help in demonstrating the commitment of the global custodian to the market. A high technology–based solution will go a long way toward reducing the dread that usually accompanies traditionally time-consuming and error-prone tasks. It will provide sophisticated managerial, accounting, and performance measurements associated with the clients' objectives.

Among client requirements are solutions that perform multicurrency accounting and track settlement throughout various countries. In at least one case, a major project was the selection of an international securities lending system.

Some financial institutions tune their global custody goals toward an income collection process in foreign markets, which is relatively straightforward:

- Funds are credited on the payable date in the markets where the financial institution operates.

- Exceptions are analyzed, including the custodian's average delay experienced between payable date and receipt in problem countries.

- Particularly prized is the ability to provide on-line, detailed reporting of income receivables.

Understanding a bank's history and the reasons for providing global custody services can unveil important clues as to its long-term commitment and senior-level support for the product. One of the critical areas is the extent to which the provision of global custody services is an important component of the financial institution's strategy.

Some banks place particular interest in finding a niche of value-added services. Others base their market strategy on professional advice. They are keen on going into their clients' offices, analyzing their operations, and helping them devise creative solutions.

From the viewpoint of an income earner, global custody fees come in a variety of packages. They may be based on the the account, its assets, income collection, execution of transaction, and reporting on receipt and delivery. They typically also include administrative expenses, telephone, telex, facsimile, and other reporting charges.

The more alert banks calculate their fees on the basis of the money they helped their client save or make. A good deal of that money comes from tax withholding and reclamation.

ADVISING ON TAXATION FOR THE TRANSNATIONAL CORPORATION

Throughout history the state's revenues have been limited by the amount of tax that it can levy, but the relation between revenues and taxes is not a straight line. Revenues are not necessarily growing in proportion to the level of taxation. If anything, revenues and taxes relate to each other through an inverted U curve.

If the amount of money collected through taxes exceeds a certain percentage of personal income, corporate income, or gross national product (GNP), a silent but most effective tax revolt begins: Tax evasion becomes a policy, while inflationary pressures build up in the economy.

Just prior to World War II, it was thought that a government could not take more than a quarter of the country's GNP through direct taxation without creating inflationary pressures. After WW II it was felt that the quota could be raised to between 35 and 40 percent, but wherever that hypothesis was tested, the result has been *stagflation*.

Stagflation is a process that combines inflation and stagnation in the most inopportune way; namely it

- Bends a company's profits beam
- Makes the citizenry poorer
- Reduces the government's intake
- Damages the economy as a whole

The effects of indirect high-taxation rates on companies and on citizenry are just as detrimental. They produce cynicism, reduce the will to be productive, and when coupled with inflation bring a shadow economy into being, which is a great detriment to the real one.

Most First World governments do recognize those negatives and try to do something about them by way of tax incentives. Typically these are applied selectively, in promoting industrialization in the more backward areas, or applied altogether in luring foreign companies into new investments or the extension of existing ones.

Governments have also concluded cross-country double taxation treaties which in their general lines are known to treasurers, but not necessarily in their details. For instance, sometimes higher rates of relief are granted in the case of substantial holdings or of a specific type of investment. This statement is valid both for companies and for private individuals. For example, there are exceptions to the 25 percent tax levied by France at source for persons residing in Switzerland.

To bring this avoidance of double taxation into better perspective, Table 4.1 identifies the rate of foreign taxes withheld at source in European countries and in North America for persons residing in Switzerland (as of March 1991). Notice, however, that mere numbers tell only part of the story. For example, Italy's 12.5 percent on interest applies only to corporate bonds issued after December 31, 1983 and government bonds issued after August 31, 1987. Otherwise the rates are from zero to 21.6 percent and for nonquoted private bonds issued beginning January 1, 1989 at 30 percent—with a corresponding relief at 17.5 percent.

Published tables do provide guidelines on the possibilities of relief according to double taxation treaties, but they are usually limited to the essential points. Since information pertaining to special cases is not included—and there are thousands of such cases—and the treasurer fails "to read between the lines" then the treasurer is not doing an excellent job.

However, some guidelines can be helpful. In general, as far as the application of a double taxation treaty is concerned, it is immaterial in which

Table 4.1 Foreign Taxes Withheld at Source for Persons Residing in Switzerland, by Countries with Double Taxation Treaty

	Dividend			Interest		
	Full Tax (%)	Relief (%)	Remaining (%)	Full Tax (%)	Relief (%)	Remaining (%)
Europe						
Austria	25	20	5	—	—	—
Belgium	25	10	15	25	15	10
Denmark	30	30	—	—	—	—
France	25	52.5	22.5	25	15	10
Germany	25	15	10	—	—	—
Ireland	—	18	20.8	28	28	—
Italy	32.4	17.4	15	12.5	—	—
Luxembourg	15	—	15	—	—	—
Netherlands	25	10	15	—	—	—
Norway	25	10	15	—	—	—
Spain	25	10	15	25	15	10
Sweden	30	25	5	—	—	—
United Kingdom	—	13.3	20	25	25	—
North America						
Canada	25	10	15	—	—	—
Mexico	0–40	—	0–40	21	—	—
United States	30	15	15	30	25	5

country the securities are deposited. On the other hand, an agreement may be applied between the country where the *creditor* or the recipient of the income resides and the country where the *debtor* resides (source country). Again, as a general rule, the total or partial tax relief takes the form of a refund or an exemption at source. Most importantly, for the general case, several countries see to it that interest on bonds issued internationally (Eurobonds) is not subject to withholding tax, but there can be exceptions.

GLOBAL CUSTODY AND TAXATION

The treasurer must appreciate that any country's system of taxation is fairly complex, some more complex than others. For instance, in Switzerland as a result of the country's federal structure, taxes are levied at the same time by three different authorities: the Federal Government, the confederated cantons, and the municipalities. Whereas the federated tax laws apply to the whole of Switzerland, those of the cantons and municipalities are only valid within their respective territories. This system ensures that both the nature and the burden of taxation in Switzerland vary a great deal from one place to another. This statement is true in regard to tax rates, as well as the method of taxation on net profits and capital, which differ considerably according to the firm's legal structure.

In respect to fiscal treatment, the three main types of companies are the operating company, holding company, and domiciliary company. An operating company is a corporation pursuing a commercial, industrial, manufacturing, or service activity.

The commercial profit and loss statement is typically used as the basis for determining the taxable net earnings. In the majority of the cantons, taxes paid can be deducted as an expense item with regard to the direct federal tax, and also to cantonal tax.

There are, however, special tax features in the case of investment firms and real estate companies. Investment firms are treated for tax purposes as having been formed as operating companies, but can also be handled as holding or domiciliary companies.

Interest on the funds with banks in Switzerland is subject to a 35 percent withholding tax. In the same way, withholding tax is applied to the debt interest of firms that are not real banks but still offer to accept interest-bearing funds from the public, or consistently accept them.

For tax purposes, real estate companies are corporations whose chief activity is the administration, utilization, and construction on their own land. Such companies must pay particular attention to the fact that their equity (capital and reserves) is not too small by comparison with assets, otherwise the excessive borrowings could be considered to be equity capital.

All types of companies may, of course, avail themselves of the tax relief according to the double taxation treaties concluded by Switzerland with other countries. This applies in particular to foreign taxes at source on dividends and interest, as shown in the preceding section.

The particularities of the tax law in one country must be multiplied by the number of countries in which a company operates, without forgetting that a certain synergy in tax laws makes the problems of optimization even more complex. It is therefore advisable to follow the lead of Japanese banks, which have been very keen in developing computer-based expert systems as advisors in legal and tax matters.*

*See also D. N. Chorafas and H. Steinmann, *Expert Systems in Banking*, London: Macmillan, 1991; New York: New York University Press, 1991.

Indeed, the best of services that global custodians can provide is to use high technology in assuring their clients of not only tax advice but also optimizations. Not many financial institutions have done the homework necessary to provide that service, or they are doing it manually in spite of the high investments they have made in networks and computers.

As global custodians who have the right preparation have learned, many of their client companies are eligible for partial or total exemption from withholding taxes on foreign income—even if they don't always know it. Therefore, the custodian should arrange to have all income received with the correct amount of withholding tax deducted, making reclamations of recoverable taxes in applicable jurisdictions.

The able organization of the tax evaluation and reclamation procedures should be carefully studied, and should become computer–assisted given the nuances of operating in countries with differing tax laws and tax exemption treaties.

This requires focused attention to ensure maximum efficiency. Procedures for filing and tracking reclaims on a country-by-country basis should be well established, with tax reclaims and receivables being an area of increasing importance.

5

Foreign Exchange Operations

Twenty years ago, forex was a mystique. People with some unique characteristics applied themselves to that job, eating lunch at their desks, being always on the telephone, and more often than not screaming. Today anybody can sign up for an on-line terminal with foreign exchange information, and the information provider feeds that terminal 24 hours a day.

From forex information scarcity we have moved into forex information abundance. Rates are available to anybody anywhere. Dealer data typically includes spots, forwards, and swaps.

The globalization of the financial markets provides a worldwide dealing system. Banks and the treasury departments of corporations set global limits and engage in exposure management. Many feature computer-based trading, and the most advanced organizations reduce vulnerability through expert systems. The forex information flow and associated growth in the number of transactions helped to develop some interesting characteristics:

1. It has created a new mindset. The evolution going on in foreign exchange trading is silent. Many people who should join it are fighting it and are engaged in a losing battle; if they do not change their culture, they will not be able to face the currency battles of the 1990s.

2. Trading has already generated an overflow of activity. To be handled in an efficient manner, dealing in forex requires intelligent networks, knowledge engineering, and *supercomputers*, which are necessary to digest volumes of forex data in realspace, to filter them,

screen them, present the relevant facts, and establish trading patterns.

3. Globality impacts on the need for greater speed, accuracy, and quality of information. Worldwide competition in the forex markets forces the need for actional information in a way that never existed before. Rapid change as well as globality is a result of market evolution and high technology, particularly of the telecommunications thrust. The world has become smaller but data overload has increased, and that calls for better solutions than those available so far.

4. The ability to handle the flow of data in a knowledgeable manner is the fundamental reason that expert systems are so important and help differentiate a bank in terms of added value. Advanced techniques in the production of foreign exchange information and its delivery are today possible. The critical ability is to process incoming data very rapidly, store what you need, get it when you need it—and do so at the end-user level without having to become an EDPier.

Knowledge and information are the critical variables. The customer acts on the information, *not* on the money. The customer needs to know exactly what happens in the market. The actual movement of the money is of lesser importance. What is truly important is to be able to make rational decisions by having the pattern of prices at hand.

THE FOREX MARKET

Billions of dollars pulsate every day through the currency channels. Trading among themselves by phone, a relatively small group collectively determines a currency's value *du jour*. No central exchange is involved in forex transactions; the market *is* the exchange.

One of the often overlooked characteristics of forex trading and its dealers is that they operate separately from the formal bureaucracy of the organization, with the shortest possible chain of command. They are the *new professional*, in the setting envisaged by Dr. Peter Drucker for the end of this century, when he compares the efficient organization structure of the 1990s to that of an orchestra. Transferring this comparison to foreign exchange operations: The conductor is the director of forex, and the orchestra members are the forex dealers.

Enriching quotations, trends, and statistics with their own educated guesses, traders instantly transmit their reactions to every twist of the U.S. trade deficit or political upheaval anywhere in the world—from New

York to Tokyo and London. Ultimately they help shape the interest rates not only on currencies but also on loans, influence the policies of central banks, and consolidate or upset decisions taken by treasury ministers.

Markets are all about personalities and psychology. Some people will do anything to gain an edge. Others are content to follow. Precisely because of the brains of their traders, some banks are market leaders, whereas others are two or three steps behind. The former usually make money, the latter are the losers.

As in any profession, there are deal makers and deal breakers. A deal maker tends to find difficult areas, gets them on the table, brings the parties together, and finds the common thread that allows the deal to be closed. In forex, this is done on-line with the voice signature being a handshake.

The more foreign exchange deals are done in realtime, the greater should be the sophistication of technological support. This means that workstations, networks, databases, supercomputers, expert systems, and visualization procedures work in synergy, as shown in Figure 5.1.

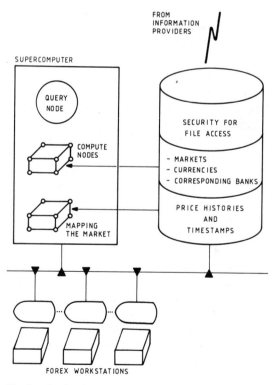

Figure 5.1 Technological support system for a foreign exchange trading desk.

Speed in number crunching and the development of patterns is not merely the best way to face the market challenges; it is the only way. Even small differences in currency exchange amount to large sums. In London alone an estimated $180 billion is traded in the average day. The amount of money traded in New York in forex deals is said to be 40 to 60 times greater than the turnover at the New York Stock Exchange.

For the last few years, exchange volume in the international monetary market is up about 20 percent per year. Volume in currency options and options on futures is up, at an even higher percentage. All of these have impact on international transfers, where statistics are impressive.

Citibank estimates that its transactions represent between 5 percent and 7 percent of the volume that goes through New York's CHIPS, and that represents 52,000 orders as an average and 80,000 as a maximum. The clearing house says that the average-value funds transfer is $3.2 million, meaning that CHIPS handles daily: 2.5 trillion dollars as an average, and 3.8 trillion dollars as a peak.

Recall that the yearly GNP of the American economy is $5.2 trillion, which means that, on average, half the GNP of the United States transits over the wires. Just imagine 240 million people working for half a year to generate one day's business in currencies.

Associated with these impressively large numbers is a great deal of risk. The $3.2 million per order may be a mean value, but not all orders are the same: Less than 1 percent of orders going through London's CHAPS represents 95 percent of value. Although not always appreciated, the risk of default is enormous. There is, every day and night, a *follow-the-sun overdraft* risk; default by one bank can snowball through the system. There are also, of course, profits that can be made.

Foreign exchange profits are good, though at times not very good. When there is lack, for instance, of dollar volatility against the Deutsche mark and yen, then the volume of trading goes down, with an evident consequence for forex profits. To compensate, dealers step up trading in second-tier currencies, such as the Australian dollar, and push into cross-rate trading. In cross-rate trading, banks sell one nondollar currency directly for another, instead of doing two separate deals through the intermediary of the dollar. As a result, they can offer better rates for their international corporate clients, who have to pay less in commissions—and banks bet on market share to support their bottom line.

In other words, it is not that easy to make money through one-way bets on a further rise or fall in the dollar, when most major currencies are nestled into narrow ranges. Instead, dealers take greater risks to earn the profits needed to cover the high costs of salaries and computerized trading rooms.

This is the reason that several years ago the president of the International Forex Association said that he was worried that stable markets might increase risk. As banks rely on foreign exchange profits, they might encourage dealers to make large bets on small rate movements.*

USING TECHNOLOGY TO IMPROVE PERFORMANCE

I have said that technology contributes toward forex dealing, and it is true all the way from the workstation and database of the trader to the intelligent network used by the information providers, who have entered the automation chores of forex trading. Reuters has developed a forex trade matching system that automatically buys and sells.

Banks and other financial institutions whose prices have so far been only a reference index—not a final offer—will commit themselves to firm quotes on this Reuters system, which keeps their identities secret. When the computer finds a match, it:

- Checks the credit rating of both parties

- Executes the transaction

- Notifies both parties

What will this do to forex trading? Speed of trading will be enhanced, and volume will go up. Most likely, we will see more activity in the market. Even minute changes in currency values can be used to make a profit or suffer a loss—depending on the technology the financial institution is using.

The message has not been lost on the topmost financial institutions, which since the mid-1980s have actively worked in bringing artificial intelligence into forex. One example, which has become popular in Japan and the United States, is the handling of unstructured telexes through expert systems subsequently channeling them into their electronic funds transfer (EFT) network.

Having acquired this experience, some banks have moved further. Citibank, for instance, extended this expert system application to handle Fedwire and CHIPS. Gaining insight from the telex expert system, Citibank rewrote it for CHIPS and Fedwire, where funds transfer traffic is high: about 20,000 financial transfers per day. The success of that expert system implementation, and the return on investment it provided, led to a policy: to build other parallel AI products according to in-house specifications.

Other financial institutions have developed expert systems that act as the trader's assistant, identifying business opportunities. An example will

*International Herald Tribune, May 30, 1988.

be shown in the next section. They are based on the following two-part principle.

- Establishing a goal, a floor, or a ceiling is a negotiating concept that works.

- Subsequently, the AI construct helps the dealer evaluate at an early time market trends and trading windows.

The executive vice president of a leading financial institution suggested that the ability to develop sophisticated AI constructs for trading separates the serious player from the phonies, who want to take part in the forex market but cannot bring themselves to formalize and structure their rules or their methodologies. To exemplify this point, Figure 5.2 shows a block diagram of a knowledge engineering solution to forex trading. The rules contained in each box constitute the second level of detail.

An approach like the one briefly outlined is particularly necessary in terms of new financial services and trading strategies. In both cases, product development activity should go hand-in-hand with the technolog-

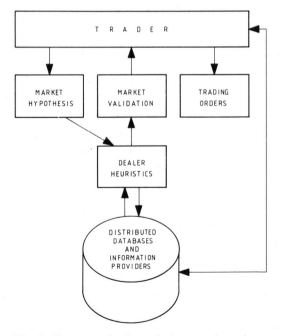

Figure 5.2 Block diagram of a knowledge engineering system for foreign exchange trading.

ical infrastructure; such a policy is being practiced in the manufacturing industry and is becoming known as *concurrent engineering.*

Most manufacturers used to develop products in a series of steps: starting with design and engineering; then contracting for various materials, parts, and services; and then finally going to production. Each step was largely independent of the others, and changes made at any post-design stage, especially after production started, caused major traumas. The late fixes would ripple back through a project, causing everything that had gone before to be reworked. That would delay the product and push its costs through the ceiling. As a result the late 1980s saw the development of a new method: doing everything concurrently. This, however, requires clear concepts regarding *products* and *processes* as well as the ability to look at them in an integrative manner step-by-step.

The concurrent engineering concept is applicable in banking, and it rests on the premise that when a project starts up the specialists involved in product design, software development, and hardware purchasing, all work side by side, comparing notes constantly. This makes for more synergy, curbs late fixes, and permits getting products out on time.

Through concurrent engineering, the total cycle time from conception to production can be vastly trimmed with obvious benefits for competitiveness. An example can be taken from forex trading where the automation of part of the trading activity made feasible through the new infrastructure is expected to relieve some of the constraints on current price information listed here:

1. *Shown rates* (Reuters, Telerate, Quotron, Telekurs) are *not* dealing rates.

2. Rates given by different banks through provider networks are only *informational*, not transactional.

3. *Effective rates* are nearest to dealing rates; but by the time they are displayed, the effective rates themselves are past.

4. *Spot rates* are close to dealing rates, but they too are past and are not *true* dealing rates.

One of the problems so far has been that nobody can provide through manual input the fast change of rates as they happen. This is being solved through the automation of trading activities, and as a result competitiveness gets concentrated at a higher level: the need to map the market into the machine—as will be seen in the following section.

Let me underline once more that simulation of and experimentation on business opportunities that exist in the global forex market, as well as trading automation, require artificial intelligence constructs. This means going beyond the "assistant" trader software that was implemented in the mid- to late 1980s by leading financial institutions.

TECHNOLOGICAL ASSISTANCE TO THE FOREX TRADER

The personality and culture of the dealers can have a great impact on how well technology works for them. At the same time, since each forex dealer has a unique personal style, we must be very careful in providing for flexibility so that he or she will feel comfortable with the system and its mechanics.

This is a long way from solutions of the past, though during the last 20 years computer screens have replaced trading floors in markets throughout the world.

- Operating since 1971, the NASDAQ electronic quotation system has been serving the over-the-counter market.

- Trading on London's International Stock Exchange has been virtually all electronic since 1986.

- Exchanges in Toronto and Tokyo today use automated trading for the less active stocks.

- The Vancouver Stock Exchange, too, replaced its floor with computers in January 1990.

These are system solutions aiming to serve both the local and the global markets. But the use of AI in trading goes beyond these approaches and beyond the one at the Chicago Mercantile Exchange: Globex, an automated international futures and options trading system designed by Reuters, is now linked to overseas exchanges with the goal of operating after the Merc's regular pit hours.*

The growing internationalization of trading has greatly propelled the ongoing automation activity. Whereas labor-intensive floor markets need to quit at night, electronic markets never sleep and are increasingly linking up with exchanges in many different time zones. Subjected to an instantaneous flow of trades, financial institutions are taking steps so as not to be left behind.

As computers and communications integrate, they become a valuable tool for the trader, supporting greater efficiency and mental

---

*This system is expected to start operating soon. For technical details see: D. N. Chorafas, *Using Technology in Treasury and Forex Operations*, New York: Wiley, in press.

productivity—a vital contribution in foreign exchange and in international commodity trading. With the systems at the dealer's disposal becoming increasingly more sophisticated, the profile of the dealer's profession itself changes.

One of the most sensitive areas in the development and implementation of new technology is *arbitrage*. It is also an important part of forex dealing. Earnings may be large, but risks are considerable and the market has to be watched carefully:

- Classically, arbitrage took place by telephone, telex, or through brokers.

- Now the bank's own network and attached intelligent workstations take charge.

Enriched with expert systems, the new wave in automation ensuring a global reach, provides more detail, integrates different financial information providers into one database, and makes feasible on-line call of trading limits for all clients. And there are plenty of challenges. For some years, the compensating effect has been calculated overnight; now the topmost banks do so in realtime; tomorrow it will be in realspace.

As explained earlier, a competitive advantage with realspace is the ability to review all transactions, both current and past, which are open (futures) no matter where they have taken place in the network of our financial institution, we can:

- Call up old, closed transactions in full detail and as a transaction

- Show the arbitrage trader his or her positions interactively including assumed risk

- Provide the dealers with immediate compensation as well as stimulation

New needs are developing every day. About every three years major banks and treasury departments must update their technologies, because they will have profitted as much as is possible—from cost reduction to on-line support and market competitiveness.

With every successive release, the applications that we are running must be significantly improved. Providing our traders as well as our clients with effective solutions implies a constant commitment. For example, today we need:

- Global networks able not only to interconnect operations but also reach a growing number of distributed databases and filter their contents

- An increasing use of artificial intelligence constructs and simulators to unearth business opportunities

- A fuzzy query system to help the dealer who wants to see the position and limits of a client but does not remember all of the codes

Automation in the dealing room must do away with the need to search for the account number, write it on paper, change the menu, and so on. Graphical presentation and exception reporting are a "must" and are still not enough. Full *multimedia integration* has become a competitive advantage and the same is true of *interactive visualization.*

Foreign exchange operations is one of the domains where interactive computational finance has to be successfully applied. In my book *Using High Technology in Forex and Treasury Operations* I discuss the *forex room* as well as supercomputers and mathematics applied in foreign exchange. A management-oriented look at the use of high technology is necessary, however, to make the point that its lack puts operations in a competitive disadvantage.

Not only is the efficient use of technology indispensable, we should also be designing a fine-grain forex support environment. In the course of working meetings with top bankers, repeated reference has been made to three issues:

- Risk monitoring

- Exposure monitoring

- Compliance control

Such services are to be achieved through a value-added layer to the forex system that goes beyond limits implementation. Such solution should take advantage of the impressive capabilities provided by supercomputers and AI. To obtain results we should exploit both the very high speed of the new generation computer technology and the more agile software structure of expert systems.

When projecting advanced technological solutions, we must carefully avoid the constraints that characterized computer implementation so far. For instance, only problems that are highly regular in nature and of a basically serial structure have been effectively handled through current DP. All other problems—particularly those data-driven—have been approached in a half-baked manner so far. Now parallel computation allows their efficient handling.

The data-driven environment that characterizes forex dealing can be seen as a graph consisting of operators interconnected through edges. Values are propagated along the edges in the form of messages. This

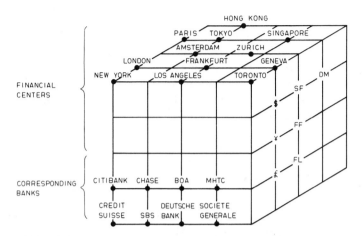

Figure 5.3 A hypercube distribution of financial centers. Each center treats in realtime all currencies handled by any other center.

specific structure is shown in Figure 5.3, which helps demonstrate how simple the solution can be on a *hypercube*-type computer.*

The example that I have taken is that of a 3-dimensional distribution of financial centers. It accounts for the fact that a forex operator works with three main reference factors:

1. Corresponding banks

2. Currencies

3. Financial centers where the operation takes place

In a graphical sense, each reference factor can be mapped onto a distinct physical processing element of the hypercube. When this is done, a high degree of parallelism is achieved. We will return to this issue later to explain the benefits that can be derived from the implementation of the suggested solution.

CURRENCY FORECASTING AND PORTFOLIO MANAGEMENT

The size of the foreign exchange and securities markets, their dynamic behavior, and pace of growth, give a good indication of future perspectives

---

*See also D. N. Chorafas and H. Steinmann, *Supercomputers*, New York: McGraw-Hill, 1990.

in treasury operations. They also lend attention to the nature of trading that will characterize the 1990s.

We concluded that treasury, forex, and securities have common elements. They also have some significant differences. Although the securities markets are sporadically in liquidity crisis, the forex markets are among the most liquid in the world. We have spoken about estimates of what daily trading represents in London.

- Central bank estimates recently put daily forex turnover on the London, New York, and Tokyo foreign exchange markets as approaching US$1 trillion, in a skew distribution in a $500 billion to $1.2 trillion range.*

- Trading in other centers, such as Frankfurt, Paris, Milan, Amsterdam, Sydney, Singapore, and Hong Kong, takes the total volume significantly higher.

- Turnover is steadily increasing. It has apparently doubled within the last five years (1986–1990).

Which product helps this business become so dynamic? Banks see swaps, options, and hedging strategies—rather than using money as a raw material—as the services that corporations will buy from them in the 1990s. They are betting on competing currencies, interest rates, futures, options, and swaps.

Key to unlocking the potential of the forex market is an in-depth knowledge of the way its mechanics work, with the right approach taken to capitalize on such knowledge and turn it into a marketable commodity:

1. *Good management* is at a premium because currency markets are huge and complex.

2. *Interest rates* for First World currencies fluctuate as a result of both market demand and central bank policies.

3. *Volatility* (see also Chapter 3) is a major characteristic of forex markets, which are often dominated by uncertainty.

4. Whereas all major transactions are conducted in a dozen currencies, *currency policy* as such is often missing or is seen as no more than the containment of risk.

5. *Currency exposure* can be both a missing risk and a profit opportunity; hopefully a highly profitable one if we are able to do the right forecasting.

---

*The $2.5 to $3.8 trillion estimate given earlier in this chapter for CHIPS represents *all* money transfers, not only forex.

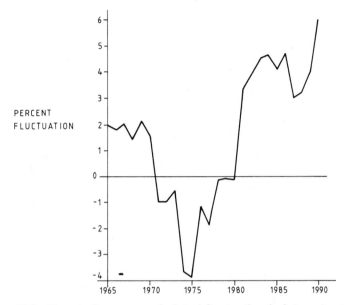

Figure 5.4 Twenty-five years of global fluctuation in interest rates, adjusted for inflation.

Good management of the foreign exchange market requires unique currency expertise, realspace information for currency trading, and a good methodological approach. As discussed earlier, technology is an able assistant. We should use networks, supercomputers, heuristics, and algorithms for arbitrage as well as for hedging. "Forex is currency trading and, as such, it is not too different from grain trading," says Craig Atkinson of Manufacturers Hanover Trust.

Figure 5.4 shows the fluctuation in *interest rates* over two and one-half decades. The statistics have been computed by Morgan Stanley and are based on fluctuation in the First World on the basis of short-term rates minus year-ago change in the consumer index. Six countries have been included: America, Japan, West Germany, France, Britain, and Canada, weighted by their gross national product.

Since the First World's capital markets are highly integrated, pressures in one market are rather quickly be felt in another. But in some cases, a spike in real rates is seen as a reflection of country-specific risk. For instance, in early 1990 the West German LBO for East Germany*

---

*Thinking by analogy, West Germany made a leveraged buy-out (LBO) for East Germany with billions of D-marks paid to the Soviet Union for liquidating control over its former satellite, East Germany.

ignited investors' fear that monetary and economic unification of the two Germanies would fan inflation there. As a result market rates shot up to 9 percent, some 5 percentage points above the current inflation rate in West Germany.

In other words, investors recognized the inflation threat to the German economy and made their returns higher to compensate for the risks they were assuming there. In the longer run, a flurry of inflation fears is abating; in the short run, however, it is obscuring the stronger forces of supply and demand that ultimately determine the direction of real rates. The imbalance created provides an opportunity for alert traders, if they are equipped to recognize it when it develops.

The *volatility* of currencies was highlighted in the 1980s and spurred the market in two ways. First, the treasurers of multinational corporations—or simply export-oriented firms—had to pay as much attention to guessing the exchange rate as to estimating cash flows. Second, the increased profitability of industrial companies led them to treat their cash as potential sources of profit.

If one reasonably safe forecast can be done, it is that volatility is a continuing feature of the currency markets for the foreseeable future. Banks, as well as manufacturing and trading companies that are well-prepared to deal with it, have an increasingly significant competitive advantage in the market.

The breakdown of the Bretton Woods agreement of fixed exchanges, coupled with the deregulation of financial markets, inflation, deflation, and oil crises led to increased volatility of exchange rates. Not only did those affect currencies, but also the environment of fixed-income securities, where private and corporate investors, insurance, and pension fund managers turn for the safer part of their investments, became as volatile as the stockmarket. This happened particularly after October 1979 when the Federal Reserve adopted a monetarist approach and a policy allowing wider moves in short-term interest rates.

The prospect of gains from the skillful management of volatility in the foreign exchange markets is attracting both investors and speculators. It brings both of them quite naturally toward institutions whose track records lie in anticipating and exploiting volatility—and this means institutions that have the best intellects, the right methodology, and high technology.

AN ENVIRONMENT FOR PROFIT

By the end of the 1980s the financial markets provided an excellent environment for skilled traders to make money. The boost came from currency fluctuations. Foreign exchange market turnover drops if the market is either too stable or too volatile; by contrast, a reasonable amount of volatility in the foreign exchange markets:

- Enables banks who know how to respond to market stimulus, to make profits on their own positions

- Provides an incentive for corporate customers and investors to use the market to hedge against potential currency losses

As many treasurers have found to their cost, currency swings can turn a successful year in overseas manufacturing and trading into disastrous financial results. But *note well* that as contrasted to commissions for trading, forex profits can be viewed as part of a zero-sum game. What one trading bank or corporate treasurer makes in terms of its positions, another one loses. This game may be getting bigger, adding new players all the time, but its zero-sum characteristic does not change.

Competition is multifaceted. An increasing number of big corporations are running their own foreign exchange departments. Securities firms, too, are moving into the forex market both on spot and on futures, underlining the need to properly support the complex system of their exposure.

- Increased competition ensures that the profit margin becomes smaller unless one truly masters the game.

- Global interactions make evident the requirements for worldwide control and consolidation.

- Sophisticated traders and customers require on-line access to all markets in the world as well as experimentation tools.

- Breakthroughs in computers, communications, and artificial intelligence help provide the leaders with global opportunities.

One of the common elements between securities and forex is that an increased use of advanced analytical techniques has been necessary to manage capably currency portfolios. Developments in computing technology facilitated the validation of market models, making them an indispensable tool in several domains of financial operations, where speed, agility, and the ability to experiment can make the difference between profits and losses. But at the same time, exchange rates forecasting, trading mentalities, and portfolio management skills can be very different. There is no guarantee that having one implies the other.

The forecaster's models aim at making investment grade decisions in forex, based on a multiplicity of information sources and client priorities defined by treasurers, whereas fees for successful trading are usually performance-related rather than fixed. Active currency management comes in a variety of forms, including public currency funds, discretionary management of credit lines, deposits, and risk-exposure administration.

Forecasting, of course, has its risks. Financial models work up to a point. The rest is politics. Prime Minister Brian Mulroney sent the Canadian dollar tumbling in international markets by predicting that the country's high interest rates were on their way down. This is not something a mathematical simulator will indicate in advance.

By contrast, simulators and heuristics can be of help in other cases such as assisting the projection of long-term interest rate movements in the world's major markets capitalizing on large databases. A similar point can be made of inflation. Long-term awareness is important as movements in interest rates and inflation spread turbulence both in the currencies and the securities markets while investors rush to the safety of cash or gold.

Of major concern to investors are the reasons for the rates rising and falling and for the potential instability that changes can trigger in asset prices. Uneasiness is fed by recollections that worldwide tightening of interest rates sets the stage for the collapse in stock prices and that in the late 1970s/early 1980s high interest rates in America made the dollar appreciate in value well beyond its historical pattern, following the Smithsonian agreement of the early 1970s.

In spite of the uncertainties which it involves, forecasting is one of the pillars of economic science. But to be able to forecast, we need metrics and reference values. In the fixed income market, for instance, the traditional measure of market risk is *interest rate risk*. This is risk caused by movements of interest rates on high-grade bullet bonds (without provision for early redemption). When interest rates rise marginally, the bond's price drops in function of its duration, thus affecting the yield-price pattern.

Another measure is bond cash flows and security attributes, which determine sensitivity to price movements as well as the dependability of the capital—adding up to the risk factor embedded in a portfolio. Such references are important in the context of a *currencies portolio* because there exists today much more background in the management of securities than in forex investments.

A different way of making this statement is that as the management of foreign exchange holdings matures wise players learn as best as they can from portfolio management, as practiced in the securities business, by exploring the parallels that exist and transferring the expertise into forex. This is in the background of Figure 5.5, which provides a strategic approach to portfolio management, albeit based on experience in the securities sector. Emulating this approach can be of great assistance in setting up a methodology for the successful management of a currency portfolio.

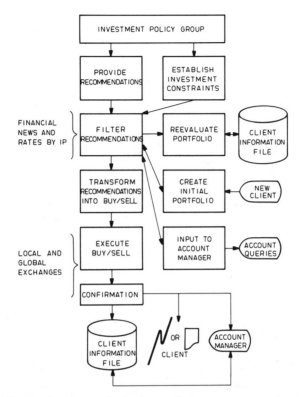

Figure 5.5 Design for a strategic portfolio management system.

Treasurers who care to learn the foreign exchange markets and to capitalize on its possibilities find themselves in a strategic position. The same is true of banks, institutional investors, trust managers, and high net worth individuals. Currency management is the response to changing times and the growing appreciation of currency risk.

The message is that not only financial institutions but also industrial companies must move up the currency learning curve. And there are growing portfolios in forex. Some corporate treasurers see the currency market as an investment opportunity that can be best approached through cross-trading in selected currencies, combined with the use of forward futures contracts to construct portfolios of short and long positions.

There are reasons to believe that *forex portfolio management* will grow significantly during the 1990s, becoming an essential resource in global diversification. Asset managers whose approach has traditionally been equity- and bond-based are getting a growing interest in it. Currency must now be regarded as an asset class and investment vehicle in its own right.

6

Swaps, Hedging, Bond Dealing, and Currency Management

When we deal in foreign exchange, as all multinational companies and many nationals must do, we have gains and losses. They become apparent when we value investments in local currencies. Sometimes, however, treasurers concentrate on local stock market performance, forgetting that for consolidation purposes foreign investment has to be converted to home country currency.

Balancing investment risk versus currency risk is one type of hedging, and one way of doing so is with *swaps*. A major phenomenon of the 1980s was the spectacular growth of interest rate and longer-term currency swaps. Directly or indirectly, they have exercised considerable influence over the volume and composition of funds raised in the international capital markets, though their aggregate size has for a long time been a matter of guesswork.

As a verb, *swap*, or swop, means to exchange, to barter, but also to strike, to move quickly, or to cut. All these meanings are applicable when we talk of swapping in foreign currency. The trader makes an exchange and must move fast to cut a deal. Often, it is a split-second opportunity.

But in a practical, down-to-earth sense, swaps and other money market instruments enable financial institutions to manage their assets and liabilities in a flexible manner. Through asset swaps investors separate their credit risks from other risks, while debtors flock to the swap market to hedge their payment obligations.

For the first time, in 1989, the Bank for International Settlements (BIS) published a study based on data collected over two years from the International Swap Dealers Association. This is an organization that brings under one umbrella virtually all major financial institutions active in swaps. According to BIS, the total swap market worldwide has accelerated: In a decade, it went from virtually nothing to about US$1.58 trillion at the end of 1988. Such a figure amounts to 45 percent of the total outstanding bank credit and bond financing of US$3.5 trillion.

During the 1980s and the beginning of this decade, the amazing growth of the swaps market helped to change the role and structure of other financial sectors. In markets where swaps have often been linked to new issues, borrowers were able to exploit a comparative advantage in different maturities and currencies.

Although such opportunities have stimulated the expansion of securities markets in a number of currencies, interest rate swaps have contributed to the demise of the market for longer-term floating rate notes. This is particularly true of the form in which they were most commonly used in the international bond markets prior to the mid-1980s. Today, in a number of cases, banks have a swap book whose value approaches that of their balance sheet. The more astute have been able to separate their funding from their interest rate risks.

At the same time, because of swaps, financial markets are being linked more tightly than before, while the distinction between domestic and international markets is eroded. The swaps phenomenon, however, did not come out of the blue sky. It has been the result of deregulation and globalization sweeping the First World's financial markets.

THE ESSENCE OF SWAPS TRANSACTIONS

As shown in Chapters 4 and 5, it is not always possible to determine the maturity of a forward transaction at the time the deal is done. But if we decide on a forward transaction with a fixed maturity date for hedging purposes, then a foreign exchange swap offers the opportunity to change the maturity to the desired date—while remaining covered against foreign risk.

A swap transaction in forex usually takes either of two forms. One is a combination of a *spot* and a *forward* transaction, according to the algorithm:

- *Spot* purchase + *forward* sale
- *Spot* sale + *forward* purchase

As an alternative, it may be structured in the form of two transactions that are both forward but have different terms:

- *Forward* purchase + *forward* sale
- *Forward* sale + *forward* purchase

It is important that the spot purchase and forward sale are concluded at the same time. If they are not, it is impossible to hedge the foreign exchange risk.

Both algorithms, spot + forward and forward + forward are examples of *long transactions*, which increasingly characterize sophisticated dealing by financial institutions and treasury operations. Long transactions:

- Demand the best of our knowledge in both information technology and in dealing terms

- Span over time and/or different places

- Can be multifunctional as well as have a variable length

Forward transactions, for example, can be shortened or lengthened by means of a swap. They are shortened when they are advanced and lengthened when they are renewed. In the first case, the original due date is changed to an earlier date; in the second, it is extended to a later date. Since a swap transaction of this kind may involve a combination of spot and forward, the calculation of swap income and swap costs is based on computing forward discounts and premiums. Swap costs represent the interest rate differential in the markets between currencies involved for the swap period.

The exact determination of the foreign exchange spot rate is of little importance provided that it is roughly in line with the prevailing spot rate. *Hedging costs* may, however, be incurred, for instance, in obtaining a currency with a higher interest rate at a later date than originally expected, whereas the determination of the forex spot rate will in every case have an impact on cash flow.

Of the total swap volume in the financial markets, the more popular interest rate swaps are of U.S. dollars, and they account for about 72 percent. The balance represents interest rate swaps in all other currencies. In terms of statistics, interest rate swaps dwarf pure currency swaps by a ratio of nearly 3 to 1 (Figure 6.1). Within this perspective, currency swaps between American dollars and another currency account for roughly 84 percent, the balance representing swaps between any two other currencies.

In terms of importance, in interest rate swaps, the U.S. dollar is followed by the yen, the Deutsche mark, and sterling. In other words, the U.S. dollar dominates the swap business mainly due to its pivotal role in international trade. Other factors are the depth of the American fi-

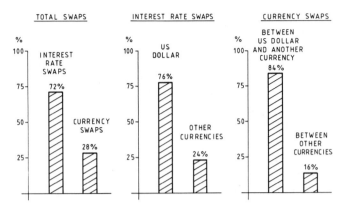

Figure 6.1   Relative importance of various types of swap
instruments.

nancial markets, and the great variety of dollar instruments available for currency swaps.

Next to the dollar, in terms of popularity, is the yen; this is attributed to the uses made of the swap market by Japanese commercial banks as an instrument for managing assets and liabilities. By contrast, business done by nonfinancial corporations and European governments is more important in the Deutsche mark.

In terms of currency swaps, U.S. dollar contracts are mainly swapped with yen, Swiss franc, and Australian dollar contracts. Both fixed- and floating-rate instruments are used. Non-U.S. dollar swaps mainly involve fixed rate instruments.

The use of swaps instruments is not limited to currencies. Practically all commodities can be handled by means of the two algorithms shown at the beginning of this section:

- Spot + forward
- Forward + forward

A good example on this fact is commodity trading at Chicago's Board of Trade (CBOT) and the Merc. Over the past 20 years, Chicago's two major futures exchanges have launched dozens of new futures contracts, many of which have not been a success. Those that stumbled were unable to attract participation by the big institutions dominating whatever commodity or financial instrument is covered by the futures.

Hedging on interest rates (see also Chapters 11 and 12) reflects the fact that corporations and government agencies make huge interest payments, and they can be hurt badly if interest rates rise. So they enter into swaps, with which they attempt to trade their exposure to floating interest rates for a fixed rate, or vice versa.

If a bank or a securities firm does not have another party ready to take the opposite side of the swap, it accommodates its corporate or government client by entering into the swap agreement itself. This, however, exposes the bank or securities firm to the risk of interest rates moving the wrong way. Financial institutions therefore like to hedge risks elsewhere, usually by making an offsetting interest rate swap with another bank. However, the hedge is only as good as the financial health of both parties involved in the transaction. If one party defaults, the bank that arranged the swap loses its protection from interest rate risk. By hedging with the Board of Trade's new contracts, a bank essentially passes along its exposure to risk takers in the futures market, where the transaction is backed by the exchange.

There is also the possibility of turning the futures swaps market into a new financial instrument. Banks can broker them to their customers or use them in their own risk-management program.

THE USE OF SWAPS INSTRUMENTS

The bad news is that swaps can be expensive instruments for trading. Managing a swaps book needs a heavy investment in computer systems and in advanced software, as well as the ability to take calculated risks. A major danger is that one of the counterparties should default leaving *our* side exposed.

Banks and treasury departments are engaging in different types of swaps. Some of them are new financial products. For instance, yen-yen swaps were born in 1986, after the Japanese Ministry of Finance started to allow Euroyen bond issues, a source of much of the debt swapped in Tokyo.

Not all swaps trades flourish immediately. In the yen-yen deals, the market took off a year later (1987), growing from nothing to become at its peak, in October 1987, the world's second biggest swap market after that for dollars.

Every swap instrument has its characteristics. *Yen-yen* swaps, for instance, are interest rate swaps: Two parties agree to exchange interest payments on each other's yen debt. This allows each to obtain the sort of loans they want, more cheaply than they could themselves, or to engage in loans they are otherwise prevented from raising because of government regulation. For instance, companies might want to turn floating-rate short-term debt into fixed-rate long-term debt.

Japan's national commercial banks, which are restricted to raising and borrowing funds of no more than three years' maturity, find swaps a useful way to let them make long-term fixed-rate loans. The wholesale trust and long-term credit banks, which are supposed to have a monopoly of long-term funding and lending, are doing the reverse by using swaps to get into the short-term market.

Under BIS rules on capital adequacy, currency swaps are considered to be far more risky than interest-rate swaps. Hence, they require more capital reserved against them. That, however, offers the better capitalized financial institutions a niche in combined currency and interest-rate swaps.

As I often say throughout this book, risk and opportunity come together. It is not a matter of being for or against the swaps instruments as they unfold. Rather, the challenge is how to identify opportunity somewhat ahead of the competitors, as well as to properly measure risk. Opportunity can be identified through the analysis of a swaps instrument in its fundamentals. We must be able to look at transactions involving different currencies stretching out over a variety of time periods.

Expert systems must show us how profitable (or unprofitable) each swap may be over its alternative, taken as a basic reference. Visualization routines should sum information to demonstrate net profit (including opportunity costs) of the whole operation.

The trader may want to see if it would be profitable to close a swap, calling not just information but patterns out of computer memory, as well as examining current prices and conditions as identified by information providers. The trader may also wish to add yields of, say, bonds in a foreign currency and instantly see whether the deal makes or loses money.

Swaps will increasingly involve both foreign currencies and equity, hence the need for AI-enriched programs like an *Expert Swap Trader*, designed for use by duration-sensitive fixed-income portfolio managers and dealers. The expert system helps optimize different buy and sell decisions; supercomputers further assist optimization faster than competitors.

Working in a multicurrency environment, an AI construct is able to instantaneously calculate prices, then estimate profits. It can do so for corporate, municipal bonds, or treasury bills. Accepting different currencies, prevailing prices, maturity and settlement dates, prepayment characteristics, and stated yield, it could calculate true yield and show volatility.

The sense of experimentation on the profitability of financial instruments inolves the trader being able to test different hypotheses by changing some of the variables. For instance:

- Specifying additional details that might affect the price, such as the call date.

- Analyzing bonds whose coupon dates are not scheduled in line with their maturity date.

- Entering tax rates on both income and capital gains, in case the trader wants to look at after-tax yields.

Suppose the dealer has to decide whether to sell a million dollars worth of a ten-year, 10 percent bond. The dealer may want to use the proceeds to buy a five-year zero coupon bond but not want to change the portfolio's duration. The system must instantly:

1. Tell how much of the zero coupon bond its user has to buy

2. Permit experimentation on how to keep either the market values or the durations of buys and sells equal

3. Show what effect the trade will have on average yield

The above calculations should be done very rapidly, in a completely integrated sequence allowing the determination of buy and sell amounts, and automatically handling trading information and bringing it into swap analysis. The programs should be networked running locally on the trader's workstation and number crunching data downloaded from databases on a supercomputer.

Applying the principle of interactive computational finance, these AI-enriched programs should work interactively with the routines designed for the investment manager. Figure 6.2 presents the highlights of such an integrated universe of operations.

Expert systems programs should be available for *dynamic value matching*, computing minimum cost and maximum return portfolios from a universe of currencies as well as bonds. The programs should:

- Match the current market value of the specified streams of cash flows (liabilities)

- Reflect the change in market value for all interest rate changes

For experimentation reasons, an expert system module should eliminate interest rate risk and perform dealer-specified operations not addressed by traditional duration matching or by duration and convexity matching. It should also optimize cash flow–matched bond portfolios under different currency perspectives.

On-line facilities are necessary to check and update forex limit utilization and position, amend instructions, and so on. Support functions for interactive inquiry and reporting must be state of the art—and this

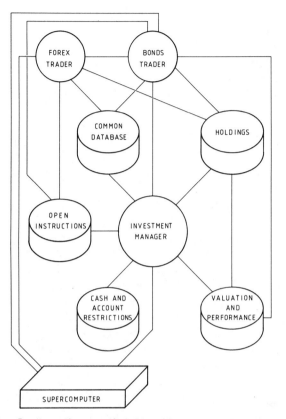

Figure 6.2 Outline of an artificial-intelligence enriched system for swap analysis.

means particular emphasis in the design of human windows (agile and user-friendly human–machine interfaces).

Valuable support requires developing the proper infrastructure with the right technology. The ability to steadily improve *our* system is essential to success as the financial markets evolve, competition stiffens, and the clients become more demanding.

HOW SECURE IS FOREIGN EXCHANGE HEDGING?

Looking to the future, BIS believes that the swap market will continue to perform a useful and growing function. This market is driven by differences in credit risk evaluations as well as arbitrage opportunities arising from tax and other regulations. An underlying determinant of swap

activity has been the desire of borrowers and investors to structure their cash flows and hedge on credit risks.

Currency hedging is an integral part of a hedging strategy and is intended to provide for diversification across foreign markets. Well-managed currency hedging can be a good way to face a currency-specific risk. Some people think of it as a tool for market-specific risk, which is true up to a point.

As we diversify into foreign markets we assume exchange rate risk; it is therefore only natural to hedge it. Today, hedging currency risk is a hot topic in equity management because of the volatility of the main currencies: dollar, yen, pound, mark, Swiss franc. This will continue being so through the 1990s.

Currency hedging may introduce complexity into the solutions that traders and investors are seeking. If an American investor is holding British securities, he or she bears exchange rate risk. A British investor holding U.S. securities also bears exchange rate risk. But if they contract forward with each other—the American investor agreeing to sell sterling buying dollars while the British investor agreeing to do the opposite—they can eliminate their exchange rate risk. Hence, exchange rate risk is not systematic, but it is present.

On principle, complex hedging problems cannot be solved with a single instrument. Therefore, solutions are sought through a combination of instruments. A good hedging transaction requires:

- The understanding of the different hedging instruments

- The trader's, borrower's, or investor's ability and readiness to assume risk

- Their learned personal opinion on future interest rate and foreign exchange developments

One of the strategies being followed is so-called *basket hedging*, which rests, as its name implies, on a basket of three or four major currencies. A basket must be properly selected, because international portfolios can often have a range of currency exposures: Currencies are held in proportions to minimize the tracking error of the basket with respect to the portfolio's overall currency exposure. Mathematically, basket hedging is an application of quadratic optimization.

Another strategy is *cross-hedging*, which amounts to active currency management. The goal is to exploit large correlations, for instance, among member currencies of the European Monetary System's Exchange Rate Mechanism (for EMS and ERM, see Chapter 8). Positions are typically taken that create a net exposure to the cross exchange rate between two

foreign currencies, neither of which is the home currency. This is not a perfect hedge, but well managed it sees to it that much of the exchange rate risk can be removed while an attractive yield spread might also be realized.

Mathematical approaches and high-performance computing can make significant contributions in currency hedging policies. Logical and analytical tools now exist to replicate currency *put* and *call* options. They are used to create more sophisticated options instruments as well as synthetic currency insurance programs.

Recently, financial institutions have started to appreciate that such developments require a great deal of experimentation. Since no two investors or traders have precisely the same goals, rocket scientists and supercomputers can help provide tailor-made solutions for high–net worth individuals, institutional investors, and corporate customers—working out imaginative approaches to hedging problems.

THE HEDGING PLAN AND THE RISK PREMIUM

Simulators and heuristic models* can help in uncovering parity states where expected returns on a bracket of securities will be equal, regardless of the currencies in which they are done. In such cases, for a contract maturing in one period, the current forward foreign-exchange rate represents the best possible forecast of what the spot exchange rate will be one period from now. A simple algorithm is:

$$\begin{matrix} \text{Expected depreciation} \\ \text{or appreciation} \\ \text{of the spot price} \end{matrix} = \begin{matrix} \text{Forward exchange} \\ \text{discount or premium} \end{matrix}$$

Uncovered parity does not mean that the spot rate will actually turn out to equal the current forward rate, every time or even any time. But uncovered parity does require the forward rate to reflect all known information about how the spot rate will evolve, taking into account everything that is known regarding the future exchange rate. In essense, hedging neither reduces nor increases the expected return of a foreign investment, but hedging does reduce the volatility of the portfolio's return.

One of the most studied relationships in international finance is indeed uncovered parity, and it is often seen as an arbitrage. The hypothesis is made that if two metrics, forward rate and expected future spot rate,

*See also D. N. Chorafas, *Using High Technology in Treasury and Forex Operations*, New York: Wiley, in press.

diverge then speculation will react to the apparent profit opportunity by buying or selling forward foreign exchange. But models and some experimental studies cast doubt on the validity of this approach.

Risk premiums have much to do with this statement because a forward exchange discount for premium equals the expected depreciation or appreciation of the spot price plus the risk premium in reference. Some currencies may be riskier to hold than others.

For nearly twenty years, currencies have been interlinked through quite dynamic relationships. Therefore, to properly identify how to hedge and whether or not to pay a given risk premium has much to do with:

- The investor's currency of reference

- A company's overall exposure, given its manufacturing and marketing network

From the investor's viewpoint, exchange rate risks cannot be eliminated merely by spreading stocks, bonds, and money market holdings among different currencies and countries. Competent investment management demands much more than that.

Investors with fixed-income securities as well as equities in foreign currencies incur the usual bond and stock risks—plus the risk that the foreign currency in question will depreciate against their base currency. At the same time, by hedging in a multinational sense they bet that some of the other currencies will appreciate, counterbalancing such risk and leaving them a profit. All this requires a significant amount of both foresight and experimentation; it cannot be done by rule of thumb. Investors must use those financial institutions best fit to serve the high net worth individuals, institutional investors, and corporate clients, that can support their advice through first-class professionals in currency hedging, assisted by rocket scientists and supercomputers as underlined in the preceding section.

From the viewpoint of the transnational corporation, currency hedging must properly map into custom-made mathematical models the international distribution of:

- Its research, development, and manufacturing activities

- Its worldwide marketing network, including projected expansion

- Its income stream and investment obligations

- The correlations between exchange rate changes and the returns to other assets

- How much compensation the treasurer will demand in order to keep under his or her control a specific amount of exchange rate risk

To the extent that these determinants change, risk premiums change too. Therefore, solutions must be sought through high-performance computing, and they must be kept very dynamic.

Sometimes treasurers miss the point that exactly because risk premiums vary so much, most of the changes we observe in forward exchange discounts probably represent changes in risk premiums, not in exchange rate expectations. That is the reason that expert forex traders think the forward rate is a biased predictor of the future spot rate, whereas the current spot rate may be a better predictor.

MANEUVERING THROUGH VARIABLE CURRENCY RATES AND BOND INSTRUMENTS

The message conveyed through the preceding sections has been that the foreign exchange markets are a more or less inefficient operation, and they could not be otherwise. There exist at least five different levels of inefficiency built into the system, from bottom to top:

1. The inefficiency of the *companies* whose equity and debt is traded in the market(s)

2. The inefficiency of the *market(s)* in which companies are quoted, as pockets of corporate inefficiency are not so easy to uncover, yet we know they exist

3. The *foreign exchange* inefficiency proper, with floating rates influenced by country risk, rate of interest in government and other bonds, but also expectations, rumors, and speculation

4. The sprawling *market-to-market* transaction process, which overwhelms practically all securities houses and forex dealers (thus providing the reason for rocket scientists as well as for intelligent networks, global databases, and supercomputers)

5. The most significant compound effect, which has been introduced by *currency risk*, because of global 24-hour trading

The complexity of this situation is being increased by the fact that there is a lack of theories on how currency risk and the associated compound effects should be handled.

What we know and account for—though most often in a rather informal manner—is that there exists considerable interaction between international investing and forex rates. This is true of banks, corporations, institutional investors, and high–net worth individuals.

Many investors are interested in participating in the higher returns available in foreign markets but face problems in selecting currencies in connection to stocks and bonds. They become aware that they have to keep in perspective the country risk. At the same time, many companies like to integrate in a transnational sense. But they face difficulties in evaluating the possible performance of their investments during a 10- to 15-year timeframe.

Some investors and quite a few corporations are primarily interested in betting on the macroeconomic fundamentals of a country or group of countries. This complicates the problem of choices, since it calls into play *political* factors that impact on both the macroeconomics, and the currency risk. The proof can be given by default. If the market(s) perceived every currency as equally risky, implied volatilities would be similar. This, however, is not the case. We should be very careful in evaluating and comparing implied volatilities embedded in currency option prices.

Another reason for the growth in international investing and therefore currency risk, is the recent development of worldwide indices. They allow money managers to compare their performance to that of others anywhere in the First World. For instance, the Morgan Stanley Capital International Europe, Australia, and Far East (EAFE) Index can be seen as the foreign equivalent of the S&P 500 in America. Such indices are structured to be comparable across countries for industry comparisons.

Some money managers have found that investing in the index derivatives of foreign countries is a good way to maintain equity exposure in the foreign stock market—being subject only to partial foreign exchange risk such as option premium or futures margin.

All these have considerations greatly altered by the velocity of cross-border investing. It is, however, good to keep in mind that different countries and markets have diverse rules that need to be understood before transacting. Collection and maintenance of legal information and compliance rules are important when establishing a multinational perspective. The study of fees of all sorts is another case in point.

For foreign trading purposes, the overall cost of clearing and settling needs to be known. The same is true about rules and pathways that permit maneuvering among financial environments, given their significant differences.

Handling a mortgage portfolio through various currencies with low or high interest rates is a good example. Although the interest rate(s) on a normal mortgage abroad may move, fluctuation regarding the principal borrowed in foreign currency or currencies for mortgage reasons can amplify. Mortgage-backed financing productizes interest rate instruments in different currencies and countries, permitting recovery of capital. Models like option-adjusted spread help give an estimate of expected lifecycle based on the propensity of home owners to redeem their mortgages.

The principle is that investment solutions must provide fairly accurate estimates of all classes of risk. In many cases, country weights have to be set according to criteria such as:

- Gross domestic product (GDP), capturing the importance of a country's economy

- Political moves made and expected to be made by governments

- Stock market capitalization as it correlates highly with trade volume

- Other country-weighting systems such as projected liquidity

Such approaches are used in the J.P. Morgan Global Government Bond Indices. Morgan's benchmark portfolio reflects very few extremely liquid (on-the-run) bonds. Its active contents consist of benchmark bonds plus other heavily traded issues.

Besides this, short-term currency deposits in a portfolio give the treasurer a pure currency scenario, which also have to be balanced in terms of risk. A sound approach involves not only the proverbial long, hard look at portfolio composition but also the impact of debt, equity, and foreign currencies.

THE BOND MARKET, THE FOREX MARKET, AND NETTING

Even though both feed on investor confidence, the *bond* market and the *forex* market should not be considered to behave in unison. Quite often, they are uncoupled. An example is given by the mid-February 1990 rout in the Deutsche mark (DM) bond market, which drove high yields on 10-year government bonds, while the DM remained very strong. By contrast, both the Japanese bond market and the yen had weakened.

During that timeframe, a rise of 0.625 percentage point in one week was a dramatic increase for the DM bond market in which a 0.25 point change was usually big news. The rise was a move by investors anticipating a subsequent tightening of policy by the West German reserve bank (Bundesbank) and an associated downgrading by the investment community because of West Germany's leveraged buy-out of East Germany.

The relatively muted reaction in the DM versus dollar foreign exchange market gave a more ambiguous message, interpreted by many that the market had not made up its mind. Other experts thought that the difference may as well be due to the fact that the bond market is essentially looking to the future, whereas the cash-oriented foreign exchange market focuses on the present.

The bond market and forex market are at the same time separate and related. Treasurers realize they can make more money by approaching in synergy their dealing in securities and currencies than handling each one alone. This message has spread through the corporate league. In Japan, Europe, and America several large industrial and merchandising companies have set up in-house banking activities aimed at managing both sides of their wealth; financial institutions are doing just the same.

For a multinational corporation as well as for an export-oriented company, currency exposure management is a must. A trading firm has to cover its exposure in receivables and payables outstanding. Every treasurer must care about the company's long-term investments in foreign subsidiaries—as well as hedge the loan portfolio.

Equities, debt, and currency exposure may occur on both accounts payable and accounts receivable, hence the motivation to *net out* these exposures for each currency, running a selective hedge on the net amount. For example, trying to balance foreign currencies against one another and versus a base currency, and including not only current assets and current liabilities but also the investment portfolio.

In its fundamentals, netting is equivalent to taking a full cover position on foreign receivables and payables simultaneously. But these are two separate decisions, and full cover may be the wrong way to go on one side of the balance sheet. More imaginative approaches are necessary for equilibrating.

Netting is usually done for currency risk management, *bilateral netting* is one of its expressions that is not always crowned by success. For instance, eight banks in London agreed to do bilateral netting only to find out that each bank had a different view of what constitutes netting. Netting is also the practice of balancing purchases of foreign exchange against sales in order to determine a concern's basic exposure. It is done largely to reduce costs by cutting the risk of adverse currency fluctuations in payments, correspondingly diminishing the need to hold liquid balances with central banks—from a financial institution's viewpoint.

Nevertheless, the operation of these arrangements in a cross-border context challenges certain critical assumptions that underlie current perceptions of the operation of international banking markets. As a result, some cultural issues need to be revamped.

One of the reasons for the constraints in the implementation of the policy that we are discussing is that quite often the treasury function is seen as a *cost center*, rather than a *profit center*. As a result, currency fluctuations are approached as a problem rather than a profit-making opportunity. Also many companies have not yet developed administrative systems that can deliver the up-to-the-minute picture of exposure needed for *active* currency management.

The central banks, too, have gotten into the act. After agreeing on how banks should account for product innovation in international financial markets, central bankers turned their attention to structural innovations in the back office. A report issued by the Bank of International Settlements* warns that efforts by commercial bankers to lower costs and minimize risks by netting out foreign exchange obligations may actually obscure management's assessment of the real exposure of their institutions.

Among practices questioned by the regulators is whether the various netting procedures are legally enforceable. As a result, the suggestion has been advanced that there is a danger netted amounts will be treated *as if* they represented the actual credit exposure between pairs of counterparties for the purposes of establishing more favorable positions in dealing and other credit lines.

There is no free lunch, of course, and as the central bankers noted, counterparties run the risk of having very large gross exposures, even though net exposures appear to be within prudent bounds.

SEARCHING FOR NEW OPPORTUNITIES IN CURRENCY MANAGEMENT

The process of netting is still in search of its proper base. There is no denying that some valid, properly experimented solution is needed while forex, securities, and treasury operations generate greater profits and risks and traditional banking lags.

Searching for new opportunities rather than hanging on to old connections, the Morgan Bank and Bankers Trust now have less than half their balance sheet composed of loans. A rising proportion of their assets is in easily sellable securities that can supply customers with short-term funds or products such as interest-rate caps. These financial products are then broken up and distributed across the financial system through securitization.

This discussion focuses on the need to actively search for new instruments and to study their possible opportunities, pitfalls, and aftermaths well before launching them in the market. As a financial institution

*Prepared by officials of the Federal Reserve Bank, the Bank of England, the Bank of Japan, the German Bundesbank, and the Swiss National Bank.

hedges its business through separate streams of revenue and uses its capital to support its most profitable activities, innovation—research and development—plays an increasingly important role. The same is true about the blending of marketing and technology—nobody said such work should be done in a blind fashion.

What some treasurers find out the hard way is that currency management requires top-level expertise in forex and thorough knowledge of the mechanics which, contrary to general opinion, can be quite simple. The first step is to learn not just trading but also:

- What *currency management* is all about

- What *currency trading* may mean to the firm given its exposure in foreign currency

Exposure advisory services include the able handling of currency overlay as well as exposure evaluation related to an equity portfolio, including the different types of loans that have been contracted.

The next step to learning the business is to experiment in order to visualize and document the solution to be chosen. Is the mass of work to be done enough to justify investments in training the treasury personnel, acquiring the appropriate software, or renting rather expensive hardware? Or is it better to work in partnership with a financial institution that has good experience in currency trading, hedging, and management?

If the mass of work justifies skill and technology acquisition, then treasurers of multinational firms have good reason in taking an active role looking at currency fluctuations. They have to watch out for movements affecting their accounts outstanding, not only covering risks but also using them as a source of profits.

An American firm, for instance, may have roughly equal payables and receivables in, say, Deutsche marks. There may be a profit opportunity in covering one side of the exposure and leaving the other open, depending on the short-term trend in Deutsche mark/dollar rate and the differential in U.S. and German interest rates. Judgment cannot be made in the abstract. It requires expertise and experimentation.

Companies that choose to do currency management by themselves typically establish a foreign currency line with their bank, equal to their maximum foreign exposure:

- For a fund, exposure is measured by total foreign investments.

- For a borrower, it is measured by the total size of the loans.

The bank may wish to formalize the deposit of underlying assets as collateral to cover foreign exchange losses. Corporations can negotiate substantial lines along this, on the basis of their balance sheet.

Some companies prefer to shop around for the right partner. All major banks are competitive in the forward markets, but, as expected, some market makers in certain currencies are better than others; also banks differ in terms of the spreads they offer.

Brokers, too, promote currency options or exchange-traded futures contracts as a way of covering currency exposure. These are more complex than simple forward transactions and can be more expensive, hence the wisdom of shopping carefully.

7

Dealing in Currencies

With flexible exchange rates, the relative value of a local currency versus a particular foreign currency, or a basket of currencies, will usually vary in inverse proportion to the variation in its domestic level of prices. *If* the rate of inflation is lower and the real interest rate higher, *then* the local currency is likely to appreciate. Theoretically, through a comparison of movements in inflation rates in the different countries and the corresponding interest rates, conclusions can be drawn regarding rate fluctuations. Practically, the situation is more complex than that, with political events and other factors entering the game. We have seen some examples in Chapter 6.

A detailed study of prices and the exchange rate mechanism must consider wage costs, productivity, and investments in a country's infrastructure. Broken down by sector, wage costs are an important criterion by which to judge the economy of a country engaged in international competition in the manufacturing, trade, and service sectors.

Since the appreciation of what is meant by competitive edge in relation to a country's currency is a phenomenon of the last 20 years, economic theory does not yet have the methods and models for accurate judgment.

- In the early 1930s unilateral devaluation was thought as the best means to increase a country's exports and thereby strengthen its economy.

- With the Bretton Woods Agreement, at least the First World experienced between 1945 and 1972 a relative currency stability, which was thought to be good for international trade.

- After the Smithsonian agreement, flexible exchange rates have led to the rise, fall, and rise again of individual hard currencies, but international trade kept on expanding.

As shown in this chapter, there is no consensus on whether it is better or worse that the value of a given First World currency is high or low relative to a basket of other currencies—and each one of them individually. Neither is it so clear if this or that currency is overvalued (or undervalued). The market sets the price.

RISE AND FALL OF A CURRENCY'S VALUE

When a given currency rises in relation to others, imports become cheaper but also exports become more expensive. As a result, the volume of imports expands and the volume of exports contracts. Eventually this imbalance in the country's current account will lead to a depreciation of the domestic currency.* In other words, a pointer toward future exchange rate movements is to be found in a country's net balance on the current account. Excluding the flow of funds not considered here, there is a tendency for the exchange rate to decline if the net balance on the current account closes with a deficit and for it to rise if there is a surplus.

The pattern of international competition is steadily changing and in so doing it affects the value of the currency. Exports, for instance, have become a significant source of economic growth for the United States, and in the early 1990s exports may be as important to the vitality of the American economy as they are in Germany and Japan.

In America, real exports of goods and services have increased 3.8 times faster than real GNP of goods and services since early 1985. As a result, such exports now account for about 15 percent of real GNP, up from roughly 10 percent in 1985 and 7 percent in 1970[†] (Figure 7.1). At the same time the ratio of imports to gross national product (GNP) stands at 11 percent, slightly higher than in Japan but much lower than Canada (26 percent), England (27 percent), and West Germany (28 percent).[‡]

These statistical references should not be interpreted as meaning that trade considerations are today the number-one factor. As will be shown later, there are counter-hypotheses to this argument but there is also no denying that trade balances and imbalances constitute an important factor.

It is conceivable that, in some cases and under model conditions, shifts in prices and exchange rates will balance each other. Such a parity of purchasing power exists if the real countervalues of the monetary units in the countries concerned are identical. In reality, this scarcely ever

*See D. N. Chorafas, *Bank Profitability*, London: Butterworths, 1989.
[†]According to a study by Dr. Edward Yardeni of Prudential-Bache Securities.
[‡]Business Week, May 7, 1990.

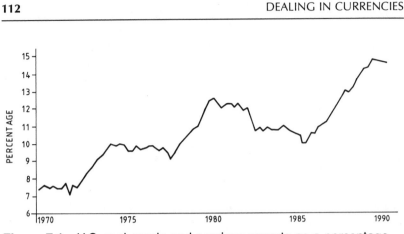

Figure 7.1   U.S. real goods and services exports as a percentage
of real goods and services GNP.

happens, as changes in different national economies usually come about
in a different timeframe.

Inflation is another determinant, itself influenced by the exchange rate.
A falling exchange rate, caused by essential imports such as oil, propels
inflation. Whether there is an increase or decrease in inflation is very
much dependent on:

1. The rate of growth of the money supply

2. The velocity of circulation of money

3. The trend in the exchange rate against other hard currencies

The role of oil in the import equation is so vital that the Japanese
consider the price of the barrel one of the six key factors (themes) that
determine the value of the yen. Figure 7.2 shows a chart that helps in
the visualization of factors affecting interest rates. (This chart was done
with British bankers during a seminar I offered in London; that is the
reason it is centered on the pound.)

The rate of growth of the money supply is typically (but not always)
in the hands of the reserve bank. The velocity of circulation of money
depends both on government policy and on consumer psychology. Whenever money is printed to cover losses, more money chases fewer goods,
and prices rise. This doesn't have to go on for long before people lose
confidence in the currency and spend it faster. The faster turnover in the
stock of money adds to the inflation rate.

Government policy may operate in any one of a number of ways to
balance or counterbalance market trends. The choice of policy depends

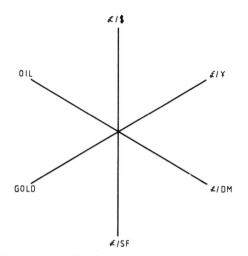

Figure 7.2   Radar chart illustrating a visualization of factors affecting
exchange rates.

on the particular circumstances and the beliefs of the decision makers.
Policies may stimulate, inhibit, or accommodate economic growth—they
do so for a number of reasons, including national supremacy.

Although prestige factors are today less pronounced than in the past,
they are not altogether out of the picture. As Dr. Charles P. Kindleberger
suggests, "Britain's ability to mobilize resources—both its own and those
of other countries—after 1688, enabled it with one-third the manpower
of France to defeat the French, unable because of dug-in interests to
reform her system of taxation and borrowing."*

The role of money and the exchange rates associated with currencies
evolves with the economic and trading environment. In the years after
World War II, and most particularly during the last 20 years, capital has
become international:

- We already said that the international money market handles about
  a trillion dollars a day. That is the money that changes hands.

- Excluding agriculture, 25 percent of the gross national product
  (GNP) in the Western World is contributed by multinational companies, which by necessity deal in a basket of currencies, though the
  dollar may still be used as common denominator.

*A *Financial History of Western Europe*, London and Boston: George Allen and Unwin,
1984.

- New exchange markets develop. Commodities futures trading is one of the fastest growing investments today. The annual value of contracts traded now exceeds $3 trillion.

- A combination of technology and worldwide financial deregulation has accelerated the trend toward an around-the-clock securities and forex market.

All this has impact on the sensitivity of exchange rates and up to a point has replaced the former emphasis on capitalistic or socialistic, conservative or big spender government policies that in the past significantly weighted currency exchange rates. From the François Mitterand policies in the mid-1980s and those of Felipe Gonzalez in Spain to the timid market economy of Mikhail Gorbachev, there is no great difference anymore among the different types of political regimes.

THE MARKET IS THE ARBITER

The market became the arbiter of currency values as business, industry, world trade, and international investments shaped up as a worldwide system of interrelated, interlocking parts able to determine the economy by country and on a global basis. Profit (including greed) is the driving force. Understandably, capital seeks employment in countries and currencies with:

- Greater stability

- Higher real interest rates

- A favorable relation to the risks incurred

If a particular country has a high level of interest rates as compared with other countries—and its ability to repay is beyond doubt—this will have a decisive effect on the standing of its currency because of the inflow of money.

Some economists suggest that the aim of monetary policy should be to influence the exchange rate rather than inflation. Interest rates, they say, should be used not to stabilize prices, but to stabilize the exchange rate.

Monetarists have argued that monetary restraint can control inflation indirectly, through the exchange rate, rather than directly: Higher interest rates push up the currency and so make imports cheaper. The snag is that a strong exchange-rate target is difficult to maintain over the longer run.

On a short-term basis nobody contests a reserve bank's ability to influence exchange rates. This, however, lasts only as long as its policy remains credible. If inflation differentials between countries persist, a given exchange rate can be maintained only temporarily. Policymakers will eventually be forced to allow the currency to fall or rise in accordance with the market's valuation, which at times may be speculative.

A country with a relatively low real interest rate (perhaps because of inflation or government policies) will suffer a depreciation of its currency as a result of outflow of money. However, in analyzing differences in interest rates, a distinction must be made between interest on *long-term* and interest on *short-term* investments. Both are factors that an exchange rate model would consider in order to provide a *forecast* on trends. Some of the variables mentioned move rather slowly, but others change fast, creating a volatile environment that can be amplified by the psychology of the moment.

The markets react instantaneously, and they do so on a global basis. To be ahead of the competition in trading and investments we must therefore have at our disposal global databases, supercomputers, and mathematical models—both algorithmic and heuristic. Together, these constitute the infrastructure. Said the *Economist* in regard to the major slide that took place in the Tokyo Stock Exchange in February/March 1990: "The big American brokerages, Salomon Brothers and Morgan Stanley in particular, have been using their computer-trading programs to arbitrage intelligently between the index-futures market and the underlying cash stocks."

The investments that will dominate in the 1990s will be neither pure currencies nor pure securities, but a combination of both. The best approach will be to define a *base currency* against which the profit and loss of an investment is measured and then to look at currencies-securities as a unified domain where decisions made in one of the two frames of reference influence the other because

- Our own actions affect *our* portfolio
- Actions of the competition as a whole affect the market

Figure 7.3 suggests a system that can lead, bottom up, to factual and documented proposals for forex trading. Quite a similar approach should be taken for dealing in securities; with the results obtained by structures at the top of the decision tree combined through the use of an optimization model.

Any movement the market makes may create opportunity. It is important to capture this business opportunity as it develops—a statement that is just as valid when we talk of currencies, other commodities, equities, or debt.

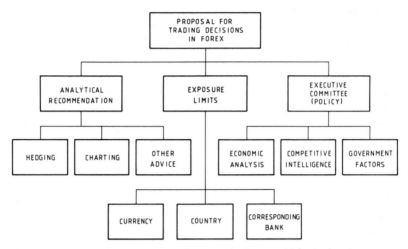

Figure 7.3   Structure of system for decision-making in foreign exchange trading.

CAPITAL FLOWS AND TRADING DECISIONS

Whether we are dealing in currencies, stocks, bonds, or any other instrument, we take risks. The same statement is valid with reference to investments, no matter how our portfolio is structured. The reference to optimization is not to weed out risk but to balance it versus the returns we obtain.

I will go further than that. Business, industry, and evidently banking must experience occasional losses. A bank that never has a bad loan or an investment turn sour never makes much profit. As shown in Chapters 2 and 3, the word *risk* has a positive as well as a negative connotation.

With a flexible exchange rate system, one of the risks in investments, as well as in foreign trade, is evidently the foreign currency risk. Currencies rise and fall as the result of several factors, including:

- Central bank intervention

- Changes in a nation's hard currency or gold reserves

- Interest and inflation rates

- General economic prospects

Therefore, any foreign investment should be viewed as two investments in one, each with its own independent risk characteristics and potential for profit or loss.

Given that for the 1990s currency fluctuations are a virtual certainty, experienced investors and wise traders sometimes employ hedging techniques to manage currency risk. Although not always appropriate, approaches such as forward sales, futures contracts, or currency options can minimize the impact of exchange rate movements.

As Chapter 6 has properly underlined, investors and traders should recognize that while reducing the risk of adverse currency movements, *hedging* both eliminates any yield advantage found in foreign interest rates and limits the benefits of any favorable exchange rate developments. Indeed, much of the allure of foreign financial markets is the prospect of the double-barreled gains that can be captured when a booming national economy sends the value of both domestic stocks and the local currency soaring.

Treasurers of international corporations have both made and lost money using this double-edged approach. It is therefore important to carefully weigh the nature of foreign transactions by isolating an underlying investment from its related currency play. Each is likely to have its own individual risks, time horizons, and outcomes.

Apart from the issues that have just been discussed regarding currency exchange pitfalls and opportunities, for a multinational corporation, risk evaluation in forex must take into account:

1. Terms of trade, that is, the relationship between export and import prices

2. Inflow or outflow of long-term or short-term capital and movements

3. Ephemeral factors that often bring about results that are the opposite of what would logically be expected

For instance, the instability of foreign exchange markets provokes an increase in speculative activities, for which there may be no rational justification one way or another of the exchange rate movement. Sometimes the same reasons are given to explain why a currency's value goes up and why it goes down. Political events also contribute to market gyrations.

The psychology of the moment will be better appreciated if we consider that international capital transfers have two aspects: One is *purely financial*, the other relates to *merchandise*. They are, of course, interrelated. The financial transfer *per se* consists of the means by which a payment is made from money of one country and received in money of another. The merchandise payment deals with the exchange of goods and services. In the days when the flow of trade governed the flow of currencies, a large trade deficit would mean that fewer people wanted to hold the country's currency because they did not need to buy goods. That is not the way the financial markets work anymore.

Today only a smaller part of the world's daily currency transactions finances international merchandise trade. The rest is made up of *capital flows*, which are largely created by institutional and other investors playing a globally networked game of chasing the highest return. Sitting in their offices they watch currency trading unfold, try to detect a pattern, and make their move.

If real interest rates on bonds in the United States are higher than on bonds in Japan, big institutional investors in Tokyo will move hundreds of millions of dollars in an instant into the United States, to get the higher return. That creates demand for dollars, so the value goes up. But the investment is made both in real interest rates and in currencies. Hence, the buyer of dollar assets bears the risk that an interest rate shift or some other factor may drive the dollar down, eroding the value of the investment.

In *capital flows*, an export surplus typically develops based on the excess savings of the lending country; the import surplus develops from the excess spending of the borrower. Other financial payments have a different origin than ordinary savings and investments. They can be subsidies, indemnities to be paid after defeat in war, financial handouts, or recycling of money—as with the Marshall Plan and in the aftermath of the 1973 oil crisis.

IS THERE PROTECTION AGAINST CURRENCY FLUCTUATIONS?

One way manufacturing companies have found to protect against currency fluctuation is to use foreign exchange credit. Depending on the size of liabilities payable in different foreign currencies, credit positions are opened in one or more foreign currencies, which are then immediately converted into the local currency.

Used in an able manner, foreign exchange credit can see to it that individual positions (credits as well as debits) are grouped in a single currency, the respective net position being afforded suitable cover. Chapter 6 describes netting, and it is good to underline, absent its other negatives, that the able execution of such a procedure requires:

- Clear definitions and methods

- Well-thought-out procedures

- Properly organized information services

- Mathematical analysis of current exchange risk situations

- A forecasting of potential future trends and associated risks

- Understanding of trade receivables in foreign exchange

- The incorporation of a whole range of different factors that influence trading

A sound methodology is often referred to as *international money management*. Banks can offer valuable service in this field especially to enterprises engaged in international business who do not themselves have the know-how, computers, expert systems, and communications power to face complex situations.

Depending on the country, effective solutions capitalize on a long-term hedge against exchange risks afforded through export guarantees. No trading model will be complete, and therefore useful, unless it reflects by country and currency all of the intricate trade promotion and capital transfer laws in addition to incentives.

All major countries feature a form of insurance on behalf of the government for the export of goods and services. Some particularly focus on attracting foreign capital. Quite similarly, the simulator to be built for currency rates forecasting should incorporate modules on hedging methods used by forex traders the world over. One of the methods of hedging is the use of *composite currency clauses*, which began in recent years for bond transactions in the Euromarket.

Another approach in hedging against foreign exchange risk is the buying of trade receivables for collection, factoring, and leasing. The basis of this service rests on the difference between the higher rate of discount change and the normal bill discount rate.

The factoring system guarantees that short-term receivables arising from the sale of goods and services are assigned to factoring institutes or banks, so that the creditor is immediately provided with funds for financing purposes. This is normally done against a correspondingly higher risk premium, with the factoring agent prepared to bear the risk of fluctuations in exchange rates.

With leasing, exchange rate risks are borne neither by the domestic creditor nor the foreign debtor. They are shifted to a third party, the leasing company, to which the exporter sells its capital goods for which it receives payment in its own currency. The leasing company tries to capitalize on exchange rate fluctuations making its own hedging.

International trade operations, whose substance is most liable to exchange risks, contain precise exchange rate clauses to safeguard against currency fluctuation.

- Under a *minimum* clause, the creditor can either claim payment of the agreed minimum amount in foreign currency or a higher amount based on any fluctuation in the exchange rate that may have taken place.

- With the *option* clause, the creditor can demand payment of a given amount in foreign currency adjusted for change in value in exchange rate, or payment in an alternative currency agreed upon in the contract.

A bilateral clause may be adopted to signify that any revaluation or devaluation of the domestic currency (or the foreign currency) will be to the advantage (or disadvantage) of either the creditor or the debtor. The amount receivable may be typically fixed in the domestic currency of the exporter.

All these financing and payment tools do reflect, to a significant degree, the growing realization that foreign markets today are becoming too important and too big to ignore. But they are also too risky to work in without the proper safeguards, which are based both on first-class expertise at defining what creates the conditions for capital flows and on the appropriate technology to support the expertise when it comes to the final decision.

The skillful use of financial instruments not only must follow the prevailing trend but also must discover fundamental factors not seen by everyone. This is a basic truth behind profitable forex operations.

INTEGRATING FOREX AND INVESTMENT PERSPECTIVES

Solutions to some of the more complex problems examined in the preceding sections come none too soon. From Tokyo to London, the deregulation of financial markets is accelerating the trend toward global trading. Post-deregulation developments have required a significant renewal of the foreign exchange and investment instruments. They also made it mandatory to revamp policies, including incentives needed to encourage the free flow of capital across borders. Stock exchanges are opening up to foreign membership. Laws are changing and are generally becoming internationally oriented. Throughout the First World, many rules are being standardized in an effort to create a truly global system.

Tokyo launched a sweeping financial reform aimed at putting it on par with New York and London as a major world financial center. In October 1986 the so-called Big Bang introduced in London a new era of British traders by abandoning fixed commissions and a number of other once common trading practices that had barred foreigners and guaranteed London firms most of the profits.

New technological solutions are vital to the development of 24-hour trading and global financial exchange. Multinational corporations are increasingly tapping capital markets in a variety of currencies, using a host of money-saving financing techniques. The integrating of interest rate and currency swaps requires banks and securities firms to have experts with:

- A worldwide view of financial markets

- An endowment of interactive computational tools

- The ability to perform experimentation in realspace

- A sharp eye for risk calculation

New powerful instruments are necessary both for enterprise and for speculation. John Maynard Keynes drew the distinction between *speculation*, by which he meant the activity of forecasting the psychology of the market; and *enterprise*, or the capitalization on the yield offered by market assets. "Speculators may do no harm as bubbles on a steady stream of enterprise. But the position is serious when enterprise becomes the bubble on a whirlpool of speculation," warned Keynes, also adding, "the actual, private object of the most skilled investment today is 'to beat the gun,' as the Americans so well express it, to outwit the crowd, and to pass the bad, or depreciating half-crown to the other fellow."*

A different and probably better way of looking at this issue is that investors and entrepreneurs play with their own money, whereas a speculator plays with that of others.

Realspace networks and artificial intelligence constructs should help protect the treasury and the bank from this passing around of the half-crown. Multicurrency investing may still be in its infancy, but it needs a firm infrastructure in order to flourish.

Not every financial institution realizes that when we talk of integrating forex and investment perspectives into one well-knit operation, we are essentially talking about something much more complex than doing two different operations simultaneously, each on its own merits. A new culture is necessary to provide the acuity necessary for integrated trades, and high technology is one of its indispensable components.

Success will not come as a matter of course; to capture the opportunities that develop in the First World's financial markets we need preparation. Such opportunities exist, as attested by an increasing variety of foreign exchange and investment instruments as well as the different options from which to choose.* International investing, foreign trade, and currency exchange are clearly some of the most exciting areas of investment specialization—but they are not everybody's cup of tea.

---

*The Economist, January 30, 1988.

Since the early 1970s when the currencies began floating freely, their rise and fall have been a constant temptation for traders, investors, and speculators. In the five months after February 1973 the dollar fell over 40 percent against the Deutsche mark, and sometimes went up or down by more than 10 percent in a week. This continued and accelerated during the 1980s. The dollar rose sharply against all European currencies and the yen then fell to half its peak value, a change which cannot be compensated by interest fluctuations in the short-to-medium run.

In late 1989 the exchange rate of the dollar to the mark was 1:2, with the dollar strengthening, and with a forecast that interest rates in the United States would be dropping, it made sense to exit German bonds and enter dollar-denominated bonds. The U.S. interest rates did drop and the dollar bonds appreciated, but in January 1990 the profits were wiped out because of the U.S. liquidity squeeze. At the same time, the price of the German bonds crashed as interest rates skyrocketed because of the projected West German–East German unification; but also the dollar-to-mark exchange rate deteriorated to 1:1.68. As a result, the dollar losses outpaced those suffered by the German bond market.

Approaches such as the use of trading forward in investments in foreign exchange can take many and various forms, none of them being risk-free. Besides, trading forward is just as essential in multinational commercial exchanges as it is in pure financial transactions, and let's not forget that there is also a speculative aspect.

In the foreign exchange context, the need to hedge currency exposures arises because of the volatility of exchange rates. There is for instance *translation exposure*, which occurs because of certain accounting rules when an organization must translate its foreign currency–denominated assets and liabilities into domestic currency on its financial statements, and/or expects to receive payment, or make payment, in a foreign currency in connection with a commercial, industrial, or financial transaction.

For buying and selling, the *spot rate* is the rate for immediate on-the-spot delivery of foreign exchange, by seller or buyer, having payments usually made with the value two working days after the deal is closed. Like spot (cash) rates, *forward rates* of exchange are given different quotations for buying or selling. (For a discussion of futures, spots, options, and forwards, see Chapters 11 and 12.)

The difference between a spot and a forward can be either plus or minus and is an expression of market opinion on future movements (forward position) of a currency.

- If a transaction is handled at a forward rate lower than the spot rate, this is referred to as *forward discount* under spot transaction. In this case, the future value of the currency in question is rated at less than the current rate of exchange, with the expectancy that fundamental reasons, technical reasons, or both, will see a downrating of this currency in the months ahead.

- A forward premium over spot means that a premium has to be paid over and above the going rate. This indicates continuing confidence in the future of the currency in question, with its current value being rated lower than its future value.

Periods of time stipulated in a forward deal or forward transaction are typically of one, two, three, or six months. A bank may, however, be willing to accommodate customers over periods other than these, including fractions of a month, such as 15 days. If deals are for longer than the normal maximum term of twelve months, there is a corresponding rise in the cost of forward exchange covering.

Forward rates do not make precise statements about what the spot rate will be at the future point in time to which the transactions refer. They simply express a current assessment of exchange rate movements that are *likely*—hence the risk that forward rates involve. Often they are based on political and general economic considerations as well as on interest differentials for individual currencies.

INNOVATION IN FINANCIAL PRODUCTS

Precisely because of the leverage factor, forward markets can involve considerable risk. This is as true of foreign currencies as it is of securities and commodities. If forward trading is an innovation, which it is, let's not forget the role of innovations in previous panics. We should always innovate, but we should also understand and control the instrument we use.

The introduction of new financial products accelerated in the 1980s. Previous centuries generated numerous financial innovations. Some of them led to speculative excesses and eventually financial panics. During the 1790s a bull market in stocks, bonds, and enormous tracts of U.S. frontier land was fueled by a then recent invention known as the *commercial bank*—the American version.

Banks in New York, Philadelphia, and Baltimore lent freely to politically powerful merchants, who sat on their boards, and often acted as speculators. Such loans allowed them to acquire millions of acres of unsettled land in the Appalachian mountains on the expectation that there would be an excess of demand.

When the projected flood of European settlers did not materialize and the land could not be sold, the speculators went bankrupt. On his way to debtors' prison, one of the richest and most powerful of these speculators scribbled this note: "My money is done, my furniture is to be sold, I am to go to prison and my family to starve, good night."

Financial engineering, as well as gambling, has often been associated with capital markets and, more recently, with currency markets. However, refinements such as options (puts and calls) and trading in futures did not develop yesterday. They developed in Amsterdam in the sixteenth century and were gradually diffused to London and Paris. In the past, gambling has played an instrumental role inasmuch as rich, young men considered it to be an investment in their future, as they sought to acquire noble status. Gambling has always been instrumental in pushing some of the better mathematical minds toward the definition of new tools, particularly in probability theory and statistics. The contributions that Jean le Rond d'Alembert (1717–1783) made in probability theory are credited to his drive to win in gambling forays.

But at times gambling moves from being a pastime to an obsession. In nineteenth century Prussia, the price of grain fell sharply after the imposition of the British Corn Laws of 1818. One of the results was that between 1837 and 1857 mortgages on Prussian estates doubled; another result was that the big land owners (the Junkers) indulged in gambling in the hope of escaping poverty and boredom.

During the bull market of the 1830s, American state governments sold large bond issues to European investors to finance transportation projects that could compete with the hugely successful Erie Canal, completed in 1825. After the crash of 1836, no fewer than nine American states defaulted on the bonds, and for a full decade European capitalists viewed Pennsylvania and Michigan with the same dread that bankers today view Mexico and Brazil.

The 1850s was the decade in which Wall Street became the center of railroad finance, as well as when the U.S. version of the *investment banking* house was invented. But ethical standards were not exalted, and well over half of the bonds that investment bankers underwrote during the railroad boom defaulted after the panic of 1857.

There are lessons to be learned from these past experiences, applicable to today's currency swap operations. When we are incapable of learning from past experience, we are condemned to repeat the same mistakes.

The euphoria that followed Bismarck's victory over Napoleon III let loose a building boom in Prussia, especially in Berlin. This gave rise to a crop of companies converted to banks: the Maklerbanken (real estate brokers' banks) and Baubanken (construction). (These interestingly enough correspond to the American savings and loan associations of our days — and look at the mess.) In a little over two years, 40 billion marks were invested in building sites and construction, but many of these quasi-banks failed.

All kinds of half-baked or full swindles took place, some involving notables on the boards of new companies appointed to lend respectability: (1) institutions speculated in their own stock; (2) most exploited the little stockholders; (3) the whole system went from boom to collapse. These three are meant to comment on real estate speculation in Bismarck's Prussia, but they are just as applicable to our days. There has been a similar real estate investment story in America in the 1970s with the Real Estate Investment Trust (REIT). Sponsored by leading banks they featured lots of investment fever and went from lust to bust in the same way.

The story of the great, bull run of the 1920s is too well known to be told in detail, but it does teach some lessons. It spawned two notable innovations: multitier utility holding companies and highly leveraged closed-end mutual funds.

Not unlike financial futures and junk bonds today, these innovations made improvements in the financial system but also created unforeseen risks. They fostered excessive specialization that ultimately ended in a financial panic.

That financial panic taught some lessons and President Roosevelt's New Deal capitalized on them to restructure the way the securities system worked as well as the means of policing it. Nothing similar has yet happened as a result of the junk-bond bubble.

Said *Business Week* on this subject: "[Michael R.] Milken's illegal aims included manipulating securities markets, evading new capital rules and cheating the government on taxes."* Milken's trial did not go on (because of his guilty plea), but it might have unearthed the machinery of the secret deals, therefore leading to new regulations to close the loopholes.

DEALING WITH PANICS

Foreign exchange and stock index futures traded in the financial markets of the First World give speculators the same degree of leverage that aggressive margin trading offered in the 1920s, when speculators could control a block of stock with little cash outlay. The value of the underlying stock traded in the futures market often exceeded by significant margin the volume of trading in the cash market.

Although futures prices normally track the values in the cash market, at critical moments the two may diverge, magnifying price swings in the spot market. This both underlines and exemplifies the capacity of financial instruments to deal with risk through:

*May 7, 1990.

- Intermediating between trader and trader, for instance, between lender and borrower

- Providing for portfolio diversification without necessarily ensuring the appropriate risk control

- Magnifying the extent of capital availability in the market, hence leading toward excesses.

Evidently the proper balance is tough to reach, and even when it is achieved it does not last long. We often forget that, just like organizations, markets stand on three pillars, as suggested in Figure 7.4. All three must be strong for the edifice to stay in place. When one or two of them crumble, the whole structure can be swept away by a major wave that feeds on vagueness, uncertainty, excesses, and uncontrollable events such as some unexpected large-scale bankruptcy, a couple of major countries defaulting, or a First World currency that capsizes because of a depression.

Major upheavals do not come overnight; they build over time: Debt dominoes in Mexico, Brazil, Argentina, Bolivia, the Philippines; the West German LBO to acquire the East German real estate; the U.S. oil patch; commercial real estate in America as well as loans to silicon valley companies; the savings and loans, whose ordeal never ends; and junk bond portfolios are examples of insecure structures that could topple as cash flows shrink in an economic downturn, spreading panic in the currency markets.

Allan Meltzer of Prudential-Bache thinks the Achilles' heel of the banking system lies south of the U.S. border: "It is clear that Peru has now

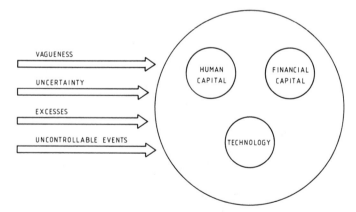

Figure 7.4 External forces that threaten any market and the "pillars" that support it.

defaulted. Other countries might follow." The loans to Latin American countries alone account for more than 60 percent of the total capitalization of U.S. banks. Meltzer adds: "If the Fed repeated the errors of the 1930s and frightened people into thinking the banking system was about to collapse, that could produce a panic."

Some economists believe that the next panic would start not from the debt doldrums but from a major agricultural debacle, for instance the former Soviet Union. Other economists are convinced that trouble could just as easily start at home. Dr. Alan Greenspan pointed to the unprecedented pileup of public and private debt in the U.S. economy. Fast-rising interest payments "make the whole nonfinancial corporate sector more brittle, less capable of responding to a sharp decline in income. Average bond ratings have fallen and the deterioration in the quality of bank assets is extraordinary."*

Or the trigger may be a computer crash. When the Bank of New York's computers went down one night in 1985, the New York Federal Reserve Board had to lend no less than $23 billion until the next day to keep the Bank of New York solvent.

Robert Lawrence suggests a panic could start in the following way: If the trade deficit failed to improve notably (or for any other protagonist reason), the U.S. Congress might throw up broad import barriers. "That would be a flat abrogation of our multilateral trade commitments, and our partners will feel it incumbent to respond in kind...attacking the United States where it is most vulnerable, in aircraft and agriculture."

A panic would be accentuated by the increased use of speculative securities such as futures and junk debt. Confidence will erode all the faster if the United States federal government is still running a large budget deficit, which would impair its ability to bail out failed banks without printing money and alarming the bond and currency markets.

Dr. Charles Kindleberger sees a possible panic as the result of a flight to quality, a massive sell-off of dubious assets by investors. That would trigger widespread defaults, which could in turn cripple the banking system. Since legislators and regulators often react after the fact, a good deal of hope should rest in trader and investor rationality. This is just true of investments as well as of the currency markets.

With so many things that can go wrong, it may seem difficult to remain an optimist. But this section has not been written to suggest a panic is truly imminent. The rational way to look at this subject is that the more we know what can go wrong, and get ourselves ready to face it, the less likely it is that a panic will happen.

*Fortune, December 22, 1986.

8

West European Currency, Political Union, and the Financial Infrastructure

The history of the European Currency Unit (ECU) started with a decision in late 1978 to set up a new European monetary system in spite of the then prevailing environment of monetary instability. After a start-up period of two years, the whole project was supposed to enter a phase of institutional development with the creation of appropriate communitarian monetary institutions.

This second phase did not take place. The European Monetary System (EMS) suffered from a halt in gestation. As a result, the use of the ECU, which was conceived in the framework of the EMS, remained for some time reserved for the exclusive (and rather reduced) use of the European Community's (EC) central banks.

Then came a rather unexpected development. A few commercial banks offered in the euromarkets an identical copy of the ECU but packaged as a financial product. They proposed it for bank deposits, loans, and Eurobond investments. This so-called *private ECU* carried the same composition in terms of base currencies as the original ECU, which from then on was labeled *official*. The private ECU received an encouraging welcome by the euromarkets. After a first ECU bond issue in 1981/82, the volume of outstanding bonds climbed, giving it a ranking of fourth, after the U.S. dollar, the DM, and the Yen. This was a good start for a new currency.

In terms of interest rates and forex rates, the ECU behaves like a weighted average of the rates of its component currencies. As a result, when the interest rate differentials between the ECU and the major European Community currencies started narrowing (on the grounds of lower and converging inflation rates), the niche that the ECU had found as a financial instrument started narrowing as well.

The law of supply and demand is in the background of this event. When the international price for the ECU's component currencies goes up, so does the foreign exchange rate at which the ECU is converted to other, non-EMS currencies—and vice versa. Some price changes, however, counterbalance one another. For instance, the weakening of the British pound (amounting to approximately 13 percent of the ECU's composition), saw the consequent weakness of the ECU in the forex markets. Then, the strengthening of the German mark against the dollar increased the price of the ECU in terms of dollars.

As with all currencies, there are other reasons that come into the price equation, such as the psychological perception of the chances for a successful achievement of the European integration and what may follow 1992. Also for some countries, like Italy, the ECU was the first alternative given to their citizens for investing in other than Lira–denominated instruments. This appealed to the small investor.

Still other factors are related to the fact that the ECU is a basket of currencies and is therefore less volatile than each of its components. Big investors like the idea that the ECU means reliance on an aggregate of European currencies and that someday the ECU is bound to become the currency of Europe.

THE SINGLE EUROPEAN ACT AND THE EUROPEAN MONETARY UNION

Established in 1986, the Single European Act (SEA) declares that all barriers to the movement of goods, services, labor, and capital are to be removed within the European Community from the end of 1992. Therefore, it seeks to:

- Abolish administrative, legal, and technical barriers

- Harmonize standards of reference

- Reduce tax differences among member states

- End national preference in public procurement

Although the Single European Act does not say so explicitly, it implies that the European Community (EC)* is after all a *market* and free competition should dominate its laws, rules, and bylaws. More precisely, EC is a market of *economically strong* nations—even if three states of its current twelve members do not necessarily fit this description.

If there are stronger and weaker states, it is no less true that not all twelve member nations of the EC are in full agreement as to goals, means, and timetables.

- Some think tax harmonization and public procurement are less important issues than the freedom from customs controls and from restrictions on capital and people's mobility.

- Others urge that the benefits of currency unification be made available now rather than later.

- Still others are more skeptical about the achievement of the demanding goals of SEA.

One of the deeper arguments (if not disagreements) concerns a common monetary strategy leading to a monetary union, which includes joint legal regulation of banking and other industrial sectors. This goes beyond ensuring conditions of free movement of goods, services, and factors of production.

A single European currency, replacing existing national monies, could radically change the structure of the EC and accelerate political integration. This is in line with the fact that the drive toward economic and monetary union (EMU) is set to gain speed. "Sign up for economic and monetary union and you are on the slippery slope to a federal Europe: You cannot have a single currency without a single finance minister," said an article in London's *Economist*.[†] Or at least this is the warning that British opponents of European integration have been iterating.

"Alarmist nonsense," reply British supporters of EC: "A monetary union should not stop governments from running their own economic and fiscal policies."

The truth is halfway between those viewpoints. The EC Executive sees EMU as the moving force behind political union, much as the 1992 program was the motor behind the political concessions of the Single Eu-

---

*Also known as European Common Market (ECM), the Common Market (CM), or the European Economic Community (EEC). Not to be confused with the European Economic Area (EEA), which came into being at the end of October 1991 and is discussed in the last section of Chapter 9.

[†] December 8, 1990.

ropean Act. Helmut Kohl, the German Chancellor, makes this connection explicit. He sees no reason for Germany to sign away the D-mark in an EMU treaty unless it gets satisfaction from political union, which for him means a great deal more power for the European Parliament.

The problem is that differences run deep among twelve European Community countries on the meaning of political union. The French are cool about strengthening the European Parliament; they put emphasis on a common foreign and security policy. The Italians want both things, while England wants as little change as possible.

There is a critical difference between a full-scale monetary union and a simple agreement on exchange rates, like the present ERM* or the Bretton Woods agreements. The latter linked most world currencies to the dollar until 1972 and was pretty successful in that mission until the run on the gold reserves at Fort Knox, which obliged the Nixon administration to drop it.

There is, however, a significant difference between a monetary agreement to be honored by the key nations and a full-fledged currency union backed by the reserves of federated—but so far sovereign—states.

- A full currency union deprives its member nations of the power to issue their own money.

- The political consequences of this are very significant and underpin the EMU debate.

Let's recall that the Bretton Woods Agreement, which was signed in July 1944, also established the International Monetary Fund and the World Bank, beyond making the U.S. dollar the principal reserve currency. Under Bretton Woods, all member countries pegged their currency to the U.S. dollar within a 1 percent band. The dollar was pegged to gold at $35 per ounce. Hence, in effect, the governments of Western countries were deprived of fluctuations in their currencies—short of explicit devaluations or revaluations—but they were left with a number of monetary and fiscal freedoms.

Depriving any government of the power to issue new money does not only prevent it from swindling its own citizens through inflation but it also imposes new limits on its ability to borrow from its own citizens, thereby subjecting all tax and public-spending policies to the ultimate control of, say, a pan-European central bank.

There exists historical precedence: Each of the 13 states that originally made up America gave up just as much, but at the time the great

*Exchange Rate Mechanism, discussed in the next section.

democracy was nascent. No strongly embedded interests existed and the bitter pill of monetary unification was easier to swallow. Still it took until the early twentieth century to set up the Federal Reserve Board as the central bank—after a late-nineteenth century effort aborted.*

The truth is that the power to print money (including funny money) is the only real guarantee that lies behind a government's borrowing from its citizens. History and economic theory both show that there are upper limits on the tax burden any nation will tolerate.

Politicians and central bankers don't miss the point, which many other people fail to understand, that governments are, in practice, immune from all the legal sanctions available against private debtors and swindlers. This principle was well-appreciated in the nineteenth century, when English judges described sovereign loans as *aleatory contracts* (*aleator* means dice-player in Latin).

If a government joins a monetary union whose central bank it cannot control, it automatically loses its privileged borrowing status in its own domestic financial market, and turns instead into an aleatory borrower from foreign investors—provided that there are any. Such a government's tax and spending decisions and its monetary policies become dependent on the supranational central bank that alone can guarantee its debts. This is actually what the great debate over EMU is all about.

THE EUROPEAN MONETARY SYSTEM AND EXCHANGE RATE MECHANISM

Many people are hearing about the ECU and the EMU, but how many know what the EMS and ERM are? They are the existing European Monetary System (EMS) and its Exchange Rate Mechanism (ERM), which groups most, but not all, EC currencies. The EMS was set up in 1979, after the recession of the late 1970s. Its goal was to curb inflation and give its members currency stability before the lifting of exchange controls in 1990. The system then spawned the ERM and the European Currency Unit (ECU).

To put this subject into a better perspective we should step back some twenty years and take a look into events which had a bearing on EMS.

- Following the Smithsonian Agreement in December 1972, which put the tombstone on the Bretton Woods Agreement on stable parities, the EC suggested that its member countries limit the movement of their bilateral exchange rates to half of the new 2.25 percent band.

*William Greider, *Secrets of the Temple—How the Federal Board Runs the Country*, New York: Simon and Schuster, 1987.

- Members of the EC voluntarily joined this system, which became known as the "snake in the tunnel" or simply, *the snake.*

The snake was short-lived. But it did pave the way for the creation of the European Monetary System (March 1979) and its Exchange Rate Mechanism. It is essentially the EMS that called for the creation of the European Currency Unit as a GDP-weighted average of the EMS currencies. Hence, periodically, the ECU composition is modified to reflect changes in the relative GDP of member nations. It also changes when a new currency is admitted to the EMS.

According to this background, the market value of the ECU is calculated by allocating a fixed share in the ECU equal to a certain number of units of currency. For instance (as of 1990):

- 0.624 D-mark

- 1.332 French francs

- 0.088 British pound, and so on

To arrive at the value of the ECU in terms of U.S. dollars, it is necessary to multiply the fixed amount of each currency by the exchange rate of that currency to the dollar. This would be a simple arithmetical exercise, if it were not for the fact that currencies change in realtime in each of the world's major markets.

Another important feature of the EMS era is the adoption by many of its members of the Exchange Rate Mechanism. Each ERM currency has an assigned *ECU central rate.* This is a targeted rate of exchange for the ECU. The central rate is measured as the number of units of currency equal to one ECU. The ratio of any two currencies' rates is defined as their *bilateral* central rate.

According to the president of the EC Executive, Jacques Delors, the advantage of the EMS framework is its ability to create a zone of increasing monetary stability. Companies can invest in new markets in Western Europe, comforted by the knowledge that any new profits will not vanish through wild currency shifts.

- Up to a point, the EMS does limit currency fluctuations.

- It has also brought inflation in several ECM countries down to German levels.

- The price has been that of dependence on the interest rates set by the Bundesbank, which correctly follows conservative monetary policies.

Another element in the EC's economic and financial momentum was the 1988 agreement on the Community budget, which fixed spending limits for the next five years. A further goal, known as *phase three*, will be an independent European central bank, committed to price stability and setting interest rates for a single currency, the ECU. Such a bank will not be an ivory tower. It will be required to support the European Commission's general economic policy, so long as that does not prejudice commitments to stable prices.

The leading thought is that a European federal bank will be modeled similarly to the U.S. Federal Reserve in terms of independence from government intervention. Its governor will both report to the European Parliament and attend meetings of EC finance ministers — *Ecofin*, in Brussels jargon. The European federal bank and Ecofin will share responsibility for exchange rate policy. One finance minister and an EC commissioner will attend meetings of the bank's council.

But aside from the fact that some EC member nations are quite negative on this concept, some important points about the extended EMS and the EMU are still to be settled. The major query is what will happen in the *transitional* phase. Another is whether poorer EC countries should get extra help for accepting EMU. They claim that EMU could hinder their development by barring devaluations and threaten to block their socioeconomic progress unless they get compensation.

Mikhail S. Gorbachev will find it difficult to put *his* claims for handouts in better terms. In the affairs of people there comes a time when demands cease being reasonable and become ridiculous.

PROS AND CONS OF THE EUROPEAN EXCHANGE RATE MECHANISM

As underlined earlier in this chapter, the key issue goes much deeper than the shallow, hat-in-hand begging and dearly affects all EC's members. Just how far will national governments have to surrender control over national *fiscal, monetary, budgetary, and macroeconomic policies*? In addition, is the current Exchange Rate Mechanism able to transform itself into the necessary infrastructure for monetary discipline in the transition toward a single European currency?

A strict interpretation of ERM operating procedures suggests that policy changes — towards stringent rules — are necessary in government decisions in order to hold together the flexible Exchange Rate Mechanism. Yet, the rules governing the ERM have been purposely kept relatively flexible, allowing difficult interest rate and other decisions to be avoided for some time.

ERM members are unlikely to set hard guidelines that are necessary to reduce tensions within the system. They are also doing little in terms of other action, such as being lenient to excessive wage settlements. Monetary authorities are hoping that the EMS takes on a more normal shape without the need for tough decisions.

Still there are several positive issues about the way ERM functions. The member countries' exchange rates are behaving well within the upper and lower control limits that have been established, and there is a notable convergence of yields among ERM–member markets.

As Figure 8.1 documents (based on statistics by UBS International Finance), during the past 10 years the convergence between bond yields among ERM members has been dramatic. As risks of exchange rate realignment in the foreseeable future continue to fade, nominal yield spreads between ERM bond markets will be more important when making investment decisions. This effect is compounded by the fact that, as the latest progress toward monetary union suggests, it is correct to discount less and less currency volatility in western Europe. In the longer term, the formal narrowing of ERM parity bands will encourage yet more spread narrowing. As a result, the higher–yielding ERM bond markets are set to outperform. Under this perspective, it is not surprising that the British government decided to take the sterling into the European Exchange Rate Mechanism. After this decision, only two of the twelve EC countries—Greece and Portugal—are excluded from it.

Let's recapitulate the key points raised in this and the preceding sections. The ERM is only one element of the wider European Monetary System, which encompasses all EC members.

Figure 8.1 Difference between long-term bond yields and average yield of several European Community (EC) currencies.

- As EC members pool part of their gold and foreign currency reserves, their currencies are used to determine the value of the European Currency Unit (ECU).

- EC membership does not automatically imply partnership in all financial instruments. England, for instance, has been a member of the EMS since its inception in March 1979, but did not participate in the ERM until October 1990.

Both the ERM and the EMS were seen by their founders as staging posts on the road to fully fledged European economic and monetary union (EMU), which will occur if and when there is a single currency and central banking authority for the whole of western Europe. Special intergovernmental conferences are arranged from time to time to determine the route toward union. Not surprisingly, this route promises to be quite lengthy.

Proponents of the European economic and monetary union argue that its advent is even more necessary when there is risk of divergence in the EC economies. Those more skeptical reply that the EC economies' performance must converge far more, before further moves to economic and monetary union take place.

THE NEED FOR A MARKET-DRIVEN EMU

The 1990 Delors plan to turn the European Monetary System into a single currency could ultimately dash volatility, the currency trader's bread and butter. But many traders and investors think that the ability of the EMS to reduce volatility, and the cost for doing so, may be questioned. A *realistic* appreciation starts with the ways and means to be put into action and passes through the very important issue of the underlying strengths in such a union. Monetary unification may be realized either through a radical move or a progression. (See also the discussion made to that effect in Chapter 9.) The radical move method is, in practice, circumvented for political reasons. Therefore, the Delors plan realistically proposed a progressive unification.

The problem with step-by-step approaches, however, is that transitional stages are potentially saddled with difficulties. Not the least of them is that distinct national monies continue to circulate during the transition.

- How would exchange rate stability be maintained without instituting a mechanism for financing a persistent disequilibrium in an EC-wide sense?

- How will transitional stages be characterized in terms of sharing responsibilities in monetary and fiscal policies?

- Will the EC Executive and the European Parliament have a say in national financial and fiscal policies?

- Will countries with higher than average inflation, and larger than average budget deficits, be *forced* to pursue tighter policies?

Most importantly, will monetary unification be a way of circumventing the lack of policy coordination? Or is it a risky enterprise if fiscal and budgetary policies are not unified along with monetary policy?

These are key questions that bankers, treasurers, investors, forex traders, and securities dealers must ask themselves and the specialists. A great deal of return on the investments they make during the 1990s will depend on the answers they receive.

There is a certain coordination in terms of fiscal, budgetary, and monetary policies worth noting. Apart from the convergence in interest rates, of which we have already spoken, during the 1980s EC inflationary pressures seem to converged (with the exception of England). This is clearly shown in Figure 8.2.

This is welcome news because the real purpose of any set of monetary arrangements should be to achieve price stability, which in practice means inflation below 2 percent, or, even better, 1 percent. That is the reason that, in the longer term, the persistent uncertainty as to the the likelihood of economic and monetary union (EMU), the nature of its operations, and the date of its implementation is unsettling. Such uncertainty is reflected in the different rates of interest paid on long-term bonds denominated in different EC currencies, and for good reason. Pronouncements and announcements alone will not make the difference. The credibility of official statements is reflected by the market through an adjustment of long-term interest rates.

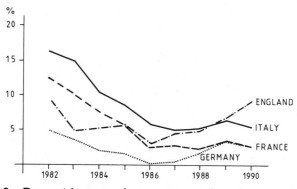

Figure 8.2   Percent increase in consumer prices (year-to-year) in several EC nations.

One approach is to turn to microeconomics, where the single-currency idea comes into its own.

- A single-market Europe would gain a lot from a single currency.
- There would be no more transaction costs of changing from one currency to another.
- There would be no worries, however residual, that exchange rates between two EC countries might be altered in the future.

There is no doubt that the United States has benefited greatly from having one dollar rather than dozens. Europe would do the same: It will find it impossible to reap the full rewards of 1992 until it has done away with its individual currencies—the ultimate non-tariff barriers to trade.

Under these circumstances banks, manufacturing, and merchandising enterprises all over the world would have an incentive to develop their business in ECU. This would give them a competitive advantage during the transition to a single currency.

But in reality it is not just a matter of EMU. The core issue consists of imaginative and coherent, stable-price economic and monetary union. Such union would introduce an anti-inflationary check on national governments that wanted to relax their monetary policies, apart of bringing the microeconomic benefits of a single monetary unit.

The bad news is that since it has been written by bureaucrats and central planners, one of the negative features of the Delors plan and its approach to EMU is that it is institutionally rather than market-driven. Yet as Robert Triffin aptly suggests:

- A successful EMU has to be market led.
- Institutional changes must be made to accommodate and facilitate market action.

The goal of market acceptance should underpin the process of creating the conditions for a uniform currency area, by closer integration through the completion of the internal market.

Together with the microeconomic factors, attention should also be paid to macroeconomic effects. In the absence of any significant imbalances of fiscal policy and balance of payments, similar monetary policies may ensure very low inflation differentials across countries.

WORKINGS OF THE ERM

Being a basket of weighted national currencies, the ECU functions as a common unit of account. As such, it is particularly useful to those who operate in different European currencies and have circular financial flows requiring financial netting. (See also Chapter 9 on netting through the ECU.)

For companies with many multinational transactions, the utility of such a common unit is obvious. At the same time, the ECU has not yet proved its role as a transnational currency. Custom and habit give a comparative advantage to national currencies—provided that their fluctuation is kept within a known range. This is the role fulfilled by the Exchange Rate Mechanism, described in the preceding section. But how does it work?

Starting with a practical response to this query, the English pound entered the exchange rate mechanism in late 1990 at a central rate, with a maximum permitted variation around this central rate of 6 percent either way. (Curiously, this central rate was expressed at 1 pound to 2.95 D-marks.) Other currencies in the system, except the Spanish peseta, operate on narrower bands of 2.25 percent fluctuation either way.

Given the ±6 percent admitted variation, the pound will be allowed to rise to about D-mark 3.13 and fall to as low as D-mark 2.78. These constitute its upper and lower limits before any devaluation or revaluation action is needed. In practice, however, this mechanism operates like a quality control chart in industry. Control action is triggering before the maximum divergence is reached.

This having been said, it is interesting to notice that when the Bretton Woods Agreements on fixed parities were abandoned in 1972, some economists suggested a similar solution for the world's currencies, but the idea was abandoned as impractical. Yet it does work.

The next question therefore becomes: How are currencies held within their bands? The answer is: through defense lines.

- The first line of defense in the ERM is intervention in the foreign exchange market in support of a specified currency.

- If the D-mark rises toward the top of its band, both the Bundesbank and the other reserve banks of the ECM sell D-marks to restrain it.

In other words, governments intervene to buy or sell currency to restore stability whenever rates overstep the 2.25 percent boundary. It took time and fiddling to get the balance right: Seven of the 11 parity alignments to date occurred during the first four years. But now the EMS is working smoothly—at least in this regard.

In case smooth operations cannot be achieved, then the next lines of defense involve market action:

- If upward pressure on the D-mark continues over a period, the Bundesbank may cut interest rates to reduce its attractiveness.

- If the D-mark is still in demand, the central bank could, in consultation with its European counterparts, arrange for the D-mark to be revalued—its ERM bands moved up.

However, the experience of the ERM has been that such realignments are rare. The last general realignment was in January 1987.

The measures to be taken will to a large extent be subject to the market's approval. Besides this, there are constraints. The central bank of any country can set a target for interest rates, or the exchange rate, but it cannot do both at the same time. Also, a good deal depends on working in unison. After a currency has settled down in the ERM, if other European central banks raise their interest rates, it will be more difficult (than it used to be) for the central bank concerned to avoid following suit.

In England, Sir Alan Walters set out what is known as the Walters critique of the ERM. He argued that the mechanism encourages a process in which capital is attracted to those countries offering the highest interest rates, which also tend to be the countries with the highest inflation. As money flows in, these currencies rise, and there is pressure for early interest rate cuts. But interest rate cuts make it harder for such countries to reduce inflation. This argument is only partly true, as it forgets the difference between the *nominal* and the *real* interest rate.

One question often asked in England after the pound's entry into ERM relates to the effect membership has on inflation. Is not participation in the ERM supposed to help in cutting inflation? In late 1990, when inflation had reached the 10.6 percent mark, the British Treasury thought that the long-term role of the ERM will be to help bring down inflation. The reason is that over any period of time the exchange rate between two currencies reflects relative inflation rates: If England's inflation does not move closer to Germany's 3 percent rate, then the pound will have to fall against the D-mark.

And indeed some eight months later (mid-June 1991), statistics indicated that British inflation had come down. Measured by the retail price index, England's inflation rate dropped sharply, pushed by lower mortgage rates and a smaller poll tax cut. Underlying inflation, however, was reduced only slowly.

Seen from a different perspective, the test of ERM entry is its ability to influence wages. In France, the commitment to a strong franc in the ERM has led to sharply lower pay settlements but also higher unemployment over a number of years.

By shifting the focus of interest rate policy to the exchange rate, ERM membership could also mean that taxation and public spending instruments have to be used more consistently to control a domestic economy. In a situation where the economy is growing too fast but the respective currency is strong within the ERM, the government could have to cut public spending to rein it back.

WEIGHTING THE ECU

The basket nature of the ECU has been a strong incentive for its development as a financial instrument. The risk-reducing character of a portfolio of currencies strengthens the wealth-preserving function of an international store of value.

Some economists, however, question whether the ECU's liquidity in the classical sense could legally extinguish debt contracts. The answer is that because of the momentum that it is developing, the ECU has started a process of "international liquidity" of its own, beyond the appearance of liquidity derived from its component currencies. As a consequence of this fact, the ECU has a relatively high external value premium. At the same time, lacking legal-tender status, it cannot be used in final consumption. Only in Luxembourg, so far, do merchants accept the ECU as a unit of payment.

As a means of transaction and in terms of holding assets, two of the reasons that give worth to money, the ECU's attractiveness is largely due to its high safety premium within an uncertain monetary environment. But which are really the components giving the ECU its worth?

We said that the ECU is a basket of currencies from all 12 member states. These contributions are weighted according to their economic strength. (As of this writing, one ECU is worth about $1.30.) Figure 8.3 gives the current weights, but Table 8.1 helps in appreciating that such weights change over time.

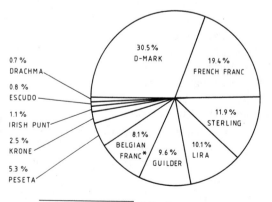

* THE BELGIAN FRANC IS ALSO LEGAL TENDER IN LUXEMBOURG

Figure 8.3 Composition of the EMU: relative weight of the 12 EC currencies.

Table 8.1 Composition of the ECU in 1986 and in 1990

Currency	1986	1990
Deustche Mark (Germany)	34.1%	30.5%
French franc (France)	19.1	19.4
Sterling (England)	12.9	11.9
Guilder (Holland)	10.8	9.6
Lira (Italy)	9.5	10.1
Belgian Franc (Belgium and		
Luxembourg)	8.9[a]	8.1
Krone (Denmark)	2.8	2.5
Punt (Ireland)	1.1	1.1
Drachma (Greece)	0.8	0.7
Peseta (Spain)	—	5.3
Escudo (Portugal)	—	0.8
	100.0%	100.0%

[a] To the rate of 8.6% for Belgium and 0.3% for Luxembourg.

Critics might say that by tying weak currencies to the strongest money, ERM, EMS, and the ECU created a system strapped to the D-mark. A fear of losing independence—and, more recently, high inflation—has been Britain's main reason for keeping the pound out of the ERM for so long. Yet, ERM and EMS have been able to maintain exchange rate stability. As we have already seen, they have exercised downward pressure on inflation and helped in the convergence of some EC interest rates.

All 12 European Common Market currencies contribute to the ECU. Although Portugal and Greece are not members of the ERM, their currencies help to make up the European Currency Unit. They are expected to join when they have a firmer grip on national economic policy.

It is only natural that along with growth and diversification of ECM's financial market the ECU cannot remain the sole property of any particular financial center. So far business has been concentrated mainly in five countries: France, Belgium, Luxembourg, Italy, and the United Kingdom. But the United States and Japan are also showing signs of increased interest in developing the ECU market.

As will be shown in Chapter 9, these developments are accompanied by a proliferation of available instruments both in the Euromarket and in a number of domestic capital markets. In addition to conventional straight issues, the following appeared:

- ECU floating rate notes
- ECU zero coupon bonds

- ECU paper with participation warrants and convertible bonds
- ECU issues with extendable maturities
- Issues with adjustable bonds

At the short end of the market came ECU certificates of deposit, both with fixed and floating rates. At present, a spreading opinion is that the role of the ECU could be further extended not only as an investment and trading vehicle, but also as a means of invoicing commercial transactions. A different way of making this statement is that, thanks to increased acceptance of the ECU by private and corporate users, the basket currency is receiving growing official recognition. The ECU is bought and sold in spot and forward transactions against practically all other convertible currencies, an additional feature being ECU futures, and ECU options trading. Slowly, transnational companies are becoming bullish on the ECU. Alcatel's accounts, for example, are tallied in European Currency Units.*

As a transnational company, Alcatel is run from Paris, but keeps its technical center in Brussels and spreads export orders among other units in Spain, France, and Germany. This geographic dispersion gives a great deal of flexibility:

- Alcatel can fill orders wherever currency, costs, and political considerations make filling the orders most attractive.

- Alcatel needs a money to unify its accounts and seems to have found the solution in the ECU.

In England, Australia's biggest bank, Westpac, maintains a 45-strong treasury team, which helps pay the bills of Westpac's European operations. It has built a strong presence in European currencies, particularly the European Currency Unit. Westpac's treasurer claims his operations capture up to a quarter of the daily ECU business, which is now ranked between sixth and seventh on the table of most-traded currencies in the London foreign exchange market. Says Tony Aveling, Westpac's chief manager for Europe: "We had a good look at where the Euromarket might go a few years on. It was obvious Europe was getting closer together and the ECU presented itself as a logical extension of that process. We followed our instincts."† The ECU's role in EC trade has been limited. Only 1 percent of EC trade is ECU–denominated. But Aveling believes this will change as the end of 1992 draws closer.

*Forbes, October 29, 1990.
† Business Review Weekly, October 19, 1990.

For his part, Michael Beales, Westpac's chief treasury manager, reports that his desk did extraordinary business in ECU after sterling went into the European Monetary System. "It was purely psychological trading," Beales said. "The ECU has nothing to do with EMS but the market just saw Europe and went for anything that was vaguely European."

While still Chancellor of the Exchequer, John Major, who brought England into the EMS, put forward an alternative proposal to the Delors plan: a dual-currency system that would enhance the status of the existing ECU, which would circulate alongside sovereign currencies.

While still Bundesbank president, Dr. Pöhl, who had initially rejected the hard ECU plan, by late 1990 became half sold on it, at least one of its versions: "I am in favor of considering hardening the ECU." But, unlike the British, Dr. Pöhl does not want the ECU to become a thirteenth currency, and he rejects the idea of creating a European Monetary Fund that would issue it. Pöhl's idea is to fortify the ECU by increasing its hard-currency component, such as the D-mark, diminishing the weight of the weaker currencies. If the D-mark's weight were to rise to, say, 40 percent, the ECU's value would gain some 40¢ to $1.73 in value (October 1990 exchange reference data).

ECONOMIC GROWTH, TECHNOLOGICAL LEADERSHIP, AND CURRENCY VALUES

In late May 1991, the news hit that Europe's trade deficit with Japan soared 63 percent in the first quarter, to $9.9 billion. In April of 1991 it had already topped the U.S. deficit with Japan.

- The new Europe is a tempting market for Japanese and American companies.

- As the world's last emerging, huge, First World market, Europe is likely to become the focal point of the world's economic-power balance for the twentieth-first century.

Many economists see the macroeconomics of ECM as a booming base from which multinationals will consolidate their financial strength and be able to capitalize on economies of scale. It comes therefore as no surprise that a three-way fight is now shaping up among Americans, Japanese, and the Europeans to determine who will reap the most benefits.

How is Europe's industrial infrastructure standing in terms of peak technologies? A mid-1991 study by *Fortune* magazine* documented that

*June 17, 1991.

Table 8.2 Leadership in the World's Peak Technologies

	United States	Japan	Europe
Processor design	9.5	5.8	4.7
Software	9.3	5.2	6.8
Displays and printers	6.0	9.6	4.1
Data networks	8.7	6.5	6.9
Chip-making equipment	7.5	9.3	4.3
Photonics (Optoelectronics)	7.0	9.0	5.1

of six pivotal technologies the United States leads in three, and Japan dominates the other three. And Europe? Table 8.2 presents the average score based on individual assessment by ten cognizant people. Whereas the gold medals (indicated by underlines in Table 8.2) have gone to America and to Japan, Europe only takes two silver medals.

In processor design, the classical leader is America, whose companies pioneered the massively parallel computers and the hypercube architecture.* Even though many ingenious ideas for new processors came from England and some of the countries on the continent, European computer companies never had transnational commercial impact and are losing market share as well as billions.

The Germans have been particularly vulnerable in this domain because of the repetitive industrial "Stalingrads" suffered by the management of their companies in the computer battlefield. The French and the Dutch have not done any better.

Whereas Americans lead in the software business, the Europeans are doing better than the Japanese in this domain—in part because of the fact that Japanese software efforts have been handicapped by linguistics. But this hurdle is by now overcome, and Kanji may turn out to be an advantage. Besides, Fujitsu, Hitachi, NEC, Sony, and NTT Data are very active in object-oriented programming—a lead unmatched by European computer companies.

Then there is the story of what *Fortune* calls *eyeball economics:* The more time people spend with their computers and TV, the more they expect in terms of sharp, clear, user-friendly displays. Here Japan is the unquestionable world leader—a huge market, all the way from business to the households.

Data networks is another area in which the Japanese work hard, and though today they are more or less in third position, many experts expect them to leapfrog to world leadership before the end of this decade. The

---

*See also D. N. Chorafas and H. Steinmann, *Supercomputers*, New York: McGraw-Hill, 1990.

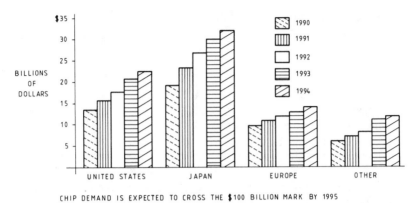

CHIP DEMAND IS EXPECTED TO CROSS THE $100 BILLION MARK BY 1995

Figure 8.4 Projected growth in semiconductor shipments by region.

future lies in *intelligent networks* with broadband channeling capacity. Narrowband used by the so-called integrated services digital network (ISDN), on which European telecommunications companies and telcos unwisely bet their fortunes, is too slow for computer users.*

Photonics (optical disks, optical transmission, optical switching) will replace electronics by the end of this decade to become the growth technology of the twenty-first century. Here the Japanese are way ahead of everybody, with Europe a distant third.

A curious story is that of chip-making equipment. In 1990, four of the top five companies in this most critical industry were Japanese. Because of this, Japan surged past America to become the world's no. 1 maker of computer chips. In America, the Semiconductor Industry Association has published projections that dramatize what this market dominance currently means. They are shown in Figure 8.4, and as it can be easily seen the gap between the leader and the followers is steadily increasing.

As far as the peak technologies are concerned, Europe is faced with the distinct possibility of losing ground rapidly and completely—and once ground is lost it cannot be easily regained. This loss of leadership bears bad omens for each of the leading European currencies and for the ECU; that explains why such a discussion fits in the particular context of this book.

---

*See also the predictions made in D. N. Chorafas, *System Architecture and System Design*, New York: McGraw-Hill, 1989.

- So far, Japan's presence is still far greater in the United States than in Europe.

- By contrast, American direct investment in Europe is greater than Japan's.

But apart from their leadership in peak technologies, the Japanese have accelerated the pace at which they plant their roots into the old continent. "In the first part of the 1980s, we concentrated our major resources on North America," says Seigo Nishino, chairman of Mitsubishi Electric Europe. "Now we have started to look at Europe."*

After buying British computer maker Apricot in 1991, Mitsubishi is hiking its investment in Europe by as much as 30 percent a year. Having gained in 1990 control of Britain's ICL, the only profitable European computer maker, Fujitsu used ICL in 1991 to buy out Finland's Nokkia Data, with a pan-European marketing network for workstations.

The Japanese have been masters in finding new avenues. They have systematically forged strategic alliances with companies short of cash and hungry for technology.

- When local production was required, they launched investments in plants, sometimes from scratch.

- Most recently they have been buying big chunks in companies outright, such as Germany's construction equipment maker Hanomag.

As *Business Week* suggested: "Add it all up, throw in a recession and high unemployment, and suddenly there is a danger that some critical European industries will be hollowed out."

- Siemens depends on Fujitsu for large-scale computers.

- Bull depends on NEC.

- Olivetti depends on Canon and Sanyo for office equipment.

- Fiat depends on Hitachi for construction gear.

For one thing, such one-sided alliances are keeping some European industries afloat in critical technologies. But the more the Japanese aim to dominate key industries, the more one-sided the alliances will be. The battle of the Yen versus ECU is just starting.

Business Week, June 3, 1991.

9

The ECU, the German Mark, and the Dollar

As stated in the introduction to Chapter 8, the history of the European Currency Unit (ECU) started in 1978 and proceeded in two phases. First, the establishment of the ECU as a unit; second, the process of making it a means of transaction within the European Monetary System. It was also stated that commercial banks took charge of turning the ECU into an investment instrument.

As of 1990 there have been billions of dollars worth of ECU in the international financial system, created by the major banks as they bundle the component European currencies together to make new ECUs for their customers:

- In Europe, over 350 banks provide a range of financial services in ECU.

- All over the world, about 1,000 banks in 30 countries are reckoned to be active in the ECU market.

Quite significantly, there are already some ECU 710 billion (US$850 billion) worth of transactions every month. This amount of money changing hands is not just good from a public relations standpoint. It is indicative of a grown market potential in ECU.

The true actors have become the European central banks, which father the ECU currency and preside over a dual increase in the number of transactions and the mean value per transaction. Both these items are important because they define the total amount of money in ECU and the netting balances such transactions call for. They are essentially the metrics of the acceptance of the ECU by the marketplace.

Criteria exist to guide such transactions. Shifts in interest rates often determine whether a particular financial package is more advantageous if denominated in ECU or in its component currencies. The financial engineers of major banks also construct special swap arrangements in which a Eurobond may be floated in ECU, but usually funds are immediately converted into a national currency that the corporate borrower prefers to have.

USING THE ECU

In mid-1988 Britain decided to switch $2.5 billion in foreign debt into European Currency Units. This created the first market for short-term bills in the composite currency, making ECUs more attractive to big investors. As trading expands, the questions posed relative to the ECU multiply:

- Which policies regarding ECU should be promoted?
- Since the ECU is a composite currency, who explodes it into component currencies?
- Should Swift or another network be used as the clearance network?
- Who compensates? Who has the last-resort responsibility?

Answers to these issues are rather urgent, as statistics by the Bank of International Settlements (BIS) in Basel show a marked year-by-year increase in the volume of ECUs created by banks since 1983. BIS manages the enlarged clearing system of the ECU, but this does not necessarily answer all queries on the role of BIS. There is a lack of necessary provision by international law not only for ECU but also for the Special Drawing Rights (SDR), which is the other international composite currency.

Where national laws favor investments in ECU, as for instance in Italy, financial institutions and investors actively look into capitalizing on favorable legal provisions for ECU-denominated instruments. This has ensured that financial activity in ECU has been on the rise in the bond market. In 1981, the first ECU-denominated bond was floated (in the Euromarkets) with the total value of ECU bonds outstanding reaching a tiny ECU 200 million. By 1985 the ECU bond market was worth ECU 9 billion, growing at 250 percent per year, but it stabilized during the subsequent years. By 1987 about 5.4 percent of international debt instruments were contracted in ECU. This is still very little considering that

65 percent of international loans are denominated in dollars—with the Deutsche mark as the second currency, though at a much lower share.

As of the late 1980s, an average of 62,000 to 65,000 payments per month took place in ECU, or about 2,300 transactions per day, with a cumulative daily average value of 13 billion ECU. This means roughly ECU 560,000 per transaction on the average, which is a very small fraction of the average dollar value of transactions transiting through New York's CHIPS.

ECU transactions are inhibited by the absence of a European bank. Therefore, to establish the ECU as unit of exchange the Association for the ECU (located in Paris) has been examining arrangements for ECU clearing both with BIS and Swift—the latter in regard to its contribution in:

- Sorting out all ECU payments

- Computing netting balance by bank (about 100 million ECU per bank)

The principle is that if a bank is not able to cover debit—either through its own reserves or borrowing—then the transaction is to be cancelled. I will return to this issue.

Promoted by the ECU Banking Association (EBA), a 1988 market study involved a number of business enterprises, who were asked: "Do you think that 1992 should go beyond market integration?" To this 80 percent answered: "Yes, beyond." To the second question "What is the key subject of beyond?" 90 percent responded: "a common currency." (This issue was discussed in Chapter 8.) A *common currency* still permits national currencies, whereas a *single currency* means only one alternative: no national currencies. This is an important issue since a common, single market implies free circulation of capital and the ability to support a Europe-wide capital market. At the present time, no member state of the European Common Market wants its currency to be the common currency, nor can a non-European currency serve this purpose. Hence, an answer is the ECU. But there remain the questions: What kind? Strong or weak?

A very strong ECU will eventually mean a single currency replacing all national currencies. A very weak one will only be an accounting unit and simple reference model. A middle scenario is that of continuing to use national currencies for domestic business while the ECU serves for international exchange—but this implies a competitive situation between the ECU and the national currencies, requiring additionally a European central bank to administer it.

Both the impediment and the opportunity are that the concept of a currency is closely related to sovereignity issues:

- The successful achievement of a monetary union in Europe will underpin European integration.

- By contrast, because national governments do *not want to* feel bound together, their failure to reach a valid currency solution will undermine European integration.

Orderly monetary solutions are fundamental for coexistence among nations and their contributions in world trade. International finance requires a well-tuned system of which the currency—hence the unit of money—is the pivot point. The principles are evident; their implementation is less clear.

ECU-DENOMINATED INSTRUMENTS

The future of the ECU is closely tied to the expectation that at the end of 1992 the major obstacles to a free circulation of goods, services, labor, and capital inside the European Community will be removed.* This is significant inasmuch as—in order of magnitude—more than half of the member states' foreign trade takes place inside the European Community, a share that will most probably increase considerably in the wake of the forthcoming integration.

At the same time, along the monetary front the EMS has proved to be a useful tool in stabilizing the exchange rates between most of the EC countries' currencies, creating the expectation that exchange rate fluctuations among EC currencies will be further reduced. With this background, we can return to the question asked in the previous section, rephrasing it in the following manner:

- Is there a need for a common currency in a single market?

- Should or would it be the ECU?

- What about ECU-denominated instruments?

- How can the way toward a common currency be paved?

---

*This and the following two sections on the ECU are based on a presentation by Dr. Gilbert Lichter, former Secretary General of the Paris-based ECU Banking Association, to the Fourth International Symposium on High Technology in Banking, which I was chairing in West Berlin in September 1988.

To the question regarding the need to have a common currency in a single European market, the answer is an unwavering yes! An integrated economic area calls for one common, if not truly single, currency. It would have been impossible, for instance, for the economy of the United States to operate with 50 different currencies—one for each state.

The first issue concerning ECU-denominated instruments now comes to the foreground, that is, the *commercial* viewpoint. The purpose of a single market is to stimulate commercial and financial flows inside Europe, capitalizing on the resulting better allocation of resources and advantages of scale induced by a home market with 320 million producers/consumers.

Currency integration would allow the European industry to develop the required competitiveness for challenging American and Japanese companies both inside Europe and in their home markets. Microeconomic dynamics are expected to generate a period of growth, but neither the monetary nor the fiscal issues can be left out of the equation.

The next reference to the ECU is that of a *financial intermediary,* in the sense of a common unit of reference. The handling of multicurrency treasuries, in particular by small- and medium-size companies, represents an element of confusion; it also implies greater transaction costs. These extra costs have been evaluated at approximately 1 percent of turnover, which talks a mouthful.

Risk is still another vital reference. An important monetary obstacle to the development of trade lies in currency risks, in particular the foreign exchange rate risk. Although west European currencies today are fairly stable, their margin of variation in the EMS is such that, combined with the extra transaction costs, they could wipe out some companies' profits.

Here again, though the larger corporations have developed the skills enabling them to live with this risk because of their global operations, smaller industries suffer a handicap. And though some might say that a multicurrency system with nearly fixed parities is good enough to tackle this problem, a big question remains: "Is it a credible system?"

Do multiparty agreements among independent nations provide enough guarantees to maintain stable rates over five years? over ten years? Five or ten years may seem to be a long time, but this is not so for an industrialist who has to decide *now* where to set up a production unit: in Germany, France, England, Spain, or any other EEC country.

A rational decision in capital investments needs to consider at what cost the products will be coming out of a production unit in five to ten years, and at what price such products can be profitably offered to the market. Planning may turn out to be quite hazardous, if one has to account for currency risks. Although we all try to hedge, the question is:

"In which way?" Industrialists have to master the risks associated with product development, production, and marketing; but the monetary risks must be taken care of by the public authorities mandated to provide a risk-free exchange environment in a common market.

Principles that have underpinned investment decisions in a *domestic* economy do not necessarily apply in the multinational landscape of a common market. The clearer the monetary policy is, the better for all concerned.

Let me say this in conclusion. Since monetary sovereignty is a major constituent of national sovereignty, it is rather difficult for national authorities to subordinate monetary sovereignty—whether partly or entirely. This is essentially what Mrs. Thatcher is saying. But the other side of the coin reads: "No common currency, no common market."

ADVANTAGES OF A SINGLE COMMON CURRENCY

Earlier in this chapter the differences between a single currency and a common currency were described. This section has been written to underline that, from the viewpoint of industry, the advantages in having a single, common currency are:

1. The ability to provide Europe with a capital market strong enough to finance the necessary investments for achieving expected economies of scale

2. The strengthening of free circulation of capital to avoid the disturbing turbulences in domestic currency exchange rates and interest rates

3. A stable financial planning reference on which industrial and commercial investments can depend

Short of this common base of reference, European Community central banks will be obliged to permanently intervene in their domestic financial markets. Eventually, this will lead to an interest rate contest or an inflationary appeasement policy in the domestic money markets.

Even if numerous coordinating mechanisms are established among the monetary authorities of Western Europe, currency competition does not appear as an appropriate mechanism. It is definitely not able to provide the economy with a stable monetary environment.

A basic managerial question is always: "Which are our alternatives?" Applied to the monetary domain within the European Common Market (with a common level of monetary reference in mind) these alternatives seem to be the use of:

- One of the existing national currencies

- A currency of a non-EC country, for instance the dollar

- A new currency, accepted as a common currency, for example the ECU

At the present stage, no actor on the monetary stage wishes his or anyone else's national currency to be the common currency—though discussions have been made about the German mark fulfilling this role. There is also a precedence of the Chinese who, years ago, proposed to use the Swiss franc for their imports/exports, but the Swiss respectfully declined. Hence, we may drop the first of the three options.

The second option seems to be rather odd, yet at least today it is the closest to reality.

- Many a European industrialist invoices his products in U.S. dollars, even when selling to other European buyers.

- Most of the EC central banks intervene to stabilize their currencies in the forex markets by buying or selling them against the U.S. dollars.

But there are also a number of European financiers and industrialists who suggest that intra-European trade should not be based on a non-EC currency. Hence the third option: the ECU.

Considering the statements made by the governments of most of the Common Market's member states, as well as the competent monetary authorities, there seems to be a consensus that a single common currency like the ECU is advisable. But there are different views of how to reach this goal and with what rapidity.

A few scenarios have been suggested. According to one of them, the *economic*, *fiscal*, and *monetary* policies of the EC member countries have to further converge until reaching a point where harmonization will render national currencies redundant. According to this hypothesis, this is the moment for a monetary reform, replacing all national currencies by a common one.

There are flaws with this scenario, starting with the thought that for monetary union states must achieve far-reaching economic convergence as a prerequisite—and that convergence is doable in our days. States may have economic divergences and still fare very well with one single

currency, provided that their monetary and fiscal (taxation, budget) policies are closely monitored and coordinated. It is primarily the member
states' divergence in taxation and budgetary policies that complicates this
solution.

The second scenario is a gradualist one, tending toward parallelism.
It calls for the national currencies to be maintained, particularly in their
domestic utilization, while a common currency, the ECU, is progressively
developed to a wider use. Eventually the time will come for it to replace
the existing national currencies.

Such a scenario implies a competitive situation between the ECU and
the national currencies in terms of market share, be it in the capital
markets, the money markets, or as a transaction currency. Hence we
again have the questions asked at the beginning of this chapter:

- What type of ECU: strong or weak?

- To be used in what areas?

- To be supported by what sort of institutional framework?

I suggested earlier that each alternative, strong or weak, has its adher-
ents. With time, practice will tell which is the best within a community
of independent nations that so far have agreed on the wisdom of togeth-
erness in commercial aspects—but not yet in political ones, where tough
decisions have to be made.

ECU CLEARING

Initially the type of clearing system devised for the ECU was next-day
value. On a given business day D, only payments carrying value date
D + 1 (next business day) were cleared. Since March 1988, however, the
clearing has been changed to a same-day value system.

The mechanism adopted for ECU clearing rests on two main functions:

- *Netting*, assumed within an agency agreement by a subsidiary of the
  Swift organization (SSP)

- *Settlement* function, executed by the Bank for International Settlements (BIS)

As a result of this two-tier approach, the daily clearing procedure is split
into two consequent stages with their relevant cut-off times: a netting

stage until 2:30 P.M. and a settlement stage from 2:30 to 3:00 P.M. (Brussels time). The netting stage has the following countdown:

- Until 11:00 A.M., customers and correspondents may transmit their ECU payment instructions for same day value to their clearing bank.
- The clearing banks then have until 1:00 P.M. (called preliminary cut-off time) to transmit to each other their payment orders for value that day by Swift/SSP messages.

For this purpose, a special netting computer (owned and operated by Swift) intercepts and copies automatically all netting-related ECU payment messages transmitted among clearing banks via the Swift network. Immediately after preliminary cut-off time, the netting computer establishes for each clearing bank a preliminary netting report, including all payments made and received by that clearing bank for value that day, as well as their balance.

Positive preliminary netting balances are considered as intra-clearing assets that may be lent or sold to clearing banks having a negative netting balance. Accordingly, money market transactions are undertaken by the clearing banks, in principle by lending intra-clearing ECUs on an overnight basis, in order to reduce the netting balances.

Immediately after final cut-off time, the netting computer establishes the final netting balances of each clearing bank, taking into account its preliminary netting balance and the payment messages resulting from the intra-clearing lending transactions. The netting computer then generates a message to each clearing bank to communicate a final netting report for the day. The BIS receives the report, which includes all the clearers' final netting balances.

The money market transactions among clearing banks, between preliminary and final cut-off time, permit a considerable reduction of the final balances that are to be settled at the end of the day via sight accounts with BIS. The use of the Swift transmission network as the technical infrastructure of the netting enables the participant banks to adapt to the system with minimal interface and message-handling problems, because they are already networked with Swift.

Initially, the clearing procedures foresaw as a possible transaction the exchange of ECUs against the basket of component currencies for reasons of reducing preliminary netting balances. The transfer of all the component currencies on very short notice proved, however, to be cumbersome. Hence, as of October 1987, the clearing banks have implemented a component currencies exchange system, operated outside the clearing, under two value days. This is coupled with an interest rate fixing mechanism for ECU-clearing overnight lendings that takes into account the liquidity supply situation for a given value date.

Other, rather unique features of the ECU clearing have to do with problems related to the need for settlement on days when one or several clearers have a national bank holiday.

For the purpose of carrying out the settlement operations, per se, the *clearing agreement* between the BIS and the ECU Banking Association foresees two accounts for each clearing bank.

1. A *clearing account* held by the BIS (outside its own book) acting in its capacity as accounting agent to the clearing: The goal of the clearing account is to register every day each clearer's final netting balance, on the debit and credit side. This account represents a record of the residual claims or liabilities of each clearing bank toward all the other clearing banks, after offsetting the day's payments.

2. An *ECU sight account,* opened in the books of BIS, with the purpose of settling each day the balance of the clearing account: This ECU sight account carries no remuneration and may not be in a debit position. The system provides two possibilities for supplying the ECU sight accounts: by transferring ECUs from one sight account to another and by transferring all the component currencies of the ECU to dedicated accounts of BIS.

On the basis of its existing funds on its ECU sight account and considering the final netting balance on a given day, a clearing bank may borrow from another clearing bank ECUs available for value that day on the latter's sight account. ECU payment orders related to those transactions have to be sent to the BIS before settlement, which is at 3:00 P.M.

Should one clearing bank be unable to provide its sight account with sufficient funds to settle its clearing balance, the system foresees the possibility of an *unwind.* In that case, the settlement is not completed; the nonperforming bank is suspended from the clearing; all the payment orders given and received by the nonperforming bank on that day are cancelled, and they are adjusted to the next value date.

INTERNATIONAL INVESTMENTS IN STRONG CURRENCIES

Shortly before the end of the gold standard, John Maynard Keynes urged the foundation of a multinational central bank. Many of his ideas have been incorporated in the IMS, World Bank, and EMS. A further development of the EMS into a European currency union may well follow the original Keynes proposal.

Dr. Keynes's concept was based on experience regarding how long goodwill organizations can last, partly in reference to the fate of the so-called Latin Monetary Union. Its main deficiency was the lack of regulation of the total money supply. After World War I, for example, France took advantage of this deficiency to solve its public finance problems. During a period of galloping inflation, banknotes were issued, even at the level of municipalities. Officially, but not in practice, the Latin Monetary Union lasted until 1927. Today, the lessons from this attempt to combine a currency union with national monetary autonomy have been largely forgotten. Yet they are very important for the future of the ECU. These lessons suggest the wisdom of:

- Applying a simple but universal definition of money

- Keeping a centralized control of the issue of legal tender

- Preventing the central banks of participating countries from being mixed up with public finances

These are fundamental steps as well as prerequisites, if we want to have both a currency union and no controls of capital movements within this union.

There could, however, be a further view of this issue if we look at the ECU as the no. 4 world currency after the U.S. dollar, yen, and D-mark. For instance, in case there develops a self-standing financial market for the ECU with transnational companies, not only doing business in this currency, like the case of Alcatel we saw in Chapter 8, but also being quoted in the exchanges in ECU.

To back up the hypothesis of a fourth major currency, the ECU-denominated stock market should in a way emulate the rise of the German stock market to world prominence during the 1980s. Let's not forget that in the mid-1960s one company's capitalization in the New York Stock Exchange, IBM's, equaled the capitalization of the whole German stock market—we are a long way from that situation.

The international interlacing of the German stock market has intensified in the 1986 to 1990 years though not at the same level as the D-mark–denominated bond market. Based on statistics by the Bundesbank, Figure 9.1 presents the fluctuation of stock quotations in Germany, the United States, and Japan in the 1984 to 1990 timeframe. Significant is the fact that during this period foreign investments in Germany reached about DM39 billion. This is roughly 250 percent more than comparable investments made between 1981 and 1985, which amounted to DM16 billion. Will ECU-denominated investments and stock market transactions reach comparable figures?

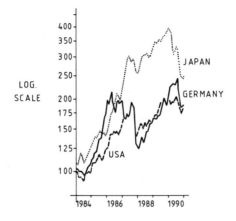

REFERENCES
TOKYO STOCK PRICE INDEX, NEW YORK EXCHANGE
COMPOSITE INDEX, AKTIENINDEX DES STATISTISCHEN
BUNDESAMTES

Figure 9.1   Fluctuation of stock prices in the United States, Germany, and Japan.

The ECU could find a niche figuring as one of the key world currencies from a portfolio management viewpoint. One of the key advantages of a global approach to stock investments and bond investments is reducing portfolio risk through diversification.

At the same time, there is no reason to believe that a composite currency, which has no clear home base, can compete with the D-mark in an investment sense. Unless, of course, the ECU becomes *the* European legal tender.

Business and therefore the financial markets are based on confidence; such confidence may take many years to build, but one major mishap is enough to destroy it. It is therefore necessary to have for the ECU both a well-defined home base and a lender of last resort. Some economists argue that the European Community could constitute itself as the ECU's reserve system.

This argument rests on the premise that such a solution does *not* need any initial capital of its own. It is enough that ECU liabilities are guaranteed by the 12 central banks.

- In the books, such liabilities consist of the ECU.

- Assets are the securities that it receives from its members in exchange for the ECU legal tender and international reserves.

To be manageable such an approach requires not only precise and binding commitments by the EC member nations but also a central board. The board should be independent of the 12 governments and have the authority to decide on:

- The total volume of ECU liabilities

- Its own central ECU reserve requirements

- Quotas for member central banks in the event of volume growth

- The standard of securities that its members (and itself) will accept in exchange for new ECU issues

These requirements more or less describe a central European bank, though they reflect a confederate approach rather than a body that can act independently of the 12 Community nations and their central banks.

Moreover, no board can be well managed if it is not endowed with a high degree of authority and discretion. Well-qualified financial management can give this solution the needed credibilities, with the result that the ECU's investment premium would rise. This is a desireable course since, as a loans and investments currency, the ECU must be able to keep in step with the general expansion of both the international and the Eurocapital markets. A number of policies will therefore need to be adopted, and lessons can be learned from the D-mark.

Since the elimination of the tax on interest, foreign buyers of D-mark–denominated bonds have increasingly moved toward *public loans*. This is particularly true of major foreign investors such as pension funds and central banks. Both prefer these issues because of *dependability* and *liquidity* compared to D-mark bonds by industrial companies. A different way of making this statement is to remember that investors take a very critical look at what they are buying. The market is a very demanding critter, and if the ECU is to be left to the market regarding its acceptance, then it has to measure up to the market's standards of:

- Security and dependability

- Liquidity

- Volatility

- Return on investment

To say that yield is very important is to state the obvious; it is not the only criterion. Other things equal, the market will focus on yield through a study comparable to the one in Figure 9.2, which reflects on yield criteria of selected strong-currency bond issues. The compound total yield index

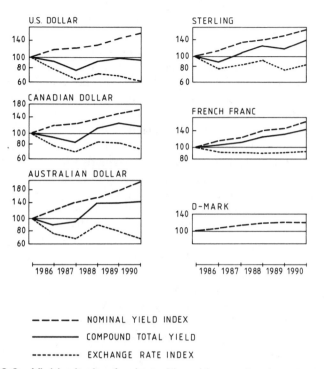

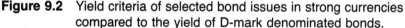

Figure 9.2 Yield criteria of selected bond issues in strong currencies compared to the yield of D-mark denominated bonds.

is the central point. It is based on the nominal yield index and the foreign exchange rate index. The total yield has been calculated with the J.P. Morgan Government Bond Index and the Exchange Rate Index of the corresponding currencies opposite the D-mark. The Yield Index mirrors the total amount of activity including reinvestment of profits.

Compiled by the Bundesbank, these statistics consider the D-mark as the base currency against which bond investments in five other currencies are measured. (The end of 1985 is taken as the 100 point.) Treasurers should particularly notice the very significant effect of exchange rate fluctuation.

COMPETITION FROM THE GERMAN MARK

The irony is that the greatest competitor the ECU has, and will have, in the financial markets is also its primary supporter: the German mark (D-mark). Since all hard currencies compete for available funds in money markets and capital markets, the major question is, which currency represents in the best possible manner the strength of the West European economy?

The confidence to be inspired through commitments made by the 12 governments of the EC is one thing. The other very important factor that can influence using ECUs as the instrument of choice is the behavior of the First World economies—and most particularly those of Europe.

Several studies provide projections to the year 2000 for the United States, Japan, Germany, France, England, Italy, and the Benelux countries. These forecasts take account of the dramatic political developments in Eastern Europe during 1989 and the events that lie ahead, which remain very uncertain. (See also Chapter 10 on the market perspectives and the risks in Eastern Europe as well as the former Soviet Union.)

In addition to the risks associated with political and social developments, the difference in inflationary pressures that exist today among EC countries ensures that exchange rate alignments will most likely take place in the 1990s—particularly if the rules of the game for the EMS remain as they have been in the 1980s.

Interest rate differentials between EC member countries appear to be consistent with this expectation. Some studies point out in their forecasts that the French franc depreciates an average of 1 percent a year and the Italian lira by 2 to 3 percent a year relative to the D-mark, because inflation is greater in these two countries than in Germany.

In general, however, there is a progressive convergence of inflation rates as well as of interest rates within the EC, as we have seen in Chapter 8. Belgium, Luxembourg, Holland, and perhaps Denmark have already reached the point—some economists think—that monetary union with Germany is feasible. That group could be joined by France within the next few years.

As the reader will appreciate, these projections seem to place more emphasis on the D-mark than on the ECU, hence the competition between the two as the opening paragraph of this section suggested. With that having been said, how strong can the D-mark be during the 1990s?

The answer is to a significant degree dependent on the response to another query: What does the new leadership of the Bundesbank have in store? Exchange markets love *tough* central banks. Whenever central banks get labeled as inflation hawks by paying only scant attention to recession fears or election posturing, financial markets buy their currencies on hopes of even higher real yields. There is a premium in being firm.

The U.S. Federal Reserve clearly had such credibility until the autumn of 1989, and the dollar rose accordingly, as shown in Figure 9.3. But tight monetary policy generally slows the economy, before it produces a dent on inflation. It is then that economists part into discrete groups with different beliefs.

Figure 9.3 Exchange rate fluctuation, D-mark versus the U.S. dollar.

The hawks want a tight stance until the gains on inflation are able to revive whatever is left of the real economy. When domestic restraint is not enough, each Group of Seven (G-7) member expresses the hope of making further progress on inflation by inducing the other members to maintain a strong currency alliance. But in reality, coordination ends where anti-inflation policies begin.

Economists tend to think that there has to be at least one loser in this inflation versus anti-inflation power game. Recently, some believe it to be fair that the loser should be the yen—the currency still with lowest inflation among G-7 members. But others are of the opinion that because of the troubles in Eastern Europe it is more likely that the D-mark should take on such a role.

A number of these economists speculate that, if the past is any guide to the future, in the 1990s the D-mark could replicate the dollar's behavior in the 1980s: going high during the first five years and running out of thrust thereafter. According to this hypothesis, the reasons for the rise and fall of the D-mark should be similar to those for the dollar a decade earlier, although their context is obviously different. At the basis of the argument is German reunification, which boosts an already overheating economy further, thus calling for added monetary measures.

In the early 1980s, in America, fears of further oil shocks prompted severe Fed tightening. This was coupled with a hands-off policy and little or no tax increases. In the case of Germany, this means that the cost of reunification will drive the public deficit much higher, putting additional upward pressure on interest rates.

Ten years ago a similar cause-and-effect sequence took place in the United States because of the belief that lower taxes would boost growth enough to lower the deficit. High interest rates ensured that the dollar received a big boost from foreign capital inflows, but concerted G-7 action eventually changed the rules.

Certain economists are of the opinion that in the second half of the 1990s the D-mark could also suffer what the late 1980s did to the dollar. By then, Germany could well be afflicted with a twin deficit, and that is when the D-mark may have to foot the bill. Other economists, however, harbor a diametrically different opinion.

"I am looking for a one-armed economist," Harry Truman once said, "so that when he gives me advice on the future course of the economy he will not say: 'On the other hand . . .'." Yet it is precisely the difference of opinion that makes a market.

EURODOLLARS AND THE ACID TEST

The second major competitor to the ECU as a financial instrument of choice is the well-entrenched and very popular Eurodollar. In the late 1950s European banks, notably in London and Switzerland, began to deal predominantly in dollars. This created a great new market.

The origin of this trading is variously ascribed to the Russians, who needed dollar reserves but were afraid that their American deposits could be frozen by a hostile administration. Others credit the Eurodollar issues to the insight of Sir George Bolton, an experienced foreign exchange trader, who saw that opportunities for trading in sterling were limited and therefore switched to dollar borrowing and lending.

Another reason given for the blooming of the Eurodollar market is the realization that Regulation Q* (in the United States) did not apply to deposits in New York belonging to foreign banks or to foreign branches of New York banks. Regulation Q has since been repealed, but the new market remains and thrives.

According to still another version, the Eurodollar market began not in the late 1950s but back in 1949 when the newly installed communist government in China, wanting to protect its dollar earnings from the Americans, placed them on a Soviet-owned bank in Paris called the Banque Commerciale pour l'Europe du Nord, whose cable address happened to be *Eurobank*. Then, this version says, came the Russian depositors also worried that the Americans would block their dollars.

No matter which might have been its origin, the Eurodollar market got a boost in 1958 when many Western European countries (though not yet Britain) agreed to allow their currencies to be convertible into dollars for the first time since World War II. This gave new freedom to dealings across frontiers. In that same year, the United States moved into deficit, with the result that dollars were flowing rapidly into Europe.

---

*Setting ceilings on interest rates payable on time deposits.

Initially, London seemed an unpromising financial center for this new business, as Britain was bogged down in economic problems after the ephemeral Suez war, which caused a run on the pound. More promising was the atmosphere of Zurich or Frankfurt. But international banking has deep roots in London. The city has accumulated a combination of trust and expertise that has survived industrial decline and lack of currency leadership, because of the pound's significant weakness. "They have got everything but the money," one American banker said at the time, "and every banker knows that money comes to people who know how to handle it." This upheld London's status even if at the time the local financial environment was morose.

One of the issues the Eurocurrency market has conclusively proved over the years is that although the world may still be divided politically, it is integrated in an economic and financial sense. International banking is a system that operates *as if* designed to exist in a certain state of economic tension. Said Walter Wriston in 1979: "The ability of anybody to attract credit depends on their management. Countries that manage their affairs well will always have credit and those that don't will not." The same is just as true of financial institutions, fund managers, and investors.

Since the end of the 1960s and even more so during the 1970s and 1980s, the Eurodollar market boomed but also changed in orientation. Even though in its beginning it played a modest role in international finance, by the 1980s it became a major independent force in the international monetary and financial markets.

To appreciate how important the Eurodollar market has become, notice that since the mid-1980s the official dollar reserves of the Western countries practically match the money at the Federal Reserve System of the United States, each standing at an estimated $250 billion to $280 billion. At the same time, the reserve banks of the Western European countries count about 800 million ounces of gold (equivalent to slightly more than 24,000 tons). This represented about $350 billion at the then going value. In other words, the total reserves in dollars and in gold of the First World were at the level of about $1 trillion, while committed funds in Eurodollars in the principal financial markets were globally estimated to be more than $2 trillion.

It is not just a matter of debits and commitments exceeding credits and assets by an incredible $1 trillion. The issue is that liquidity is at a level that would have been totally unacceptable for any private corporation. The acid test:

$$\frac{\text{Current assets}}{\text{Current liabilities}}$$

stands below 0.5, whereas for most companies in good financial health this ratio typically hovers around 2.0, and any time it falls beyond 1.0 the company is considered to be insolvent.

Today in an international financial sense, the principal function of monetized gold is to be a reserve for extreme, unforeseen cases. If gold were suddenly monetized, the official reserves would have covered only one-sixth of the amount of dollars in circulation. Alternatively that means that the price of gold should be raised to $2,400 per ounce if it were to be used as a guarantee of paper money, as it had been prior to the Smithsonian agreement.

The dollar, Eurodollar, and petrodollar markets do not seem to pass the acid test, as discussed in this and the preceding chapter, but the 1970s and 1980s saw two collective international currencies, each carving a share of financial transactions:

- The Special Drawing Rights (SDR) of the International Monetary Fund (IMF)

- The European Currency Unit (ECU) of the European Common Market

Hence the suggestion was made that we look at them quite carefully. We did so by examining what a composite currency, the ECU, may have in store, including the challenges, opportunities, and risks that are involved.

THE EUROPEAN ECONOMIC AREA

Before too long, the ECU's role may be changing while the European Community as a whole is undergoing a major evolution. Underpinning this statement is the European Economic Area (EEA) treaty approved on October 22, 1991, by the twelve EC members and the seven-nation European Free Trade Association (EFTA).

The EC-EFTA agreement, which has been reached after long negotiations, is an *acquis communautaire* of over 1,000 pages with another 12,000 pages of 1,500 European Community laws appended to it. The pillars on which it rests are the four freedoms for the movement of:

- People

- Goods

- Services

- Capital

Through the agreement, the EFTA national (in alphabetic order: Austria, Finland, Iceland, Norway, Sweden, and Switzerland) are subscribing to the EC rules, helping to create a market of 380 million consumers;. This market accounts for 40 percent of world trade.

Table 9.1 presents the statistics on population, gross domestic product (GDP), as well as income per citizen, applicable to each of the two market groups. The population of the EC is by order of magnitude larger than that of the EFTA, and GDP growth is somewhat faster; but the EFTA is richer—its income per capita is 44 percent higher.

The figures in the table are of course averages. Therefore they can be misleading in terms of representing the health of each of the six EFTA economies. The Austrian GDP grows by 4.6 percent; by contrast, that of Finland, Iceland, and Sweden stagnates in the 0.0 to 0.3 percent range. Norway's GDP growth stands at 1.8 percent; that of Switzerland at 2.6 percent. But Austria is the poorest of the six EFTA partners with income per capita at $20,650, and Switzerland is the richest with income per capita of $33,550.

The careful reader would not miss the fact that the EC-EFTA treaty is not a full economic union. Aside from the fact that EEA must still be approved by the European Parliament and ratified by the parliament of each EC and EFTA state, there are also constraints stipulated by the treaty itself:

- EFTA countries will not be able to vote on EC legislation.

- The EEA Council of Ministers will decide by consensus whether to extend new EC legislation to EFTA.

- There will be reviews of treaty and clauses every two years; the first will be at the end of 1993.

But as currently stipulated, the EEA treaty does guarantee the free movement of products in the EEA from 1993 onward, though the EFTA

Table 9.1 Vital Statistics of the EC and EFTA

	EC	EFTA
Population (in millions)	345.0	32.6
Growth in gross domestic product (GDP)	2.3%	1.9%
Income per capita (in U.S. dollars)	18,320	26,480

and the EC must agree on a system for classifying which goods will be regarded as originating from within the EEA. Special clauses will cover food, fish, energy, coal, and steel.

There have been compromises in working out the mechanics of the European Economic Area, for instance, on fish. It was tacitly understood that Iceland had special claim to reserve to itself a good deal of the fishing rights, which provide most of its livelihood. Norway has had to concede, but not much. The EC's share of what is now a 215,000-tonne (metric ton) quota for Norwegian waters will rise from 2.14 percent to 2.9 percent. The main beneficiary is England, which gets about two-thirds, with Germany and France taking the rest.

On the subject of transport, Austria has agreed to issue 1.3 million transit licenses for EC heavy trucks. This freezes the level of permits for all members except Greece, which gets a 29 percent increase to 60,500 licenses a year. Since the Greeks insisted on 62,500 permits, Austria agreed to the addition on condition that Greece compensates by using rail shipment through Austria twice the equivalent amount of additional road traffic.

Austria will also expand transit rights through a new system of *Ecopoints*, rewarding low-pollution vehicles in a scheme to reduce emissions by 60 percent over the 12-year life of the transit agreement (which starts in 1992, a year earlier than EEA proper). For its part, Switzerland agreed to unlimited passage for EC trucks up to 28 tonnes. In addition, a maximum of 50 trucks of up to 38 tonnes will be able to transit daily each way through Swiss passes, provided they are:

- Under two years old
- Carry perishable goods
- Carry *just-in-time* components for manufacturers

Correctly, the Swiss insisted on rail usage to minimize environmental damage, and this led to bilateral agreement between Switzerland and Austria to promote rail transport in its full capacity.

Switzerland is to build two new railway tunnels through the Gotthard (50 km) and Loetschberg (30 km) mountains, which together will cost more than the Channel tunnel. This had been labeled "the contract of the century," and the Swiss government opened it up to international competition—a move that did not particularly please Swiss construction firms.

Forecasting major growth in traffic flows, Austria and the EC will co-finance a new tunnel through the Brenner pass. The European Community has also undertaken to create combined transport links in Germany, northern Italy, and the Netherlands.

Most importantly, in regard to financing, the EFTA nations agreed to supply ECU 2 billion ($2.4 billion) in soft loans, with a 3 percent interest subsidy and 2-year grace period, and an ECU 425 million ($510 million) in grants as a contribution to the EC's structural funds. The aim is to help poorer nations like Greece and Portugal catch up with the rest of the EC.

But the EC stood firm against EFTA attempts to secure a more than marginal voice in shaping European Community policy and law or, for example, against the alcohol monopolies run by most of the Nordic states.

- The EFTA will assume EC rules on company law, consumer protection, education, the environment, research and development, and social policy.

- The EFTA will also adopt EC competition rules on antitrust matters, the abuse of a dominant position, public procurement, mergers, and state aid.

By contrast, the EFTA countries can maintain domestic farm policies, rather than join the EC's Common Agricultural Policy. An independent, joint court will deal with EEA-related disputes and all appeals on competition policy.

This can be said in a nutshell: From 1993 people would be able to live, work, and offer services throughout the EEA. There will be mutual recognition of professional qualifications. Capital movements will be freed up, but there will remain restrictions on investment in some types of EFTA real estate and on some direct investments as well.

An educated guess is that the next major issue on which negotiations will focus is the ECU. To what degree the ECU will become EFTA currency will largely depend on EC nations' decisions in adopting it as such. The interlinking of currencies, such as the one long standing between the Deutsche mark and the Austrian schilling, will help promote not only economic but also financial integration.

10

Economic Planning
and the East European
Transformation

A forecast, according to Webster's, is a foresight, forethought, prediction, or prophecy. It can also refer to the process of estimating and calculating in advance, to foresee the consequences of our actions and those of our competitors.

The establishment of planning premises necessarily involves the making of forecasts: What kinds of markets will there be? Which products? What costs? Wage rates? Quantity of sales? Prices? Tax rates and tax policies? What new plants? Policies with respect to dividends? How will expansion be financed?

Forecasts are based on facts but also on opinions, estimations, and appreciations. For instance, many executives today appreciate that one of the key problems in Europe is the lack of rapid exploitation of markets, particularly at world standards. This rapid exploitation is an area where the Japanese excell—and the availability or lack of it should surely influence forecasts and plans.

Planning premises include far more than basic forecasts of demographics, prices, costs, production, schedules, market potential, and similar issues. Some premises project decisions and policies that have not yet been made. Others naturally grow out of strategic decisions or already established plans. Quite often, the emphasis is on the direction of decisions and actions—not on the fine grain of events.

"I feel the real thing in this world is not so much where we stand, as in what direction we are moving," said Oliver Wendell Holmes. Planning is connected with the concept of the organization as an agent of change, and the plan prescribes the direction of change.

Dr. Peter Drucker points out that people have not always regarded business in this way. "Up to the seventeenth century it was the purpose of all human institutions to prevent change. The business enterprise is a significant and rather amazing novelty in that it is the first human institution having the purpose of bringing about change." But even today this concept is not a universally accepted one.

Whether we talk of the level of enterprises or of national governments (to which the larger part of this chapter is dedicated), the fact remains that the planning infrastructure does increase an organization's capacity to change. Managers tied to current operations have at their disposition a tool permitting them to make important changes in goals and policies. But they are more likely to formulate meaningful change if they stand back from operations and think ahead.

"Planning," Dr. Kenneth Boulding suggests, "is not really a prediction of the future. What I think you can plan for is change itself—and this is quite important. If you think of planning in terms of an organization's flexibility in preparing for the unknown and of anticipating possible crises and system changes, then this really seems to be the essence of it." We may reach our immediate goals without a great deal of forecasting. But we cannot build vitality for the years to come without plans, because the process of planning helps to deeper understand our problems.

This is the perspective from which we should examine the ongoing social, political, economic, and industrial transformation in Eastern Europe—as well as the plans we may be making in that regard. The reason that this issue is most relevant in a book on treasury and forex should be found in the fact that it constitutes one of the best examples of how attentive treasurers and traders should be to political and socioeconomic factors. Once the political euphoria is gone, the economics it leaves behind can be grim.

THE FOUR COMPONENTS OF A LONG-RANGE PLAN

Long-range planning owes part of its rise to the growing status of economic research. As economic research and financial research outlays have multiplied, so has the number of options: from new products and processes to new markets and new financial tools.

The development of alternatives in the options ahead of us, and subsequent optimization, mean better investments in the future. At the same time, our society has become more demanding, and its technology is more complex. Payoff times for new investments have lengthened, and the choices to be made require a polyvalent approach.

This all too familiar picture has been a strong, practical incentive to plan farther ahead. Strategic plans are long range, and there are four fundamental components in any master plan:

1. A *financial strategy* must be established, in spite of uncertainties and turbulence, to protect and increase our economic resources.

2. A *human resources strategy* aims to identify, recruit, train, and motivate key members of management and the professionals corps.

3. A *marketing strategy* focuses on market drives and directions as well as on the development of a plan.

4. A *product strategy* addresses itself to the products and services we offer to the market, how we price them, sell them, and support them through after-sales service.

Both endogenous and exogenous factors influence the master plan. As of early 1992, for instance, exogenous factors suggest that we are probably on course toward a global recession of uncertain magnitude, and whose size is likely to be determined by the trade policies of the First World.

There is a body of opinion that holds that the 1930s were exceptionally severe because of the trade warfare that occurred. If this view is correct, we could be facing once again a serious situation in terms of economic downturn. Given such a possibility, astute management would place particular emphasis on the company's financial staying power, making such a policy an integral part of its plans.

What detailed planning really involves is how we are going to attack the problem of *survival*. This is true whether we talk of persons, corporations, or nations—and the lack of detailed planning is one of the fundamental weaknesses that finally spelled the death of communism.

Whether we talk of the treasury duties or those of the ministry of finance, planning represents an intellectual movement of change. Ever since administration became a subject of teaching and analytical writing, scholars have emphasized the need to break away from managing by the seat of the pants. As long as administrative decisions were made by instinct or impulse there was little hope for the kind of probing and reflective thinking that characterized older fields of learning. Now, few management activities are so immediately and intimately related to an approach that is both as intellectual and pragmatic as planning is.

There are indeed six major functions in management, starting at a highly unstructured information environment with forecasting, and continuing through planning, all the way to control. Control action is exercised in a highly structured information environment as shown in Figure 10.1. By contrast, the forecasting environment is fully unstructured.

As every free enterprise businessperson knows, though some tend to forget, forecasting attempts to find the most probable course of events, or at least, a range of probabilities and possibilities. But the treasurer's (and the dealer's) problem is to know the unique event that will alter the possibilities within an entrepreneurial perspective that focuses not on a physical but on a value universe. The central contribution of a business spirit and the one that is rewarded with profits is to bring about the *unique event*, the innovation that changes the probabilities.

Treasurers and dealers, but also presidents and prime ministers, should appreciate that long-range planning does *not* deal with future decisions. It deals with the futurity of present decisions—whose implications extend into the future. For instance, when a dealer or treasurer says that a certain trading decision was made when the market was different, or when the communist leadership of the former East European regimes, the Soviet Union, China, or Vietnam find the excuse of unexpected developments, they forget that decisions exist only in the present. The question that faces the able manager is not what he or she should do tomorrow. It is what must be done today to be ready for an uncertain tomorrow. For every professional, the critical questions are the following: What perspective needs to be factored into present thinking and

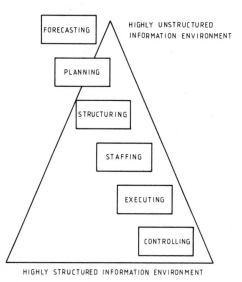

Figure 10.1 Spectrum ranging from highly structured to highly unstructured information environment.

doing? What time spans must be considered? How are they merged into a simultaneous decision in the present?

America, Britain, and Japan are skeptical about the murky plans of the former Soviet Union. They are right to ask for factual and documented clarifications about Gorbachev's and Yeltsin's changes—if they are to receive economic assistance from the First World. Most particularly for Gorbachev the queries become the following: Does he understand the difference between assistance and handouts? Has he really abandoned his subsidies to his clients like Cuba? Did he stop diverting scarce economic resources to the military? Is he *really* in charge?

Any finely tuned decision-making process is essentially a time machine that synchronizes into one present time a great number of divergent time spans. On the contrary, the defective approach tends toward the making of plans about something one will decide to do sometime in the future. This is a futile exercise.

When in the following chapters we talk about *options* and *futures* we will see that treasurers and traders make their decisions only in the present, while considering aftermaths. The core of the matter is that neither companies nor governments can make decisions for the present alone. Any decision in dealing, or in allocating resources, may commit us on a long-term basis, if not permanently and irrevocably.

There is as well the rather common misconception that long-range planning is an attempt to eliminate risk. This is patently false. Planning is not even an attempt to minimize risk, because such an attempt may lead to taking irrational risks and to disasters. Existing means of production will yield greater economic performance only through greater uncertainty, that is, through taking risks. As every treasurer and minister of finance should recognize, the central fact about economic activity is that, by definition, it commits present resources to future courses—to highly uncertain expectations. To take risk is the essence of economic activity.

A different way of looking at this issue, albeit a controversial one, is to say that the end result of successful long-range planning must be the capacity to take greater but controllable risks. This is the only way to improve entrepreneurial performance. To do this, we must *know* and *understand* the risks we take (see also Chapters 2 and 3). We must be able to choose rationally among risky courses of action, rather than plunge into them on the basis of hunch, hearsay, dogma, or seat-of-the-pants experience.

PLANNING FOR COMPETITIVE ADVANTAGE

In a book selected for the 1954 Council of Europe Award, Dr. Fred Polak develops the theory that the future of a civilization, a country, a company, or an individual is determined in large measure by the images of the future. His thesis is that it is possible to alter or adjust these images, thus guiding a nation's or company's future toward positive goals. According to Polak, if a society has optimistic ideas, dynamic aspirations, and cohesive ambitions, it will grow and prosper. If it exhibits negative trends, unclear ideas, and hesitant plans, then it is in danger of disintegrating.

Looking into the decade of the 1970s for examples has the advantage of abstracting from present conditions, taking a more objective view of the severe losses suffered by large corporations. Table 10.1 brings under scrutiny the twenty largest losers of the early 1970s, with all figures having been converted into 1991 dollars.

Italy's Montedison leads the list, but Penn Central can steal the show if we account for the fact that in 1967 it had another major ($690 million) loss. Indeed, the company lost money in eight out of the nine years between 1967 and 1975. The combined net loss (reduced by a 1968 profit) was $5.53 billion in 1991 dollars.

Another star performer in the game of losses and mismanagement has been Itel which, in 1980, announced losses of $1.2 billion (roughly $2

Table 10.1 The Twenty Largest Losers of the Early 1970s

Loser		Losses in Millions of 1991 Dollars
1.	Montedison (1972)	2.088
2.	Penn Central (1971)	1.560
3.	Penn Central (1970)	1.256
4.	Montedison (1971)	1.036
5.	Anaconda (1971)	996
6.	Singer (1975)	950
7.	Ataka (1977)	946
8.	National Coal Board (1974)	782
9.	Volkswagenwerk (1974)	718
10.	Usinor (1975)	668
11.	Northwest Industries (1970)	666
12.	Sacilor (1975)	654
13.	AEG-Telefunken (1974)	602
14.	Penn Central (1972)	596
15.	National Coal Board (1973)	576
16.	Chrysler (1975)	545
17.	CNA Financial (1974)	496
18.	Penn Central (1975)	460
19.	Boise Cascade (1972)	456
20.	Penn Central (1974)	456

billion in 1991 dollars). At the time, this left the company with $200 million in "negative assets."

Gorbachev can take heart in these statistics. His bankrupt economy and his negative assets are nothing new to the First World. But they do happen in the former Soviet Union on a much more grand scale.

There are plenty of reasons that a business gets into trouble, and they are just as valid as those for governments: lack of forecasting and planning, changes in the marketplace, changes in technology leading to process and product obsolescence. Further reasons are:

- Incapable management

- Short supply of professionals

- Uncontrolled increases in the cost of production

Quite often, the company's or the government's business is growing beyond the skills of management. This is what has happened in the communist countries — where renewal has been a dirty word.

Internal conflicts, obsolescence in know-how, and inadequate control systems have been in the background of many failures. Other major contributors to downturn are a tarnished image in the marketplace, and management short of guts to chop off deadwood.

Essentially all this amounts to a lack of *competitive advantages*. If an industrial or financial organization, or the nation as a whole, fails to take immediate advantage of its know-how, its products, and its processes, the market will pass it by. In this fierce, competitive environment only the steady innovator and lowest-cost producer with top-performance products and a well thought-out strategic plan can survive.

Management without clear objectives is the sign of a business in trouble. Companies and nations incapable of providing for creative thinking and planning have fallen behind the time. "The plan is nothing," Dwight Eisenhower once said. "But planning is everything."

When it comes to the exploitation of competitive advantages, plans come in graduations and so do planning processes. As Figure 10.2 demonstrates, at the top of management's preoccupations should be the far-out plan, whose aim is to give direction:

- What will our company (or our country) be doing 15 to 20 years from now?

- Where will we get the income to enable us to face our obligations?

- Do we have the human resources and the products to generate that income?

- Are we overcommitting ourselves?

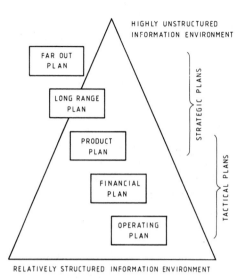

Figure 10.2 Short-term and long-range planning placed within a structured information environment.

Taken together, far-out planning and long-range planning reflect the strategic approach to organizational behavior—as contrasted to the tactical one, which is used more day-to-day.

Since managers became more conscious of the importance of goals, planning took the form of a valuable educational tool, helping to see the folly of exploiting long-term trust and goodwill for short-term gains. In this sense, the process of dynamic planning is evidence of confidence in the economic and political stability of a society, permitting our horizon to reach well into the future:

• Promoting the conscious determination of courses of action

• Enabling us to base our decision on concrete purposes

• Providing evidence of having correctly considered the aftermaths

This course of action, obviously, should not be confused with the routines of the so-called central planners in Moscow or Peking, which are exercises in yesmanship. I am quite sure that if there were hundreds of societies just like those of the First World today with exactly the same economic, social, and political conditions, there would still be no success in any of them if one crucial, priceless ingredient were missing. That is the personal interest of top management and the motivation of the professionals entrusted to do the planning job. It is also the skill they bring to their mission, their independence of mind, and the technology they use in support of the duties they have been entrusted with.

FROM KARL MARX TO ADAM SMITH

After the end of World War II, Western Europe prospered, and today it has a strong currency, the ECU, as well as strong national currencies— because, like America, it followed the word of Adam Smith. More precisely, both America and Western Europe followed not just the original Adam Smith teachings but those that have often been revamped and restructured; hence they have renewed themselves as a function of time and of economic developments.

By contrast, Eastern Europe tied itself for 45 years to the hairy thoughts of Karl Marx. The Soviets did better than that in terms of timing; they sank for nearly three-quarters of a century into Marxist ideas. During that time, there was no renewal in economic thought, yet the world's economy had tremendously changed. As a result, there was no adaptation to the new environment, just a monolithic bureaucracy orchestrated by Marx's apostles, with a vested interest to maintain the status quo.

The lessons from the fortunes of Asia's four tigers and the misfortunes of Eastern Europe is that national prosperity is created, not inherited. Whether personal or national, prosperity just does not grow on trees. Prosperity requires hard work and has much to do with human resources, investments, interest rates, currency value, and most importantly, with leadership.

A nation's competitiveness depends on its capacity to *innovate* and *upgrade*. In a similar manner, companies gain advantage against the world's best competitors because of their ability to face the challenges as they occur. They benefit from having:

- Strong domestic rivals

- Aggressive international competitors

- Sophisticated and demanding customers

- The willingness to renew and renovate themselves

The central Marxist theory, which until two or three decades ago held uncontested, was that revolution represents a crucial phase in the process of change from feudalism to capitalism. Although Karl Marx pointed out that such progress was in fact a triumph of bourgeois society, many socialist fire-eaters (in the East as well as in the West) saw in it a revolution "by the masses for the masses," against an entrenched capitalistic authority. They judged wrong and now pay the damages.

Adam Smith wrote: "To found a great empire for the sole purpose of raising up a people of customers, may at first sight appear a project fit only for a nation of shopkeepers. It is, however, a project altogether unfit for a nation of shopkeepers, but extremely fit for a nation that is governed by shopkeepers." The shopkeepers of Adam Smith's time have today become the multinational corporations in finance, manufacturing, and merchandising.

These are the companies that today are dearly interested in treasury operations, liquidity, global risk management, exchange rates, interest rates, cash flow, return on investment, return on equity—not just profits in an accountancy sense. And this answers the statement typically made by socialists: We don't want to entrust our future to people whose chief concern is what comes through the cash register—which is totally out of place and context.

There is a change of heart among former socialists after finally realizing that the system of deciding through a centralized bureaucracy what, how much, and how to produce was incredibly wasteful of resources. The attempt to run an entire country's economy by dictate has been unable to keep pace with the requirements of a modern society.

Traveling through the East European countries and the former Soviet Union brings to mind the immediate post–World War II economy, characterized by nearly universal rationing and black markets. It will take time for people to learn how to compete in rough-and-tumble free markets, without government subsidies to cover repeated mistakes.

Businesses eager to reap a benefit from the reconstruction of Eastern Europe should therefore constantly remind themselves of the prevailing risks and uncertainties. Only the former East Germany offers somewhat better prospects, and this is due to the massive West German economic and financial help—but, even there, investments should be very selective.

This is practically what Peter Munk and his Toronto-based Horsham Corp. plan to do in East Berlin. Their aim is to replace vast sections of the aging city with Western-style offices, residences, and shopping centers. "The existing buildings are totally unsuitable," says Munk. "This provides unparalleled opportunities for the right players."*

Moving along with its plan, Horsham purchased from Treuhandanstalt 500 acres just south of Berlin for $12 million. Treuhandanstalt is the state agency responsible for privatizing East German assets. The stated goal is to transform this farmland into a modern business park, betting on the transfer of the German capital to Berlin and the fact that this will act as a sponge for office space.

With the eastern half of Europe hurriedly dropping communism and embracing the free market, Adam Smith's ideas have become much in

*Business Week, October 21, 1991.

vogue. Yet he was no proponent of unregulated business. In the 900 pages of his *Inquiry into the Nature and Causes of the Wealth of Nations,* published in the year of the American independence:

- Adam Smith extolled "the invisible hand" that, left alone, regulates trade and markets generally for the common good.

- He also believed that when a man is left alone to pursue his own interest, he "frequently promotes that of society more effectually than when he really intends to promote it."

The whole sense of free enterprise is in the two preceding sentences, to which American experience added a third: The freedom to enter a business and *fail.* When the state sees to it that nobody can fall hard, then there is no place for anybody to prosper.

THE ROLE OF POLICIES AND REGULATIONS

Policies and regulations, Adam Smith thought, should do more than ensure that "every man, as long as he does not violate the laws of justice, is left perfectly free to pursue his own interest in his own way, and to bring both his industry and capital into competition with those of any other man, or order of men."

The role of government should be *regulation,* not substitution. Governments and their central planners should not create for themselves a state supermarket, wiping out private initiative. These are precisely the conditions that both the Soviet Union and the countries of Eastern Europe made for themselves over the years. By contrast, the ingredients of prosperity—in spite of the ongoing changes—are still missing.

That explains why I don't think that, until the laws of these different countries have changed, providing for a truly free private enterprise, there is much that can be done in turning their economies around. Financial assistance will be like throwing money into a bottomless pit, just like it has been done in Latin America and other parts of the Third World, where an oligopoly (not a communist monopoly) has been running the show.

Until the current governments, or those that follow them, move boldly to make the following changes, no amount of aid will save the Eastern European and former Soviet economies:

- Contain inflation

- Force market discipline on enterprises

- Collect taxes

- Create the preconditions for meaningful investments

Just as it happened in the past, for instance in Poland, foreign capital will be used to grease the transition to an uncertain status of fake prosperity. In the absence of market incentives, much of this capital will be wasted.

- Factories will continue producing third-rate products.

- Make-work projects with no payoff at all will mushroom.

- Foreign debts will boom, to be eventually written off because of inability to repay.

Correctly, President Bush is counting his beans in terms of aid to Eastern Europe and also refuses major outlays for reconstruction purposes to "Russia." There is no restructuring that can be done until the *current laws*, bylaws, policies, and *overall culture* change. This will eventually come, but not very soon.

Neither is there a reason to rush in with private money when the governments are thrifty. Precisely because private investors are not that interested, the European Bank for Reconstruction and Development has only state participation and will grant loans, not handouts—with investments requiring a good documentation and associated guarantees. These will not come that easy.

With the exception of eastern Germany for which the western Germans made a leveraged buyout and now start the reconstruction process, the other Eastern European countries and former Soviet republics will take some time to turn around. To do so, they will have to slash the huge bureaucracies and put in key-decision posts persons who are free from stereotypes. The needed transition from Karl Marx to Adam Smith could not be described in more lucid terms.

The more successful examples of such transition rediscover the mercantile policies that flourished a few centuries ago. *Business Week* published and article about Vladimir V. Yudin and his Siberian plant complex: "To get consumer goods for his workers, Yudin constantly puts together complex barter deals. In a convoluted scheme to get scarce products, such as baby food or cheese, he may start out with timber, exchange it for cement, and then find a factory that has an excess of baby food but needs cement."*

But not all deals can be served through barter, particularly when the financing requirements are huge. The Soviet aviation minister was

Business Week, October 21, 1991, pp. 24–25.

recently saying that Aeroflot, which is absolutely vital to the economy of so vast a region as the old Soviet Union, faces the sudden "block obsolescence" of its entire 2,524-plane civil fleet. And the situation could worsen dramatically if aircraft repair facilities do not immediately improve: Up to 130 civilian airliners are said to be grounded daily for lack of engine parts.

Servicing the massive restructuring of large economies poses unforeseeable challenges in terms of financial requirements as well as of human capital able to run the new landscape. Therefore, those who think that Eastern Europe and the former Soviet Union can manage to convert themselves to free markets prior to year 2000 are long on enthusiasm but short on judgment.

Let's also not forget that the liquidity crisis that hit the First World at the end of 1989 and early part of 1990 did not start in the United States, as many people think, but in Europe. The trigger was the crumbling of the Berlin Wall, which made apparent the huge financing requirements western Germany will have to face to rescue eastern Germany—and investors got immediately worried about what this may mean regarding interest rates of the German mark.

Precisely because of projected private and public capital investments primarily by western Germany, it is presently estimated that what used to be East Germany may triple its gross national product during the 1990s. But the other Eastern European countries and Russia will move much slower, and at a variable pace. In the overall:

- State lending from Western Europe will go on, but private investments will be very selective.

- Banks will think twice before coming forward, being cautious because of the Third World lending experience (among other reasons).

- Both state and private investment will move faster when the local laws change in the former communist bloc, permitting the ownership of property with no strings attached.

- The privatization of the banking system in each country will be regarded as a milestone, and for good reason.

- The more the wings of the central planners are clipped, the more confident the outside investors will get.

In short, the basic criterion for turnaround is the creation of a market economy. This will not come overnight. And although no single measure taken by the East European governments will create a quick fix, all of them together will be examined as a pattern that can open doors.

EASTERN EUROPE, THE COMMON MARKET, AND THE UNITED STATES

Let's now look at the other side of the news. Since the communist world says that it wants to embrace capitalism, it seems only proper that capitalists should respond by embracing the worn-out and impoverished peoples of ex-communist countries. This seems even believable after decades of loudly proclaiming the superiority of the free market—but we have seen the reasons that such embracing cannot happen so fast.

Considered from the longer term, the Second World of the ex-communist countries offers a historic opportunity: a market of 380 million consumers, each with a great appetite for goods and services taken for granted by Westerners. Just as important, the East European countries and most of what used to be the Soviet Union are full of educated professionals and skilled workers who for some years will toil for relatively low wages.

All this looks fine, but the preceding section already underlined that pouring loans and grants into these heavily indebted countries will not make sense. Solutions call for courage and vision not only from Western business leaders, but also, if not primarily, from the people and the governments of the East European countries themselves.

Today, the countries of Eastern Europe and the former Soviet Union are not facing the physical destruction of plant, equipment, and human resources that prevailed in Western Europe in the mid- to late 1940s. However, the existence of physical plant can be deceptive, particularly if one wrongly believes that quality production can be increased by making use of existing physical plant in a more efficient manner.

No realistic estimate of the situation can forget the fact that the entire operating infrastructure and associated social fabric have been destabilized, especially the accountabilities between owners, managers, workers, and consumers. With the death of European communism, the old structures have been abandoned, or are in the process of being dropped, but the new ones have not yet been described, much less defined. At the same time, there is lack of professionals in engineering, law practice, marketing, accounting, and management who really know how a free market works and what makes it tick.

As the *Economist** suggested: "Unless, or until, they establish all the paraphernalia of capitalism to go with their new-found enthusiasm for free markets, the risks for foreign investors are likely to grow, not shrink. The obvious exception is East Germany, whose transition to a free market

---

*June 16, 1990.

economy will be faster precisely because it will adopt West Germany's economic and legal system wholesale."

Additionally there is the fact that Eastern Europe cannot be judged from a distance as a more or less homogeneous landscape. Every country has its rules, its opportunities, its constraints, and its problems. Hungary, for instance, seems to be ahead of Poland and Czechoslovakia—and way ahead of Yugoslavia, Bulgaria, and Romania.

From one country to another, reaction to privatization varies. Unlike the Poles, the Czechs have so far shown remarkably little resistance to the idea of their best firms being sold to foreigners. Most appear to accept that this is the fastest way of acquiring the know-how to reestablish their industry's international reputation.*

The Poles got a break when in March 1991 the organization of Western creditor states agreed to cancel 50 percent of Poland's $33 billion government-to-government debt as a reward for Warsaw's economic reforms. But that reduction broke a longstanding Paris Club tradition of not canceling but restructuring debt, and the move annoyed several member nations.

Chief among the negative reactions was that of Japan, which retaliated by placing a $500 million loan to Warsaw on hold. "In principle, we cannot extend new money to a country whose debts are written off," said a finance ministry spokesman in Tokyo. The write-off also dismayed private banks around the world, making Poland a less likely recipient of future loans.

How far has reform gone? Every East European country and the former Soviet Union too still face a tough list of established tax regimes, contract laws, nonexistent capital markets, and lax environmental, safety, and employment rules. And much of what has to do with the free market is lip service:

- Dismantling and selling state-owned monopolies is an immense job, which no government has yet attempted to effectively think out.

- Deciding about wealth distribution and the size and role of the state are not easy problems to resolve—not even the surface has been scratched.

- Particularly in regard to the former Soviet Union, its great size, the past mismanagement, ethnic strife, and the depth of its problems dwarf any conceivable package of grants and loans.

In the short to medium term, the huge problems are much more visible than the business opportunities. And as a matter of principle, both

*Financial Times, June 13, 1991.

Western banks and corporate investors are aware that in new markets those who invest later rather than sooner may reap the biggest rewards. The mortality rate of investment pioneers can be high.

The handful of East European companies with an exportable product or respected brand name have already been sold or are being negotiated. General Electric owns 50 percent of Hungary's Tungsram. But as for the 380 million consumers that some American and West European companies are talking about, this is still a fragmented and impoverished market which, in the end, could prove just as chimerical as China's.

As a matter of fact, a study by the United Nations indicated that worldwide global economic growth is expected to slow, with Russia and other East European countries acting as the major drag on global output. Until the state supermarket is dismantled, things are not going to change greatly—and dismantling seems to be much slower than many people thought.

In the former Soviet Union and Eastern Europe, the UN said, economic growth fell sharply from 4.1 percent in 1988 to only 1.2 percent in 1989. Then a forecast was made for 1990 pointing to a *negative growth* of 1.2 percent, followed by minuscule positive growth of 0.2 percent in 1991. If we also count for population growth, 0.2 percent is a negative statistic, a retrenchment.

Rarely has the UN been so accurate in terms of direction, though its forecast was an underestimate. The 1990 statistics now available document that in 1990, Eastern Europe's and the Soviet Union's GNP fell about 7 percent, and there is no reason to believe that the 1991 statistics will be much better.

There are deep reasons behind that fate: the lack of managers and professionals who know how to plan and run a free market economy and an undue amount of resistance to change by the state supermarket's bureaucracy.

In the case of Poland, Hungary, and Czechoslovakia, the state still owns about 80 percent of production assets. In Poland, however, as of July 1991 the government decided to hand over to 27 million adults the majority ownership of 400 state-owned factories. This only *sounds* wonderful. These Polish factories represent some 25 percent of the country's industrial sales, which still leaves the government with majority control over the industrial base. It takes many years to get rid of the bad habits of the past. As a result, old methods of R + D, production, distribution, and marketing continue to hamper recovery. An uncertain trumpeter heralds the major change ahead, resulting in loss of public confidence—and, after all, that is what business is all about, *confidence*.

In Czechoslovakia, for instance, a two-year program of half-baked reforms resulted in a 54 percent inflation rate and a 12 percent drop in industrial output for the first quarter of 1991. (A large part of the drop is due to the reduction in exports to the former Soviet Union.) Unemployment keeps rising; about 1,000 jobs are lost every day.

If these are the results of partial change, no change at all is far worse. No East European economy is more sick today than that of the former Soviet Union, with stagflation being rampant and the economy clearly going beyond repair. The same is true of the majority of countries in the Third World.

These are the facts that led the First World's leading commercial bankers to the conclusion that they have no taste for increasing lending to the former Soviet Union or Third World countries, which are already in substantial arrears in their Western bills.

While expressing sympathy and understanding for the need for additional credits, bankers at the International Monetary Conference of June 1990 in San Francisco suggested that additional lending to Moscow was now a matter for Western governments rather than private banks. And we have seen what this means in terms of government loans.

"A liquidity crisis may be looming," Hilmar Kopper, Deutsche Bank's chief executive said at the San Francisco meeting. "It is time to establish arrangements to avoid that." He then called for a concerted effort from First World governments to establish "whether it is desirable and possible" to provide joint official guarantees on new loans to Russia. John S. Reed, chairman of Citibank, concurred: "We recognize how difficult the economic situation is." And he added that new lending is "a political decision."

Dr. Paul A. Volcker, former chairman of the Federal Reserve Board and currently chairman of the investment banking firm James D. Wolfensohn, warned that "trillions of dollars" would be needed to bring developing countries up to Western living standards. From where will come these trillions?

"THE ONLY CURE IS TO GO COLD TURKEY"

The title of this section was the essence of an interview Jeffrey Sachs of Harvard University gave to the *Herald Tribune* of Paris, as well as the headline of the article in which this interview was published.* Let's follow the highlights.

The first question regarded the similarities between Latin America and Poland. Said Sachs in reply: "When you arrive in a country with hyperinflation they explain why they are different. But you see the same distortions." Grains and medicine get the lowest priority and exchange rate, and "if you compare Poland's multiple exchange rate system with Peru's, you would get a perfect match."

*January 17, 1990.

One of the common characteristics of countries in deep trouble is that they have bankrupt governments, very high inflation, and distorted and closed trading systems. The private sector is highly regulated independently of whether or not the regime is communistic. Ironically, in such decaying environments the central planners pride themselves on a heavy bureaucratic intervention that characterizes state-led industrialization.

If this is the state of affairs characterizing countries that are as different as Argentina, India, and Poland, could Dr. Sachs give some significant differences among them? "In Eastern Europe," he answered, "the bureaucratic systems were brutally imposed and the private sector was thoroughly repressed. There is no financial system, and the laws and institutions that support a market economy are just now being developed."

The assessment is right. At various degrees, this is true all over Eastern Europe and Russia.

- Accounting systems are a joke

- Profits are purely notional

- Productivity levels are a deep unknown

Maybe these conditions explain why even people bent on long-term planning, the Japanese, have announced no sizeable investments in that area. By most yardsticks, southern Europe and Southeast Asia look like safer and more promising bets.

The thought of helping the new democracies is nice. It is a larger challenge than was the Cold War, as Howard H. Baker, Jr., the former Senate majority leader and former White House chief of staff, suggested. Instead of a monolithic adversary, the United States will face dozens of difficult and trying situations as the new democracies around the globe struggle to ascertain their existence and survive.

What is the best way to cross the divide from central planning to market systems? First, says economist Ronald I. McKinnon of Stanford University, both the fiscal and monetary sides of these economies must be stabilized in spite of the fact that government deficits are large and growing.

- The money that used to be available to the government as it appropriated the surpluses from state enterprises is disappearing, since businesses are being privatized.

- The various wild subsidies and giveaway programs of the state supermarket are difficult to slash, because neither the governors nor the governed have yet learned that "you can't have it both ways."

- The money that individuals had stashed away over the years, for lack of goods to buy, is threatening price stability primarily in Russia and to a lesser degree all over Eastern Europe.

Not only must the monetary and fiscal policies be properly worked out, but also hard budget constraints on government and on enterprises must be imposed as a critical precondition for price reform. At the same time, the temptation to use capital inflows to postpone economic adjustment, as was done in Latin America, should be resisted at all costs.

It is a matter of a new culture—not the matter of throwing money at the problem, because this often tried strategy brings no tangible results. It is useless to say that the $380 million that George Bush proposed to bolster economic growth in Eastern Europe is "barely enough to bail out a failed savings and loan institution, much less to jump-start national economies that have been dead for decades." Or useless to say that "the U.S. Congress should seize the initiative and set aside up to 1 percent of the military budget as a catalyst for East European reconstruction" because the preconditions for a new Marshall Plan are not yet in place. The vast empire put together by the Tsars and then expanded by Stalin's iron fist is crumbling, and its substitute has not yet formed.

Communism did not die in 1989 as many people like to think. When in 1968 I conducted a series of seminars in Moscow and Leningrad at the invitation of The Russian Academy of Sciences, I often heard the Moscow radio drumming "Marxism-Leninism-Automatism." But "Marxism" was nowhere around to be seen—nor for that matter was "Automatism."

By contrast, "Bureaucratism" and "Immobilism" were to be seen wide and clear. Nothing was moving in any direction, and twenty years later this ossified state supermarket came crumbling down. The regimes put together in 1918 and in 1945 supposedly to satisfy the workers' needs ended up the other way by creating the privileged class of "*Homo bureaucraticus*."

Alexander Melnikov, the conservative Communist Party leader from the Kuzbas mining region in western Siberia admitted in an interview* that "the situation in his region may become really explosive if the Government does not take urgent measures to satisfy workers' demands." In 1968 I found the Russian intellectuals against "Marxism-Leninism." In 1990 the militants against the regime are the workers.

Melnikov said there was a complete power vacuum in his region, and food supplies were being denied by the agricultural sectors of the Russian republic. No meat was being delivered from Krasnodar, Voronezh, Lipetsk, Stavropol, and Tambov, all traditional suppliers. The region was also short of pork, poultry, and eggs because of inadequate supplies of fodder. Money alone will not solve that sort of problem.

Russian economic performance was abysmal in 1989, the worst since Mikhail Gorbachev took over. By now, the prospect of even a modest economic recovery appears to be remote at best. The economy is in such an

*Financial Times, June 5, 1990.

unstable state that it could shrink as much as 20 percent over the next few years if pushed by a single major event, like a prolonged strike or new ethnic unrest.

Farm production is far lower than official figures indicate, and the system of distributing food and other products to consumers has almost completely broken down. As an example, of the 90 million tons of potatoes harvested annually by Russian and Ukranian farmers, only 24 million get to consumers because of transportation and storage problems.

The overall milieu has led to a decreasing motivation for work, and no scenario indicates a way out of the deep crisis in the near future. The vast empire is falling apart without a visible succession—other than the different republics going their own way, the alternative is civil war.

THE DIFFICULTY OF CULTURAL CHANGE

Everybody knows that communism is on the wane, but not everyone appreciates what exactly this means. The aftermath of decades of blind complacency is that some 1.5 billion people will have to learn painfully— over the next ten to twenty years—that bureaucratic mediocrity can never triumph over market forces.

Communism is giving ground to more competitive economic thought, just as the twenty-first century is dawning on the First World and me-dieval times are prevailing in most of the underdeveloped countries. But let's not kid ourselves that the change to a free economy and to democratic regimes will be rapid or that it will happen like a miracle. A longstanding tradition mediates the opposite way.

Communism was not born with Lenin, and surely not with Stalin, who was a right-wing dictator.

- The word was first used in the *Commune* of Paris, which was set up following the disastrous (for France) French-German war of the 1870s.

- The concept framed-up in the late 1890s, which witnessed an at-tempt at radical socialism to wipe out the economic and political changes brought by capitalism in central Europe.

Economic and social pressures aggravated by industrialization and na-tionalism, acted *as if* to provide justification for an oppressive political ideology. Ten years prior to the Russian Revolution, Franz Kafka described in unparalleled fashion this spirit.

In its roots, like fascism and nazism, communism (in the Stalinist version) is Kafkaesque. It is also directed at eradicating the ill-perceived deficiencies of two great trends: capitalism and liberalism. This sort of gruesome spirit is still alive and well today: look at Romania. Racism has not disappeared either. We cannot finance Poland and at the same time see its government so lenient to the rebirth of anti-Semitism.

Therefore, as many people fail to realize, a return to capitalism in and of itself is no guarantee of economic and social progress. American and West European business and government decision-makers should remember the lessons of East European history and develop their strategies accordingly.

Nor can we accept the silently growing principle that, on the economic front, the gravitation of Eastern Europe from Karl Marx to Adam Smith would more or less automatically boost living standards in those countries. Taken all together, their population is 123 percent as big as the European Common Market. This would mean a significant reduction in the standard of living of Western Europe and America. No democratic regime can sell this bitter pill.

The whole premise in an accelerated change in the living conditions of the Second World, Eastern Europe, and Russia, is "if and when somebody else pays the bill." Nobody should be willing to pay the bill for the mere reason of being polite. As in the ancient Greek tragedies, god only helps those who help themselves.

The East European countries and Russia cannot afford to underestimate how far self-help should go. *If* they do not get active and really help themselves out of the current bind, *then* their problems will prove to be insurmountable, as the recent Polish experiment with a Solidarity-led government will quite likely demonstrate. And the concomitant economic growth at any price is likely to have highly negative effects on the environment.

There will be no ECU for Eastern Europe because government policies cannot sustain it; the central planners have produced more misery than goods. And though in Russia reformers are demanding that the Communists give up their monopoly on power, this is not happening readily.

A political commentator said that, "In 1989, Western Europe celebrated the anniversary of the French Revolution. In Eastern Europe they more or less reenacted it." There are somber overtones to this comparison. A little over two centuries ago, the French Revolution was followed by civil strife, widespread assassinations, and thereafter a new autocratic regime that ended with the Napoleonic Wars. It took nearly 100 years for France to find a democratic equilibrium. Let's hope Russia and Eastern Europe will do it faster.

11

Commodities and Futures Trading

Commodities are goods, wares, merchandise, currencies, and in general everything that is bought and sold. Because of their wide distribution, universal acceptance, and marketability in commercial channels, certain commodities have become the subject of *trading* on various national and international *exchanges* located in principal markets.

Traded commodities include, but are not limited to: metals, financial instruments, foreign currencies, grains, and meats. Commodities are usually sold in conveniently predetermined lots; for instance in a 100-ounce gold contract. But who is to regulate commodity markets and the financial futures industry? Let's follow an American example.

As of early 1990, a fierce battle was starting on the issue of who should regulate America's financial futures industry, which accounts for 45 percent of the world's futures trading. The pivot point has been the cozy arrangement for Chicago's futures industry, where securities come under the Securities and Exchange Commission (SEC) and futures under the Commodities and Futures Trading Commission (CFTC).

The push for reform has been led by the Treasury Secretary Nicholas Brady, a former chairman of Dillon, Read (a Wall Street investment bank) and former U.S. senator. Brady has worried about regulation of financial markets ever since; as a senator, he was chairman of a task force studying the October 1987 stock market crash.

An effective regulatory mechanism can be provided if we do not just respond to circumstances, but take the proverbial long, hard look. And though regulation is a "must," we all know that it does not come cheap: It imposes constraints; its study and establishment should not exclude any reasonable possibility of the regulated system getting out of control.

191

When the New York stock market crashed in October 1987, some observers were quick to point an accusing finger at the futures markets and portfolio hedging strategies. Others faulted the system of selling short, through which companies could short baskets of equities anonymously through the futures market. Such hedging tactics, they suggest, contributed to the market's sharp decline.

The focal issue is one of jurisdiction. The basic argument is that the stock market and stock-index futures should come under the same regulator and that margin requirements should be harmonized between related cash and futures markets. Who should be fulfilling this mission?

THE COMMODITY FUTURES TRADING COMMISSION (CFTC)

The *Commodity Futures Trading Commission* has been set up by the U.S. government as an independent regulatory body empowered to regulate commodity futures transactions and other commodity transactions under amendments made to the Commodity Exchange Act (CE Act). Its goal is to regulate:

- Trading in commodities

- The exchanges on which goods are traded

- The individual brokers who are members of such exchanges

- Commodity professionals and commodity brokerage houses that trade in these commodities in the United States

The CFTC has been an independent governmental agency that administers the CE Act and is authorized to promulgate rules thereunder. A similar statement can be made about the *Securities and Exchanges Commission* (SEC), which regulates the stock exchanges. Hence there is the split responsibility.

In March 1990 Nicholas Brady said that other countries accepted the reality of *one market* by putting shares, options, and futures under one regulator, whereas America divided the regulation by reason of "historical accident." He then outlined three possible ways of ending this:

- Merging the SEC and CFTC. Separate SEC and CFTC divisions could then be maintained within a new umbrella agency.

- Putting all financial futures (for instance, stock-index futures, bond futures, currency futures) under the SEC. The CFTC would be left to regulate physical commodities, such as foodstuffs, energy products, and precious metals.

- Shifting stock-index futures to the SEC, which would then become the only agency dealing with stock market matters.

Any transfer of regulatory authority will require legislation by Congress, and the two Chicago futures exchanges, the Board of Trade (CBOT) and Chicago Mercantile Exchange (Merc) including the International Monetary Market (Merc/CME), have seasoned lobbyists in Washington, with powerful political supporters. They succeeded in averting moves to put them under SEC regulation following the October 1987 crash.

Apart from the principal commodity exchanges, the CBOT, Merc, and Merc/CME, trading in the United States is also conducted on the New York Mercantile Exchange (NYMEX) and the Commodity Exchange, the Kansas City Board of Trade (KCBT), the New York Futures Exchange (NYFE), the Philadelphia Exchange, the New York Cotton Exchange, the MidAmerica Exchange, the Minneapolis Grain Exchange, and the Chicago Rice and Cotton Exchange.

The Merc and the Board of Trade, where financial futures account for 80 percent and 75 percent of business, respectively, are putting forward two arguments:

1. That securities are very different from futures. A shareholder owns a piece of equity. A person who owns a stock-index future or a treasury-bond future owns nothing except an obligation to pay up or receive payment at some future date.

2. There is turf in the power to set margin. In the American futures industry this is done by the exchanges themselves (self-regulation), changing the rules constantly to reflect fast-moving markets. In principle, the more volatile the market the higher the required margin. The conflicting goal is that a low margin makes hedging as cheap as possible.

This, however, contradicts financial prudence. It also somehow waters down the CE Act, which is designed to promote the orderly and systematic marketing of commodities and futures contracts while preventing fraud, speculative excess, and price manipulations. The CE Act makes unlawful any device, scheme, or artifice to defraud a customer or participant in a commodity pool. It also prohibits any transaction, practice, or course of business that operates as a fraud or deceit upon any current or prospective customer or participant.

MONITORING VOLATILITY IN THE COMMODITY EXCHANGES

A function of the CFTC is to implement the objectives of the CE Act in preventing price manipulation and excessive speculation and in promoting orderly and efficient commodity futures markets. Hence, it has adopted regulations covering, among other things:

- Designation of contract markets

- Monitoring of U.S. commodity exchange rules

- Establishment of speculative position limits

- Registration of commodity brokers and brokerage houses, floor brokers, and principal employees engaged in nonclerical commodities activities

- Segregation of customers' funds and record keeping

- Periodic audits of commodity brokerage houses and professionals

The goals are not unlike those of the SEC, and the Bush administration wants to give the SEC power to regulate some financial futures now under the purview of the rather lax CFTC. Many financial analysts believe that the CFTC-SEC division hampers enforcement efforts, stifles market creativity, and hinders U.S. regulators in negotiations with their foreign counterparts.

There are good reasons for compelling brokerages to disclose more information about major stock trades. And in a move designed to prevent surprises, such as the bankruptcy of Drexel Burnham Lambert Inc., regulators should demand data on the financial health of brokerages' parent companies.

Such regulatory activity does not need to upgrade or downgrade the existing markets. The CE Act provides that futures and options trading in the United States must be done on exchanges designated as *contract markets* by the CFTC. Commodity exchanges provide centralized market facilities for trading in futures contracts and options on such contracts and on physical commodities.

Members of, and trades executed on, a particular exchange are subject to the rules of that exchange. It is the rules that need tuning. Revision and updating of regulations are also necessary because of technological effects and operational changes.

The CBOT expanded trading hours by opening the trading sessions for all financial futures contracts earlier and establishing an evening trading session to trade in its U.S. Treasury-bond and Treasury-note futures contracts. The CME has entered into an agreement with Reuters to create a global, after-hours automated trading system, which may include other exchanges.

Technological and operational changes left aside, the heart of the CFTC-SEC controversy is the concern that stock-index futures contribute to *volatility*. When index futures contracts are at a sufficient discount to the underlying stocks, program traders sell off stock and buy futures. Therefore SEC Chairman Richard C. Breeden wants the authority to raise the margins for index futures, perhaps to 20 percent.

Supporters of consolidation also argue that split jurisdiction stifles product innovation. As things now stand, the CFTC has to approve any instrument with a futures component.

The courts blocked stock exchange efforts to offer hybrids known as index participations, which combine the features of both stocks and futures. But handing futures regulation over to the SEC is no guarantee of innovation either.

Opponents point out that consolidating market jurisdiction might stifle growth.

Another issue regards clearing. Commodity exchanges in the United States generally perform a clearing function, whereby at the end of each day's trading purchases and sales of all contracts are matched against each other. Once the matching process is completed, the clearing house itself is deemed to have accepted the trades and becomes substituted for the buyer and seller of each contract.

Among the plans advanced for the modernization of commodities trading in the exchanges is dumping the pencil-and-card system to record deals, using instead portable electronic trade recorders held by each trader in the pits. The exchanges have already spent millions on computers to speed the flow of customer orders to the trading floors.

As it happened in London with the International Stock Exchange (ISE), as soon as technology is brought to the state-of-the-art, the American commodities exchanges will pit their *open outcry* trading style against the *computerized trading systems* they are developing but currently limiting to after-hours use. By letting the computer-based systems run around the clock, traders on the floors would be encouraged to give customers the best possible price with the simultaneous trade executed by computer.

THE CONCEPT OF FUTURES CONTRACTS

A *future* is a binding contract to buy or sell a commodity or financial instrument at a specified price on a future date. There is today a growing market for 24-hour trading of futures financial instruments.

Futures contracts are made on or through a commodity exchange and provide for future delivery of agricultural and industrial commodities, precious metals, foreign currencies, stock index instruments, Eurodollars, and so on. In the case of the Eurodollar, futures contracts also provide for cash settlement.

Futures contracts are uniform for each commodity on each exchange but vary with respect to price and delivery time. Futures are standardized contracts for a specified underlying instrument with the obligation against the clearing house.

- An initial margin has to be paid.

- A variation margin is calculated daily and can be called.

The specific provision made by futures contracts concerns the delivery or receipt at a future date of a specified amount and grade of a traded commodity at a specified price and delivery point, for an agreed settlement. A commodity futures contract should be distinguished from the actual physical commodity, which is termed a *cash commodity*.

Futures contracts are but one category of organized commodity trading. Two other classes of commodities transactions are *spot* contracts and *forward* contracts (see also Chapter 4). Both of these are varieties of cash commodity transactions, as opposed to futures transactions, in that they relate to the purchase and sale of specific physical commodities. They differ from each other with respect to quantity, payment, grade, mode of shipment, penalties, risk of loss, and the like.

Viewed from a trading perspective, futures are promises to either buy or sell a certain amount of goods at an agreed price within a fixed period of time. Brokers are often pushing the potential for spectacular gains with futures, but they typically forget to tell their customers that the downside can be quite slippery.

- The risks of steep declines increase as prices rise.

- Although market reactions to either side may be brief, there is no guarantee they will not last.

- Downside reactions can produce large losses for speculators without ample financial reserves to meet margin calls.

A *margin* is a good-faith deposit with a broker to ensure fulfillment of a purchase or sale of a commodity futures, or, in certain cases, forward or option contract. Commodity margins do not usually involve the payment of interest. The margin indicates the percentage of all outstanding outright deals and futures of a counterparty or counterparty-group, which must be covered by assets.

Minimum margins are usually set by the exchanges. *Margin calls* demand additional funds, after the initial good-faith deposit, required to maintain a customer's account in compliance with the requirements of a particular commodity exchange or of a commodity broker. Thus margins are not permanently fixed but can vary over time for the same commodity or type of contract.

- Whenever the CFTC has reason to believe that a market emergency exists, it is authorized, among other things, to set temporary emergency margin levels on any futures contract.

- Brokerage firms carrying accounts for traders may impose margins, whether or not otherwise required, and may increase the amount of needed margin as a matter of policy in order to afford themselves further protection.

- In contrast, margins with respect to transactions on certain foreign exchanges generally are established by member firms rather than by the exchanges themselves.

- The International Commodity Clearing House Limited (ICCH) requires margins and deposits from its members, and such members generally ask their clients to put up amounts at least equal to the ICCH charges.

The payment of a margin is made with a commodity broker in order to initiate or maintain an open position in a futures contract. In the United States and on most exchanges in other countries, when futures contracts are traded, both buyer and seller are required to post margins with the broker handling their trades as security for the performance of their buying and selling undertakings and to offset losses on their trades due to daily fluctuations in the markets.

Upon delivery of the commodity in satisfaction of the clauses of a futures contract, the entire contract price is generally payable by the buyer. The buyer may immediately resell this contract or take delivery of it. In the case of precious metals, the ingots are left in the vaults of a trust bank.

Commodities usually fluctuate rapidly and over wide ranges. The commodities market is subject to the many psychological factors working on each buyer and seller, as well as various fundamental factors.

Any prediction of commodity prices is necessarily subject to market factors, any one of which may change at any time. Only by constant

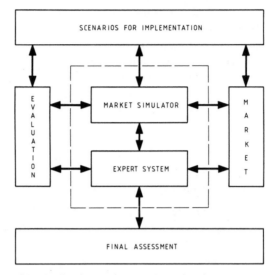

Figure 11.1 Block diagram of a market simulator program enriched with artificial intelligence.

updating of information relating to these factors or by technical analysis can reasonable forecasts be made for commodity prices.

Computer-based mathematical models can help make predictions on market demand and price fluctuations, and several brokers as well as investors use them for this purpose. Figure 11.1 is a block diagram of a market simulator enriched with an artificial intelligence construct.

CURRENCY FUTURES AND INTEREST RATE FUTURES

Currency futures are mainly traded in three exchanges: the International Monetary Market (IMM) in Chicago, the London International Financial Futures Exchange (LIFFE), and the Singapore International Monetary Exchange (SIMEX). The volume of currency futures traded on the IMM has greatly increased in recent years, but such contracts have not yet become commonly used in Europe despite their introduction on LIFFE.

Typically, currency futures are forward transactions in foreign exchange with designated maturities and standardized contract amounts, which are traded on an exchange. For instance, Swiss franc currency futures contracts traded on LIFFE are standardized in terms of unit of trading and maturities.

- In major contrast to forward transactions, at the present time only a few currencies can be hedged with currency futures.

- LIFFE, for instance, accepts sterling, yen, D-mark, and Swiss franc, against the U.S. dollar.

Also, unlike a forward transaction, the buyer or seller of a currency futures contract does not deal with a bank as counterpart, but with the clearing house of the related exchange. In this sense, the Clearing House acts as the intermediary for the processing of transactions between sellers and buyers.

Margins do exist with currency futures and work the way shown in the preceding section, in regard to other commodities. An initial margin must be paid to the clearing house as a guarantee. The payment of the initial margin is mandatory for each participant at the exchange; it can be effected in cash or by depositing collateral. In the case of LIFFE, for example, this margin is currently US$1,500 for each currency futures contract.

Similarly, just as with any other commodity traded in futures contracts, the daily price movements cause the value of the open positions to change constantly. Rules see to it that the initial margin is maintained at all times. Therefore, in order to maintain the initial margin, a *variation margin* must be paid up daily if any losses arise in a position.

The position and the variation margin are monitored by the intermediary, for instance a bank or broker. Paper profits are credited daily to the account. The conclusion of a currency futures contract involves the transaction costs incurred in connection with buying or selling a contract.

To traders and speculators, the appeal of a currency futures contract is its significant leverage, since the initial margin, hence the capital to be employed, is very low relative to the contract size or unit of trading. But leveraging can also end in very negative effects.

Like currency futures, interest rate futures are traded on the IMM, LIFFE, and SIMEX, but also the Chicago Board of Trade (CBOT). Contrasted to currency futures, interest rate futures have become well established on the existing markets and offer an alternative to classical money market instruments. Interest rate futures can be used to fix interest rates in advance. The best way to look at them is as forward contracts traded in an exchange,

- Emulating short-term investments

- Helping in money market and capital market dealing

- Characterized by fixed maturities and standardized contract sizes

Contracts for about 10 money market and capital market instruments are currently traded, the key ones being based on 3-month Eurodollar deposits, U.S. Treasury bonds, U.S. Treasury bills, and 3-month sterling deposits. Interest rate futures have fixed units of trading:

- $1 million in the case of contracts for short-term deposits, such as 3-month Eurodollar deposits

- $100,000 in the case of contracts for long-term, fixed-interest securities, for instance U.S. Treasury bonds

Interest rates derived from the prices of interest futures contracts are not equal to the current interest rates for the related instruments, but represent expected interest rates for future periods.

Typically, such contracts are not held until delivery but are often closed out before maturity through countertrades. It is always good to know that a borrower is protected against rising interest rates by selling interest rate futures, and an investor hedges against falling interest rates by buying interest rate futures.

An underlying position with existing or future interest rate risks is hedged by building up a long or short position in the futures market. In regard to its nature and scope, this corresponds as closely as possible to the underlying position. Through this procedure, trades are able to fix in advance the future interest rate, making it immune to market fluctuations.

In principle, gains or losses on the underlying position are compensated by an increase or decrease in the value of the futures contract. However, an exact compensation will hardly ever occur since the amounts and the maturities of the underlying positions usually differ from those of the contracts, and the spot and forward market developments do not always match.

In terms of financial instrument design and associated trading decisions, the underlying position to be hedged is the critical factor for the selection of a contract.

- If this position is based on a money market placement, it is advisable to choose a contract with a short-term underlying instrument, for example a 3-month Eurodollar deposit.

- If the objective is to hedge a capital market operation, a contract with a longer-term underlying security is preferable, such as a U.S. Treasury bond.

The settlement of purchases and sales of interest rate futures is done through the clearing houses as in the case of currency futures. Both the initial and the variation margins again play an important role in covering the liabilities assumed by any purchase and sale. A commission is payable for the execution of an order to the exchange.

Notice should also be taken of forward rate agreements (FRA). These resemble an interest rate futures contract and make it possible to fix in advance the interest rates of futures interest periods. However, because the agreement is traded in the interbank market and not on exchanges, there is no normalization of procedures. Hence, an FRA can be seen as an interest rate hedging tool that may be tailor-made with respect to amount, currency, and interest period.

In principle, an FRA can be concluded in all hard currencies, subject to minimum amounts. The interest rates applied are London Interbank Offered Rates (LIBOR).* A special feature is the fact that there is never any transfer of principal. Only the interest differentials are paid out on the principal amount on settlement day.

TREASURY AND MONEY MARKET INSTRUMENTS

The foregoing section made reference to Treasuries as an investment vehicle. When an individual or a company buys a U.S. Treasury bill, note, or bond, a loan is made to the U.S. government. The main difference in the three types of Treasuries is how long it takes before the government pays the investor back:

- Treasury bills mature in a year or less.
- Notes mature in 1 to 10 years.
- Bonds take 10 to 30 years to mature.

One more difference is that Treasury bills are sold every week at what is called a discount rate that affects the true yield. Bonds are auctioned quarterly by the U.S. Treasury, and yield calculation is more complex. When interest rates are creeping up, and buyers are scarcer, bond yields spike up.

When the two aforementioned conditions are in synergy, investors have a chance to lock in very attractive yields on a safe investment. They can do so for as little as $1,000 a pop—without paying a commission if they buy directly from the Treasury. Investors can also buy from banks and brokers, but then they pay a fee.

---

*LIBOR is the offered rate for deposits among first-rate banks in London and is frequently used as reference basis for financial transactions.

The purchase of Treasuries can be made directly at one of the 37 Federal Reserve Banks or branches, or by mail. There are two kinds of bids: (1) *competitive*, for which the bidders must specify not only what amount they want to buy, but also what yield they will accept (companies choose this channel, but they risk getting shut out if the yield they bid is too high); and (2) *noncompetitive*, which is the route most individual investors take. The smaller investor does not have to outguess the multimillion-dollar players and is guaranteed to get the average yield from successful competitive bids. The individual investor is also well placed to buy as many securities as desired.

Table 11.1 identifies the three classes of Treasuries, dividing the Treasury notes into two categories depending on maturity. The usual schedule for auctions is also outlined.

Table 11.1   Treasury Securities: Minimum Investment and Time Necessary Before Receipt of Face Value

	Maturity	Usual Schedule
Treasury bills: $10,000 minimum, $5,000 increments	13 weeks	Every Monday except holidays
	26 weeks	Every Monday except holidays
	52 weeks	Every fourth Thursday
Treasury notes		
A. Notes maturing in less than 4 years: $5,000 minimum, $5,000 increments	2 years	Monthly, on a Wednesday
	3 years	First week of February, May, August, November
B. Notes maturing in 1 to 10 years: $1,000 minimum, $1,000 increments	4 years	Late March, June, September, December
	62 months	Last Wednesday of February, May, August, November
	7 years	Late March, June, September, December
	10 years	First week of February, May, August, November
Treasury bonds: $1,000 minimum, $1,000 increments	30 years	First week of February, May, August, November

The good thing about Treasuries is that they are safe, since the investment is backed by the full taxing power of the U.S. government. For this reason, however, Treasuries tend to pay an interest less than other bills and bonds that involve some sort of repayment risk.

Such differential in rates also takes account of the fact that interest on Treasuries is exempt from state and local income taxes, a consideration for investors who face high tax rates. But a basic question in management is always: What are my alternatives? There are alternatives to Treasuries that offer higher yield but also greater risk.

- The alternative to Treasury bills is the money market

- The alternative to Treasury notes and Treasury bonds is the capital market (see next section)

The money market consists of accepting and investing short-term funds for periods of up to 12 months. This contrasts to the capital markets, which operate in the timeframe of one to several years.*

The money market flourishes in many countries, but in others, such as Switzerland, it has attained only minor importance because of fiscal duties like the stamp tax. For this reason, Swiss banks conduct their money market operations primarily abroad, with the larger share transacted on the Euromarket denominated mostly in U.S. dollars.

Money market instruments are available to hedge against interest rate risks. The strategies followed typically depend on the currency and the amounts involved. Money market deposits bear interest at Euromarket rates and can be obtained in any freely convertible currency. Time deposits are typically placed with a fixed term and a fixed interest rate.

Call deposits with 24-hour or 48-hour notice are funds invested for an indeterminate period but can be increased, reduced, or called as the case may be with, respectively, a 1-day or 2-day notice. However, attention should be paid to the fact that, in some countries, deposits in all currencies are subject to withholding tax at source.

The interest rate applied to money market advances is fixed on the basis of the London Interbank Offered Rate, plus a margin depending on the credit standing of the borrower and the term of the advance.

Concerning money market advances, it is also good to differentiate between those *fixed* and *on a roll-over* basis. Both can be obtained in all hard currencies by corporations accepted in the Euromarket.

A foreign currency advance can for instance be an alternative to local currency credit for the financing of imports or exports in another foreign country. A fixed advance is a short-term credit instrument with a fixed

*See also D. N. Chorafas, *Bank Profitability*, London: Butterworths, 1989.

term of up to one year, but the borrower cannot give notice to terminate the loan prior to maturity.

Advances on a roll-over basis are medium-term credits (two to five years) whose interest rates are based on the short-term interest rates in the Euromarket. The interest rates are based usually on "LIBOR plus," the "plus" being a margin depending on the borrower and the term. Contrary to a fixed advance, the roll-over advances can feature partial repayment or calling prior to maturity. This, however, is not true of the liabilities arising within an interest period.

TRADING IN SECURITIES AND COMMODITY FUNDS

International sales and trading of securities has grown rapidly over the last five years. It will continue doing so, according to reactions by leading money managers, traders, and corporate finance officers. At the same time, there will be a worldwide, continued consolidation in the financial services industry.

Such consolidation has its prerequisites. One of the key issues is uniformity in international settlements and payments for stocks and bonds traded on individual national exchanges. In an increasing number, corporate treasurers predict that by 1995 those selling *bonds, stocks,* and *commercial paper* in a multinational market orientation, will be in the majority. This is very significant, as during 1990 only 29 percent of the treasurers of American corporations issued equity in foreign markets, whereas 36 percent publicly traded debt overseas.

American statistics are a good indicator inasmuch as U.S. corporations are expected to account for a large share of the increase in the global trading and selling of financial instruments, reflecting both the need for foreign capital and the growing familiarity of the U.S. companies with foreign markets. A similar statement can be made about Japanese, German, British, and French firms. Recent discussions tend to indicate that there will be a threefold increase in the number of American companies planning to sell equity abroad in the next five years, and about 33 percent of them expect to issue bonds that can be converted into stocks or other hybrid securities (up from 16 percent in 1990).

Many financial analysts are also predicting that heavily indebted U.S. corporations will have to deleverage in the 1990s in order to become more profitable. As a result, the private-placement market for debt and equity is projected to boom. The number of companies:

- *Selling debt* on private markets is predicted to nearly double to 58 percent, from 33 percent now.

- *Selling stock* privately will grow to 34 percent, from half that number at present.

However, the inconsistencies among national clearing and settlement practices and the technological inadequacies associated with the payments process in many financial markets pose a major impediment to the evolution of globality in trading and sales. This is seen as the primary reason that the aforementioned projections may take longer to materialize.

Capital markets also feel the competition from racy commodity funds that are increasingly proving to be a refuge of sorts. Such funds:

- Invest in a variety of leveraged future contracts

- Actively look for diversifying portfolios and bolstering returns, when stock or bond markets decline

The theme of greater diversification and improved returns is attracting many investors, but it often leaves them grumbling. They find themselves paying stiff fees for flat or negative performance, at a time when stock and bond markets were posting strong gains.

This pattern has been observed in the 1980s but seems to have changed with the 1990 downturn of the stock market. Commodity funds are countercyclical investments. Even though the Morgan Stanley world stock index flashed a 25 percent loss for the first 10 months of 1990, on average commodity funds are up a hefty 20 percent.

- Commodity funds perform well when there are wide price swings, either up or down.

- Portfolios in stocks and bonds generally do well only when prices rise.

- Hence many of the trends that hurt stock and bond investors help commodity funds investors by cushioning their losses.

But commodity funds should be used with caution, mainly as hedging instruments, because of a good portion their profits comes from betting against the stock markets themselves.

Whereas strong price swings help futures, the economic and political calm that allows stock and bond markets to rise frequently work against commodity funds. Furthermore, though assets under management in commodity funds have more than doubled between 1988 and 1990 to $3 billion, the industry remains small because investors fear the riskiness of futures.

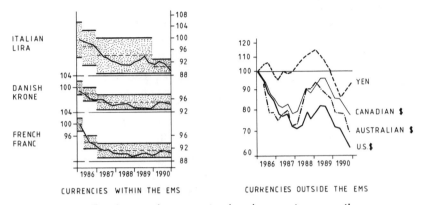

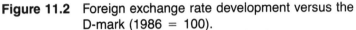

Figure 11.2   Foreign exchange rate development versus the D-mark (1986 = 100).

As it is never too much to repeat, the potential size of losses in leveraged futures markets is practically limitless. The cautious investor knows that the way to control risk is through hedging, thereby focusing on diversity that is closely followed in terms of results. And as the preceding chapters have underlined, hedging in the capital markets is inseparable from currency exchange rate fluctuations. This is further dramatized in Figure 11.2, which shows exchange rate developments in the 1986 to 1990 timeframe (based on statistics provided by the Bundesbank). The left side of the figure focuses on the decline in the price of the Italian lira, French franc, and Danish Krone against the D-mark. The permitted range of variation is also shown. The right side exhibits the fluctuation against the EMS by the U.S., Canadian, and Australian dollars, and the yen. In both cases, the exchange rates at the end of the first quarter of 1986 have been taken as equal to 100.

It is furthermore a wise policy to follow commodity metrics like Goldman Sachs Index, measuring a basket of commodities, which was developed in 1991. This index seeks to weight the value of a range of actively traded commodities and is constituted as shown in Table 11.2.

The Goldman Sachs Commodity Index would have outperformed government bonds and the S&P 500 share index over the past 20 years, says a spokesman for the investment house; Goldman Sachs is negotiating to have the price of the index quoted regularly in major newspapers around the world.

TRADING IN COMMODITY FUTURES

Trading in commodity futures contracts means dealing for future delivery. A contract to buy or sell may be satisfied either by making or taking deliv-

Table 11.2 Using Commodities as a New
Financial Investment

1.	Energy: 48.0 percent	
1.1	Crude oil	18.7%
1.2	Gasoline	16.6%
1.3	Heating oil	12.7%
2.	Livestock: 24.7 percent	
2.1	Live cattle	14.7%
2.2	Live hogs	10.0%
3.	Agriculturals: 18.3 percent	
3.1	Wheat	5.6%
3.2	Corn	3.9%
3.3	Cotton	3.2%
3.4	Soy beans	2.2%
3.5	Sugar	2.1%
3.6	Coffee	1.1%
3.7	Cocoa	0.2%
4.	Industrials: 6.7 percent	
4.1	Aluminum	3.3%
4.2	Copper	2.5%
4.3	Zinc	0.9%
5.	Precious Metals: 2.3 percent	
5.1	Gold	1.8%
5.2	Platinum	0.3%
5.3	Silver	0.2%

ery of the commodity and therefore payment (or acceptance) of the entire purchase price—or by offsetting the obligation with a trade containing a matching contractual obligation on the same (or a linked) exchange prior to delivery.

- A futures contract to accept delivery (buy) generally is referred to as a *long contract.*

- A contract to make delivery (sell) generally is referred to as a *short contract.*

Commodity exchanges individually or (in certain situations) in conjunction with foreign exchanges provide a clearing mechanism to facilitate the matching of offsetting trades. Until a futures contract is satisfied by delivery or offset, it is said to be an *open position*. The aggregate amount to open positions held by all traders for all delivery months in a particular contract is referred to as the *open interest* in such a contract. This is a factor contributing to such a commodity's volatility.

Commercial companies, banks, other financial institutions, and farmers, who market or process commodities, use the futures markets for hedging. As already discussed, hedging is a protective procedure designed to minimize losses that may occur because of price fluctuations. The commodity markets enable hedgers to shift the risk of price fluctuations to speculators. The usual objective of hedgers is to protect the profit that they expect to earn from their financial operations, rather than to profit strictly from their futures trading.

Hedging can also be seen as a facility to check whether it is cheaper to finance, say, a foreign exchange position from the bank's own money desk or in the market. Here again simulators and expert systems can be of significant assistance to the trader in reaching decisions.

- *Hedgers* are typically investors who risk their own money.

- *Speculators* play with the money of others, including highly leveraged deals, with the hope of making profits from the price fluctuations in futures contracts.

This action by speculators contrasts to the hedgers who seek to offset potential losses, measured as the difference between the price at which they had hoped to buy or sell and the price at which they are eventually able to buy or sell. In this sense, they act in the hope that losses in futures trading might be offset by unexpected gains on transactions in the actual execution of commodity trading.

In other words, the aim of hedgers in trading futures is not to make money at all but to guard against adverse price moves. Flour millers, for example, who buy wheat will sell wheat futures short to protect against a drop in the value of their grain inventory.

Hedging may involve a variety of financial instruments. Its effective execution requires current information, rapid computation, on-line experimentation, and networking to keep the database fully updated. For instance, the dealer experiments to evaluate whether it is more profitable to finance a foreign exchange position from the money market desk or with an external customer.

Prior to doing a hedge deal, alternatives must be analyzed, and their aftermaths evaluated. If a hedge deal is made, data entered should be used to update the foreign exchange and money market position, while needed bookings are generated.

The maximum permitted daily price *fluctuation* in the price of a commodity is imposed by commodity exchanges. As such, it affects the futures contract for a given commodity, by putting limits on prices that can occur on a commodity exchange on a given day in relation to the previous day's settlement price. However, maximum permitted fluctuations are subject to change by the exchange from time to time:

- In the United States these limits, including changes thereto, are subject to CFTC approval.

- Such limits generally are not imposed on option contracts or outside the United States.

The higher the prices rise, the more likely it becomes that exchanges will expand the limits that prices are permitted to move above or below the close of the preceding day. When the slide comes, traders either have to pump in more cash or are forced to sell prematurely to meet margin calls.

Position limit is the maximum number of futures or option contracts in any one commodity (on one contract market), imposed by the CFTC or a United States commodity exchange, that can be held or controlled at one time by one person or a group of persons acting together. These limits generally are not imposed for trading on markets or exchanges outside the United States.

The preceding section described limits as typically indicating the maximum of the outstanding liabilities for a counterparty, counterparty-group, or currency. For *outright* deals, limits for maximum tenor are set up. Outright is the case when delivery of the dealt instrument takes place on another date than spot.

The *contract month* is the month in which a futures contract may be satisfied by making or accepting delivery of the underlying commodity. Most hedgers and speculators in the futures market have absolutely no interest in either acquiring or delivering the commodity they buy or sell. As stated in the preceding section, they rarely take delivery of the *cash* or *actual* physical commodity in the futures market, closing out their futures positions by entering into offsetting purchases or sales of futures contracts.

Since investors may take either a long or a short position in the futures markets it is possible to earn profits or incur losses regardless of the direction of price trends. In addition to hedgers and speculators, there has developed a group of commodities market participants which, though not literally hedging their cash positions or requirements, use the futures and forward markets:

- For reduction of risk

- Pursuant to strategies designed to reduce risk

Generally speaking, price swings tend to be more extreme as the contracts near maturity. Hence, the rules of the futures and options game require that aside from having the financial resources and, perhaps more important, the frame of mind willing to assume the loss, hedgers and speculators must have access to market information all day.

Particularly with agricultural commodities, besides responding dramatically to weather changes, prices are affected by export sales, governmental agriculture department reports, and even news articles. Even with buying stocks, the investor must watch market reactions, but not every minute. Trading and hedging in commodities futures intensifies the requirement of being steadily informed on price movements and market mood.

12

Dealing in Options

An *option* is the right to buy *(call)* or deliver *(put)* a specified underlying instrument. It can be dealt and expire at a fixed date. For instance, a stock option is a right to buy or sell 100 shares of a given stock at a specified price by a future date.

Chapter 11, describes puts and calls in connection with futures. Now I will expand on this notion in a trading sense.

- Investors use stock options to reduce their risks in the stock market or to speculate on price movements.

- Options are also employed to hedge a position or for trading. Such trading positions have to be watched very carefully.

- Stock-index options involve baskets of stocks, like those represented by Standard and Poor's 100 and 500 indexes.

But as many traders know, stock options can be dangerous, often taking the speculators' money with them as they die.

Stock options are just as risky as any other commodity, and much depends on expectations—right or wrong. During the recent Middle East crisis, for instance, an oil trader in Singapore plunged into the market in the expectation that a Gulf war would drive oil prices substantially higher.

The day before fighting started the trader bought 100,000 barrels of Brent crude in the forward market at 28.70 U.S. dollars for March delivery. In the space of a few hours after the war began, the price jumped to $33. However, he did not sell and take the profit because, like most traders, he thought the price was going higher. When he arrived in his office on January 18, 1991, Brent was trading around $23. By the time he found a buyer, the price had dropped to $21.20. The deal cost his company $750,000.

In a way similar to other commodities, the rights to buy and sell options on shares usually are granted for a few months, but their value can double or halve in just days. The latest variety, with a life span of nearly two years, began trading on three American exchanges in 1990, where officials hope to attract traders.*

Most series of short-term options have several strike prices. The person who sells, or writes, that option does have an obligation. He or she must buy or sell the stock on the option holder's request.

One type of stock option, known as long-term equity anticipation securities (Leaps), was designed to appeal to investors and speculators with a longer-term horizon. Except for the longer trading period, the new options work exactly the same way as their shorter-term counterparts. A buyer has the right, but not the obligation, to buy or sell a stock at a set price by a fixed date.

Whether shorter or longer term, options have limited life spans. This is usually tied to the delivery or settlement date of the underlying futures contract. As an option nears its expiration date, the *market* and *intrinsic value* typically move into parity. The difference between an option's intrinsic and market values is referred to as the *time value* of the option.

LONG AND SHORT CONTRACTS

The use of interrelated options and futures positions provides a means of risk management and permits a trader to retain a futures position in the hope of additional appreciation in that position. At the same time, it allows the trader to limit the possible adverse effects of a decline in the position's value.

An option on a futures contract (or on a physical commodity) gives the buyer the right to take a position at a specified price (strike or exercise price) in the underlying futures contract or commodity. As opposed to an obligation, this right is specifically to call or put a given quantity of a commodity or a futures contract for a specified period of time at a specified price.

- A *long contract* is a contract to accept delivery of (to buy) a specified amount of a commodity at a future date at a specified time.

- A *short contract* is a contract to make delivery of (to sell) a specified amount of a commodity at a future date at a specified price.

*The Chicago Board Options Exchanges (CBOE) and the American and Pacific stock exchanges trade long-term options on 33 issues.

- An *open position* is a contractual commitment arising under a long or short contract that has not been extinguished by an offsetting trade or by delivery.

- A *premium* is the price paid to purchase an option.

The buyer of a *call* option acquires the right to take a long position in the underlying futures contract or commodity, receiving from the seller the underlying instrument at the fixed terms represented by the option. The option can be bought or sold at a price depending on offer and demand. If the option is not used until its maturity date, it expires.

The buyer of a *put* option acquires the right to take a short position in the underlying futures contract or commodity, delivering to the seller the instrument at the fixed terms represented by the option. Once again, this option can be bought or sold at a price depending on demand and offer—and if not used until its maturity date, it expires.

Spreads (or straddles) characterize a transaction involving the simultaneous holding of futures and/or option contracts dealing with the same commodity but involving different delivery dates or different markets. In the case of a spread, the trader expects to earn profits from a widening or narrowing movement of the prices of the different contracts.

Spreaders (straddlers) do not care whether prices rise or fall because they simultaneously buy and sell the same commodity with contracts that expire on different dates. What they hope is that one leg of their spread will make more money than the other loses.

Another instrument is the *premium* deal. This is a special type of forward or option deal in which the buyer or seller can withdraw from concluding the transaction by paying a premium.

The purchase price of an option is referred to as its premium. The seller of an option is obliged to take a futures position at a specified price opposite to the option buyer in the underlying futures contract, at the striking price, in the event that the buyer should exercise that option. The seller of a put option, on the other hand, must stand ready to take a long position in the underlying futures contract at the striking price.

When a trader purchases an option, the *premium* must be paid but there is no margin requirement. When a trader sells an option, for example an option on a futures contract, he is required to deposit a margin in an amount established for the futures contract underlying the option, plus an amount substantially equal to the current premium for the option. The customer's margin deposit is usually treated as *equity* in his or her account.

A change in the market price of the futures contract will increase or decrease the equity. If this equity decreases below the *maintenance margin* amount (generally 75 percent of the initial margin requirement), the broker will issue a margin call requiring the customer to increase the account's equity to the initial margin. Failure to honor such a margin call generally results in the closing out of the open position.

If at the time such an open position is closed the account equity is negative, then the equity in the customer's remaining open positions, if any, as well as the customer's cash reserves, will be used to offset such debit balance. In case such equities and reserves are not sufficient, the customer is liable for the remaining unpaid balance.

A call option on a futures contract is said to be *in-the-money* if the striking price is below current market levels. It is *out-of-the-money* if the striking price is above current market levels.

Most ledgers and speculators have a *strategy for options*. This includes interest rates, forwards, and menus. Some dealers have written simulators and expert systems able to emulate customer strategies leading to factual and appealing offers to their clients. Among the criteria used to evaluate computer support in option deals are:

1. The ability to manage options

2. A quick response to trader requests

3. Simultaneous calculation of risk in options

4. An integrative presentation to make corrective action feasible

From a broker's viewpoint emphasis is increasingly placed on *quality client service,* where a leading edge can be achieved. The next goal is the integrated treatment of exposure as well as an enhanced ability for all activities related to measurements, compliance, behavioral simulation, and acceptance testing—including all factors affecting performance.

CURRENCY OPTIONS AND INTEREST RATE OPTIONS

Chapter 11 describes currency futures and interest rate futures. Similar concepts can be outlined regarding currency options. Buying currency options makes it possible to guarantee the purchasing price (call) or the selling price (put) of foreign exchange positions without forgoing the opportunity to benefit from favorable exchange rate trends—but also taking the risk of adverse developments, other than those foreseen.

The purchaser of a currency option acquires the right, but not the obligation, to:

• Buy or sell a given amount of foreign exchange

• At a rate and at a date specified in advance

The buyer pays the seller a premium for this right. It is, however, proper to differentiate between two types of currency options: *put* and *call*.

The buyer of a call option gets the right to purchase a defined amount of a certain currency on a stipulated delivery date, at a specified strike price. By writing a call option the seller takes obligation to deliver a defined amount of a certain currency, at the strike price and on the delivery date, at the request of the buyer.

By purchasing a put option the buyer acquires the right to deliver, on the delivery date, a defined amount of a certain currency at the strike price. By writing a put option, the seller ensures the obligation to buy on the delivery day a specified amount of a certain currency at the agreed price. This is done at the request of the option buyer.

There exist minimum contract sizes customarily employed in the market for these option varieties, for instance, $50,000. But on demand options can also be bought or written for other currencies and for individual contract sizes.

Typically, the purchaser of an option must pay an option premium to the seller immediately after the option has been written.

- If the bank is the buyer, it will credit the premium to the account of the customer.

- If the customer is the buyer, the bank will debit the premium to the client's account.

The size of such a premium is determined by supply and demand, a major role being played by *intrinsic value*,* interest rate differential between the two currencies, term of the option (1, 2, 3, or up to 12 months), and volatility of a currency.

Currency volatility is calculated in terms of its daily exchange rate fluctuations against another, specified currency:†

- If the option is being exercised, this must be done no later than the time on the settlement slip on the expiration date.

- The expiration date is two business days prior to the delivery day of the trading month.

In a general sense, options can be exercised at any time. The exercise of the option must be expressly declared to the trading agent, otherwise the customer is subject to a number of regulations.

---

*The difference between the strike price and the market price.

†Remember that *beta*, the volatility factor, is equal to the standard deviation of the price distribution.

For instance, options sold by the bank to third parties—that still have a value at the time of expiration—are closed out at current market prices. Options bought by the bank from third parties, which still have a value at the time of expiration, are deemed exercised at maturity—even if no express notification is made by the bank.

For this purpose, the third party authorizes the bank, in advance, to debit and credit the respective accounts. As a rule, options are not exercised until expiration, in order to allow optimal use to be made of the option right and the related advantages. Typically, currencies are delivered with the value date and terms that have been agreed upon.

Conversely, investors or speculators may be inclined to sell currency options if they believe the course of events will be favorable. However, they face the risk of having to deliver or buy the currency underlying the option at strike price.

The seller receives a premium for the right he or she grants the option buyer. The option buyer orders the option seller to deliver (or buy) only if he or she can buy a currency cheaper than on the market (call option) or sell it at a higher rate (put option). Selling (writing) options can produce attractive returns if the markets are stable. But because of market volatility, this operation should not be looked upon as a hedge for existing foreign exchange positions.

Like any kind of trading, selling currency options requires the ongoing monitoring of the position. The potential loss is leveraged, like the opportunity—and it can be great if no action is taken during a strongly negative price movement to right the balances.

Interest rate options practically exist on the most commonly traded interest rate futures contracts. Besides this, the interbank market provides interest rate options in the form of caps, floors, and collars.

In trading, a collar (also called a *fence* and a *range forward*) is a combination of a long position in a put option and a short position in a call option: the latter is usually struck at a higher price than the put. The idea behind a collar is that the investor derives downside risk protection from the put at a cost that is subsidized by the proceeds of the sale of the call.

Also in the specific case of interest rate options, a collar is a combination of cap and floor:

- The bank may be willing to sell, at a premium, an insurance policy, which guarantees the treasurer that in the worst case the interest rate will not exceed a certain cap. Hence, there is a hedge against higher interest rates through the definition and contractual fixing of a maximum interest rate.

- To reduce the necessary premium, the treasurer may accept a floor to the interest rate, which will benefit the bank in the worst case—if interest rates drop significantly. The floor, too, is a hedge; but it is against falling interest rates through the fixing of a minimum interest rate, which binds both parties. There is also a *currency insurance*, that is, a program creating a synthetic currency put option through dynamic hedging.

Cross hedging is an exchange rate risk–management approach that involves taking exposure to a cross exchange rate. This is frequently used by foreign exchange dealers and by investment managers seeking yield enhancement. A typical cross-hedge can consist of a long position in a high-interest rate currency, combined with a short position in a low–interest rate currency.

Conversion is another technique used for hedging interest rates, as well as for other reasons. A conversion creates a synthetic currency put option by combining:

- A long position embedded in a call

- A long position in a zero coupon bond with present value to the strike that matures on expiration date

- Borrowing the present value of the principal quantity of foreign currency, with repayment due at expiration day

In addition to employing interest rate futures, it is possible to hedge against interest rate risks with exchange-traded interest rate options. These entitle, but do not oblige, the buyer to receive or to pay an agreed interest rate, also called strike rate. This is essentially a call and put deal on a designated date.

The treasurer of a corporation, or any other investor, will think of buying call options on interest rate futures if interest rates are expected to fall; hence futures prices are expected to rise. But it would be advantageous for a borrower expecting falling futures prices and higher interest rates to buy put options on interest rate futures.

As with every transaction, the option buyer will pay the option seller a premium. Such a premium is determined by supply and demand with key factors being the following: the difference between the strike rate and the current market rate; the maturity of the option contract, and the volatility of a certain reference interest rate.

Investors and traders have the choice among different strike prices with corresponding option premiums. Since such strike prices are quoted, market participants can choose between in-the-money, at-the-money, and out-of the-money options.

In the case of a call option, in-the-money means that the price of the underlying contract is higher than the strike price of the option. By contrast, with a put option the price of the underlying contract is lower than the strike price of the option.

At-the-money means that the strike price is equal to the price of the underlying contract. An out-of-the-money call option is one in which the price of the underlying contract is lower than the strike price. With an out-of-the-money put option, the price of the underlying contract is higher than the strike price.

Given that options on interest rate futures are actively traded, positions can be closed out at any time. For the most part, maturities of option contracts run parallel to the interest rate futures contracts. The most heavily traded running period covers the two nearest trading months of the futures contracts.

Currency options are automatically closed out on the last trading day. Closing guarantees that the buyer of a call or put option is credited with the positive difference between the strike price and the prevailing price. At the same time, the seller (writer) is debited with that amount. Conversely, if the difference between strike price and prevailing price is negative, the option expires without value and the deal is closed.

SPOTS AND FORWARDS FROM AN OPTIONS VIEWPOINT

The concept of spot and forward is introduced in Chapter 4. In a *spot* transaction, current price dominates. Reception and delivery of the dealt instrument takes place two working days after deal date, or as agreed when the transaction is done.

A spot *contract* is a cash market transaction in which buyer and seller agree to the purchase and sale of a specific commodity for immediate delivery. Risk is more limited because the current exchange is simple, the conditions are visible, and commitment is made immediately.

Delivery is the process of satisfying a commodity futures contract, an option on a physical commodity, or forward contract by transferring ownership of a specified quantity and grade of a cash commodity to the purchaser thereof. *Open delivery* regards commodities or financial instruments already booked but not yet delivered physically, or vice-versa.

A deal is done *outright* when the receiving and delivering of the dealt instrument takes place on a date other than spot. With *fixed outright*, conditions are fixed when paying, with receiving taking place at a specified future date. With *variable outright*, conditions are fixed when paying; receiving takes place at a specified date. But redemption, or partial redemption, is possible during a fixed time period.

Precious metal spot deals typically concern exchange of currency and precious metal and take place two business days after deal date. This contrasts to *precious metals outright,* in which conditions are fixed but exchange of currency and precious metal takes place at a specified future date.

A *stop order* is an order given to a broker to execute a trade when the market price for the contract reaches the specified stop order price. Stop orders are utilized to protect gains or limit losses and are the triggers that launch computer action in program trading.

A *stop loss order* is an order to buy or sell at the market when a definite price is reached, either above or below the price of the instrument that prevailed when the order was given. A *disposition list* is the list of all the pending exchange orders not yet executed.

Revaluation is the determination of profits or losses, for instance, on foreign currencies.

- Spot and forward revaluation are differentiated.

- Foreign currencies and precious metals are periodically valuated at inventory rate.

- A revaluation list shows the details of revaluation for each currency spot and forward.

As shown in Chapter 11, a *forward contract* is a cash market transaction in which the buyer and seller agree to the purchase and sale of a specific quantity of a commodity for delivery at some future time, under such terms and conditions as the two may agree upon. In a *forward deal,* price, quantity, and quality of an underlying instrument are fixed today. Paying and receiving takes place at a specified future date.

In recent years, the terms of certain forward contracts have become somewhat more standardized and may, in lieu of requiring actual delivery and acceptance, provide a right of offset or cash settlement. For example, foreign currencies may be purchased or sold for future delivery in the international foreign exchange market among banks, money market dealers, and brokers.

The bank, broker, or other institution generally acts as a principal in such forward contract transactions, including its anticipated profit and cost in the price it quotes per contract. Such forward contracts bear substantial similarities to exchange-traded futures, but are not generally regulated by the CFTC.

Although United States banks, which are major participants in the forward market, are regulated in various ways by the Federal Reserve Board, the Comptroller of the Currency, and other federal and state banking officials, banking authorities do not regulate forward trading in foreign currencies. Likewise, forward trading in foreign currencies is not regulated by any foreign governmental agency, although exchange control restrictions on the movement of foreign currencies are in effect in many nations, particularly in order to protect the value of their currencies.

Since the risk of loss in trading foreign futures and foreign options can be substantial, it is proper to carefully consider whether such trading is suitable in light of one's financial condition. In evaluating whether to trade foreign futures or foreign options, investors, hedgers, and speculators should be aware of some basic facts.

Participation in foreign futures and foreign options transactions involves the execution and clearing of trades on or subject to the rules of a foreign board of trade. For these reasons, persons and companies who trade foreign futures or foreign options contracts may not be afforded certain protective measures that are provided, for instance, by the Commodity Exchange Act (the Securities and Exchange Commission's regulations), by the rules of the National Futures Association, and by those of any domestic exchange.

Investors, hedgers, and speculators should also be aware that the price of any foreign futures or foreign options contract may be affected by any variance in the foreign exchange rate between the time their order is placed and the time it is liquidated, offset, or exercised. This has evident impact on potential profit and loss.

If a bank's or broker's client is truly unable to meet the terms of a forward deal on the maturity date, the forward deal can be offset by a corresponding spot deal at current rates. If these rates differ from the agreed forward rates, the client has to bear any resulting loss.

Should a client be able to fulfill the deal as such, but cannot meet the required maturity date, the possibility to extend the deal is utilized. The original buying or selling agreement is executed on the due date while the foreign exchange is sold or repurchased at the prevailing spot rate. The latter becomes the basis of the extension. Gains (or losses) as a result of the extension are credited (debited) to the client. This amounts to a form of swap transaction. Should a forward deal for any reason lose its validity, it can be balanced at any time by a reciprocal contract equivalent in amount and maturity to the existing agreement.

If no date is set for payment of a claim or debt in foreign exchange, with periods of time stipulated instead of fixed maturity dates, a forward deal with a set forward date cannot be concluded. By contrast, there is the facility of foreign exchange options.

The starting date of the period of a forex option may coincide exactly with the date of conclusion of the option deal. With a forward forex purchase, the client has the right to receipt before the termination of the contractual period, since he has already paid the premium for the whole of the period up to the maturity date. Although the deal is a contract with a set date, it is in effect a form of option.

Techniques important in a normal forward contract, such as position closing and extensions, can be equally applied to foreign exchange options. The common link can also be executed as a combination of spot and option deals.

A currency swap agreement is an attempt to exchange and re-exhange at a future date two sums of foreign currency. Intermediate exchanges of currency can also be done to account for interest rate differentials.

OPTIONS ON PRECIOUS METALS

Precious metal futures, traded primarily at the New York Mercantile Exchange (NYMEX) and the Commodity Exchange (COMEX) in New York, are forward transactions for the purchase or sale of a standardized quantity of a precious metal at a standardized maturity, traded on an exchange. Quotation is in U.S. dollars with delivery months January, April, June, August, October, and December. In a way similar to currency and interest rate futures, an initial margin as well as a variation margin must be paid.

The most important precious metals traded today are gold, silver, platinum, and palladium, with a difference made between the primary market and the secondary market. This distinction is important as far as investors are concerned.

- In the primary market, producers sell their precious metals to banks, brokers, and bullion dealers.

- In the secondary market, the banks, bullion dealers, and brokers sell the precious metals to the investor.

Precious metal dealing is structured in a different way from that prevailing in foreign exchanges and money markets—though spot forward and options are part and parcel of dealing.

One of the key questions treasurers and investors ask themselves concerns the potential for long-term, sustained gains in the precious metal of choice: gold, silver, or platinum. Any significant potential is likely to attract speculative interest.

Such interest could also develop on any early test to price ratios. For instance, a gold-to-silver ratio of 100:1 will represent a major price slippage for silver.* Inflation fears and financial panics also boost precious metals' prices but typically tend to favor gold.

*From 1970 to 1990 the gold-to-silver price ratio moved from 18 to 95, having held in the 30 to 40 bracket for nearly eight years. In the year 3500 B.C., according to the Egyptian code of Menes, the two metals were at parity.

Part of the interest in this type of indicator is due to market psychology. Another has its origin in the fact that, to a good measure, the supply of precious metals is price-inelastic. There are up to 20 years supply of above ground stocks both visible and invisible, and the market continues to generate a year-to-year surplus.

Part of the supply is for industrial purposes, but the slowdown in economic performance hampers offtake growth. As a result, supplies continue to outstrip demand, and prices remain depressed.

Figure 12.1 gives a glimpse at silver prices over the decades of the 1970s and 1980s, including 1990. Notice that, adjusted for inflation, the price of silver is at an all-time low.

Precious metals transactions can be spot, forward, or subject to options. The investor has a choice of instruments. In the case of a spot transaction, the precious metal is bought or sold at a fixed price. It must, however, be specified to which place the metal must be delivered or collected from, stored or withdrawn from, and debited or credited.

A precious metal forward transaction has embedded in it the obligation to buy or sell at a later date a specified quantity. Forward transactions can be conducted in the most important precious metals in all major currencies. Unlike spot transactions, the commitment of a forward transaction and its fulfillment (that is, delivery and payment), are clearly separated in time. Although a forward transaction cannot be canceled, it can be closed out by repurchasing or selling the relevant quantity of the same metal.

Profits or losses arising from price changes are realized on the maturity date. The basis for calculating the forward prices is provided by the spot price of the underlying precious metal and the Euromarket interest rate

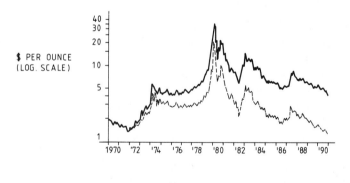

Figure 12.1 Long-term spot silver prices, quoted and real.

for currencies and maturities concerned. This essentially represents the financing costs from the time the contract is concluded to the time of delivery.

Margin cover is analogous to forex forward transactions, but the margin itself can vary by decision of the exchange and of the regulating authorities.

• Forward sales are used for hedging existing precious metal positions.

• Forward purchases are employed by industrial firms and by investors expecting higher prices.

A precious metal advance typically sees an agreed quantity of a precious metal being credited to the account of the borrower. He or she can dispose freely of this quantity of precious metal, but the bank or broker charges interest for this advance. The rate depends on the supply and demand for the physical precious metal. Typically, advances to investors are granted for 6 to 12 months, though in some cases longer terms can be agreed upon—with the interest rate usually reset every 6 months. Interest can also be paid in the form of a specified quantity of a precious metal. Another possibility is to pay interest at an average price of the precious metal draw.

Precious metal loans are made available as a rule—at the one-year level—to the manufacturing industry. By contrast, longer-term loans are requested by mining companies for the financing of new mining projects. In these cases, the repayment of the advance is often out of current production.

Precious metals options have similarities to currency options. The buyer of a precious metal option acquires the right, but not the obligation, to buy or sell a specified quantity of precious metal at a previously agreed price and time. The purchaser pays a premium to the seller of the option for this right. The transaction is fundamentally characterized by puts and calls.

Minimum contract sizes are customarily used in the market for options: gold at 100 ounces and silver at 1,000 ounces. However, the real amounts can be somewhat higher or lower, and the price of the contract is adjusted accordingly. The option must be exercised not later than at the time listed on the settlement on the expiration date. For instance, two business days prior to the delivery day. The expiration date is the third-to-last business day of the trading month.

Similarly to currency options, precious metal options can be exercised at any time, but only with the delivery day as value date. Should the option be exercised, the precious metal will be credited by the bank to a precious metal account—the client being thereafter charged for safekeeping. Precious metal transactions can be handled as book entries through precious metal accounts. Such accounts are kept by weight in troy ounces or grams, or by number of coins. The difference between transactions carried out by physical delivery and through book entries is that in the case of book entry processing, the customer has a claim to a specified quantity of a precious metal in the form of goods delivery: standard bars or coins at the account-keeping bank.

Correspondingly, the physical delivery of precious metals or coins in a client deposit gives the buyer title to the deposited items. For normalized valuables, unallocated or collective custody is used. Numismatic coins are typically safeguarded in individual custody on an allocated basis.

DEVELOPING AN OPTIONS TRADING SYSTEM

The design of an options trading system that can provide significant assistance to traders and clients should start with the fundamentals. The first is to define options and attributes of options. The next step is that of rating options on attribute scales, weighting the attributes. This essentially means (1) assessment of utility and profitability and (2) evaluation of risk. Then comes the calculating part using computers for monitoring the movement of prices as they happen, networks to carry these prices from information providers, and databases to store them.

To spot bargains, we must compare in realspace the prices of stock index futures contracts that have begun trading (for instance, at the Chicago Board of Trade), with the prices of the actual stocks traded in New York. This ensures that decisions reflect pertinent information instantly and that business opportunities can be explored.

Developing a strategic options-trading system means effectively integrating front desk and back office but also focusing knowledge-engineering talent on building strategic systems that help the organization compete more effectively. For growth and survival, there is no alternative to the cutting edge of technology.

System architecture and system design* must be *marketing-oriented* and very sensitive to customer-driven requirements. A huge wave of demand is feeding the financial industry's growth: Corporate customers have finally realized that they do not have the time to develop all the financial solutions they need. Nor do the banks and securities houses have the

*See also D. N. Chorafas, *System Architecture and System Design*, New York: McGraw-Hill, 1989.

resources to build all applications themselves, if they spread themselves thin on old data processing rather than look toward the future.

Any self-respecting financial institution should capitalize on the opportunity to pass some of the most time-consuming software developments, now projected for implementation on classical mainframes, to the more efficient AI and supercomputer environment. The possibility for restructuring is always there if we know how to exploit it. We should take what has been done so far, identify which components have had shortcomings, work together with a top professional of the team of futures and options traders to correct them, and revamp and restructure the approach for handling through AI.

A leading New York bank followed this policy with options and found it valuable for learning a great deal about how to make the system much more efficient. Said a senior executive: "In investigating the AI application we were forced to examine the whole issue from a business viewpoint—for instance, improving the current operation through expert systems and graphics."

Another benefit from the project just referred to has been the restructuring of the bank's databases. Until this study had taken place, for every channel: forex, commodities, securities, and treasuries, there was a different programming solution with its associated information elements, as shown in Figure 12.2a. Although full integration of largely incompatible database structures and programs was not feasible, bridges have been provided through expert systems, and common-ground applications were fully restructured (Figure 12.2b). That, too, is an interim solution until virtually homogeneous solutions can be developed, integrating the presently heterogeneous environments.

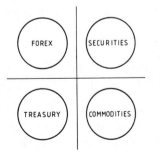

Figure12.2a Non-integrated databases and programming products.

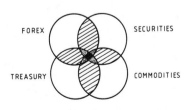

Figure12.2b Nearly integrated databases and programming products.

A CONTRIBUTION BY KNOWLEDGE
ENGINEERING TECHNOLOGY

"The most valuable part of anything we did in technology is the knowledge-engineering part. It proved to be a good productivity tool," suggested a shrewd executive.* This integrative work has overcome organizational dichotomies from past structures that made no sense under current operating conditions.

What another financial institution wanted to do with AI was to support trading decisions. For a number of reasons, it did not succeed in fully automating all of the trading decisions, but in the process it learned how to do the knowledge engineering of the trading application as a whole. Thus a *Futures Trading* (FT) application evolved as a product of research and development work on financial instruments.

Management underlined the following basic reasons for the AI orientation:

1. Futures and options essentially involve managing money—and they are an integral part of a diversified portfolio.

2. There is a whole range of available types of futures markets, trading in anything from pork bellies to the Deutsche mark.

3. Many of the components of these markets react to specific economic conditions uncoupled from one another, unlike the stockmarket where stocks all tend to rise and fall together.

4. Selling short presents its own opportunities, profiting from declines as well as rises in commodity markets.

5. Futures markets trade in standardized contracts and are rather liquid, with large volumes of business transacted quickly.

6. Because only a small percentage of the value of the commodity being traded need be committed at any time as a deposit, there is leveraging—but also high risk.

7. There is today a body of knowledge in AI that permits the development of state-of-the-art approaches—hence an opportunity.

The "trader's assistant" application comprises both a simulator and an expert system that acts as optimizer. Simulation software is used to evaluate thousands of trading data and associated rules, subjecting such data to rigorous analysis in order to determine how successful the rules

*See also D. N. Chorafas, *Knowledge Engineering*, Van Nostrand Reinhold, New York: 1990.

in use have been historically and estimate the probability that trading success will continue in the future.

A historical database covers the last 10 to 20 years (depending on the commodity) of price behavior in the markets being followed. This enables trading approaches to be subjected to a wide variety of market conditions, in order to isolate those that were most consistently successful.

To attune the forecasting system to a given market, the results of all possible permutations of critical parameters for each market are analyzed as a *pattern* and subsequently displayed as in Figure 12.3. The intensity at the intersection of each pair of parameters in the matrix represents the probability of a system being profitable in any given annual period. Parameters being optimized in the matrix of Figure 12.3 represent the amplitude and period of price patterns being sought in the dollar/pound exchange rate. The search is done for groups of profitable factors clustered together rather than for solitary, "lucky" approaches.

When experimentation reveals crucial parameters, then the computer-based knowledge engineering construct, which acts as the trader's assistant, can flash out business opportunities associated with futures markets, whether they are trending up or down. There are, however, a number of further steps necessary in order to create a stable and reliable investment.

Use is made of *weighting* scales—from the commodities entering a diversified portfolio to the relative weightings of the individual markets— determined by the degree of correlation between them. Account is also taken of varying *volatilities* of the futures contracts.

A critical part of the analysis is the estimation of the expected risk and return in a diversified portfolio, which includes: currencies, interest

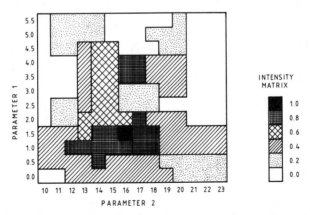

Figure 12.3   Pattern analysis of exchange rate fluctuations as a function of two parameters.

rates, base metals, precious metals, oil, other energy, grains, livestock, and industrial. New products and/or new markets are researched and added to the system as they meet criteria for liquidity, maturity, and profitability.

The solution just described emphasizes the value of investment vehicles whose performance potential is independent of traditional equity and bond market trends. It provides for diversification, which has the ability to return profits under all market conditions, provided such conditions can be sufficiently controllable, and they are controlled through computer-run knowledge-engineering models.

THE OPTIONS TRADING TRAINING SYSTEM

In November 1988 Nikko Securities put in operation the Options Trading Training (OTT) expert system. In its first version, OTT was used for futures and options *training*, but even at that level it was a sophisticated solution, rich in graphics and simulation. Subsequently, OTT was converted into a futures and options-dealing support system, timed to operate with the opening of the Osaka futures market in June 1989.

In its training version, the OTT system fit the structure of the course it was designed to serve, providing online support in terms of basic knowledge and application-intense training. The basic knowledge addresses itself to beginners, teaching them how to develop strategies and do position hedging.

The advanced simulation is applications-intense, often used for retraining mature traders, offering them new skills and tools. Hence, it uses real-life data to test performance and includes yen, dollars, Eurodollars, and other currencies, U.S. Treasury-Bonds, stock indexes, interest rates, and so on.

Originally the OTT implementation covered the Chicago Board of Trade and Chicago Mercantile Exchange. Japanese brokers and banks use the Chicago futures market for Eurodollar trading, being connected to it through satellite channels.

The OTT trading system consists of two major parts, having been a development from the original training solution. These two parts can run independently:

1. *Simple simulation*, which is designed for people with little or no experience in options trading.

2. *Advanced simulation* is for people who have some experience in options and futures trading.

The modules for both simple and advanced simulation underly trading operations on four classes of securities:

- *Stocks*, focusing on S&P 500

- *Bonds*, Treasury bonds, options, and futures

- *Currency*, yen, options, and futures

- *Interest rate*, Eurodollar, options, and futures

With simple simulation the trader-to-be learns how to select a strategy and simulate the position by going through various menus. With advanced simulation, since he or she has sufficient knowledge of the characteristics of each strategy, the trader will set up a position simply by choosing to sell or buy options or futures contracts through the *trading window*.

As Figure 12.4 explains, the trader has available on the screen a help menu and an input section. The latter provides multiple windows, and its operation can be assisted through further pulldown menus.

Another major difference between simple and advanced simulations is the number of different contract-months that the trader is allowed to select for trading. In simple simulation, there is only one calendar that deals with the next month contract type. Hence, the maximum number of contract types for trading is two: nearby and the next contract month. Advanced simulation has three contract months: nearby contract months, the next contract month, and the next-next contract month.

For instance, if the entry date that the trader has specified is 14.1.90 for T-bonds, trading is possible on March 90 contracts as nearby con-

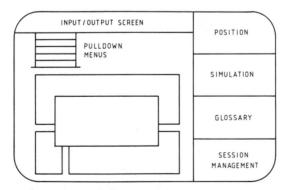

Figure 12.4   Multiple window presentation as used in the Nikko OTT expert system.

tract month June 90 contracts as next contract month and September 90 contacts as next-next contract month.

A sequence of menus leading to a focused choice is shown in Figure 12.5. The model's forecast will be communicated to the trader in a graphical presentation with bullish, not-so-bullish, rather bearish, and bearish alternatives.

The OTT trader's assistant system operates on-line with real-life data. Its use by the Nikko traders is not compulsory, but with the rhythm with which the market works they want to use it, because they cannot be very efficient in their work without it.

The expert system provides the trader's position and P + L through histograms and tables. It permits the saving of data on request for experimental purposes, helps in controlling operations, assists in self-improvement, and, after interacting with information providers, gives four prices to the trader: high, low, closing, and current.

Nikko has developed an intelligent chart-analysis module enriched with knowledge-based constructs. It also has *Swap-CAD*, which acts as intelligent assistant to the design of new swap instruments. To these

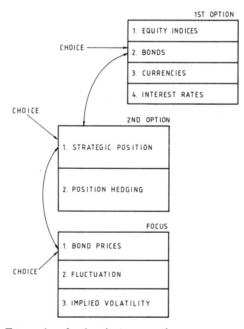

Figure 12.5   Example of a basic transaction as presented in the Nikko OTT expert system.

should be added an impressive range of other AI projects some of which involve neural networks and fuzzy-set theory.

Nikko Securities is not alone in the emphasis it places on the use of artificial intelligence in futures and options. In other Japanese securities houses simulators help the trader to select a strategy from a set of specific strategies that are organized in a table. The trader does so based on the expectation from the market to be bullish or bearish, volatile or stable. Before setting up a position, the trader has access to market price behavior as well as the implied volatility index of the past 20 days. Before making any transactions, he or she specifies an *entry date*, which identifies the starting date of the simulation and the available contract months for trading.

In all applications elaborated by Nikko Securities, the end-user communicates with the expert systems and simulators interactively. Wherever the system wants an input it prompts the end-user. The latter can simply click on an appropriate *icon* for responding to the system's request. Only in a few exceptional cases does the end-user have to type in a number.

Help windows present name of position, brief explanation (when needed), and calls "you should buy" and "you should sell." Based on previous data, the expert system comes up with short-term interest, implied volatility, and market price. Then, based on market price, it flashes buy and sell prices. The model responds in the event of input, or logical mistake, and it gives analysis of *risk* exposure; a graph shows profitability (Figure 12.6) as well as daily variation based on market price.

Other AI modules evaluate the trader's positions through algorithmic and heuristic approaches:

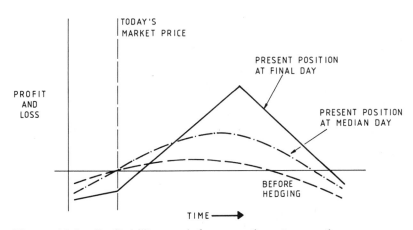

Figure 12.6 Profitability graph for an options transaction.

- The trader must hedge to improve the position.

- If the trader makes a mistake, for instance, selling rather than buying under current conditions, the system tells him or her so.

- If he or she makes an error in product mix, the system says so.

As shown in Figure 12.6, the expert system communicates in a graphical manner what happens after hedging; it also reflects on the fact that as time passes the effects of hedging dissipate.

In other words, suitable measures have been taken to give guidance to the trader should any inappropriate action take place. Such measures include meaningful warning messages and in many cases help screens. Whenever the system expects a response from the end-user, a help icon is provided. If necessary, before the trader responds to a system query, he or she can click on the help icon to get guidance.

Expert system modules provide interim as well as final control and commentary, greatly increasing the trader's possibility to experiment. Support by a 24-hour network makes it feasible to trade both in Osaka and in Chicago.

13

Arbitrage, Spread Management, and Gap Analysis

To *arbitrate* is to decide a dispute as an arbitrator, or arbiter, selected to settle such issues and fully authorized to judge or decide. Disputes subject to arbitration do not need to be solely between persons; they may be price differences in the financial market, and in this case the arbitrator is typically self-appointed to set them through arbitrage for profit.

In financial terms, arbitrage means buying something in one market to sell at a higher price in another. The principles of arbitrage can be applied to many areas:

- Currencies

- Commodities

- Bond portfolios

- Equities with yields

Financial arbitrage is a profession as old as civilization, from barter agreements in old times to hedging and speculation in today's markets. What is relatively new is the *global convergence* in arbitrage; it will be one of the more important trends of the 1990s.

As the major industrial economies become more interdependent and integrated, the spreads among interest rates, currency rates, and inflation rates around the world tend to narrow. Should this happen in a consistent manner, in the longer run exchange rates are likely to become less volatile, with a certain level of stability replacing the big swings in relative currency values that characterized the foreign exchange markets during the 1970s and 1980s.

Still, short-term currency swings will exist creating opportunities for arbitrage operations, as well as for the exploitation of spreads and gaps. Technological support is fundamental in unearthing opportunities hidden in such swings as well as in profitable switching operations.

Switching is the practice of trying to increase the return on a portfolio of investments by selling certain bonds and stocks then buying others, without adding cash or taking it out. *Policy switching* means moving between debt and equities that are very different in term and therefore have different sensitivities to changes in interest rates. Such a move is done with the aim of producing a portfolio that performs better if a predicted change in interest rates takes place.

The essence of *anomaly switching* is that of moving between bonds and stocks that are similar in term and coupon, with the goal of exploiting the small pricing anomalies that occur from time to time. For this purpose the financial markets must be analyzed as to their price and deviations — whether steady or transient. Simulators can be very helpful in anomaly switching by permitting both forecasting and experimentation. Heuristics has a major role to play in all arbitrage operations.

THE ESSENCE OF TECHNOLOGY-ASSISTED ARBITRAGE

The role of technology-assisted arbitrage is to provide intelligence for strategic investment policy decisions and to help set guidelines for action on the trading floor. One example is decision support assistance in calculating the effective yield to maturity of bond issues based on their current trading price (quote). This yield will often differ from the original interest rate paid on the bond issue value and will frequently deviate from the current market interest rate — hence the need for computer support.

If the bond is selling at a price less than par, its effective yield is higher than the stated rate, and the issue may present the opportunity for financial leverage to a buyer. This is particularly true when other conditions exist, such as when a lottery system redeems bonds at their 100 percent rate, realizing a capital gain over the purchase/maturity price and replacing it in the portfolio with an issue of higher yield.

The experimentation necessary in arbitrage operations is in reality more complex than this example. A properly studied application has to consider many factors, including the cost of trading commissions, as well as alternative methods of valuation.

Both experimentation and product enhancements can be done through algorithms and heuristics, always maintaining a close relation with the database for the evaluation of:

- Actively traded issues not being held
- Dormant issues with high arbitrage potential
- Current portfolio in hand
- Switches to be made to improve upon overall performance

An example is provided through anomaly switching, which, as stated, is an arbitrage operation within the bond and equities markets. Basically one looks for investments that are cheap but give a high return. This is done through a two-level computer-assisted process:

1. *Elimination:* Weeding out too low coupon and too high coupon (the latter because of high risk, junk bond–type investments).

2. *Similarity screening:* One algorithm uses as a basis a 1 percent difference in the coupon. If such a difference is greater than 1 percent, then it is an indication of a possible strategic switch.

Enhanced through on-line expert systems, the arbitrage expertise is used to define similarities and differences, looking at similar maturities and the risk factor involved in a switch.

When we talk of arbitrage switching we must keep in mind that most financial markets are steadily watched and analyzed. As a result, there exist price structures from which individual bonds and stocks do not deviate much. We are therefore talking about very small profits, perhaps 0.5 percent of the money invested, with benefits provided as long as profits are in excess of costs and commissions.

Arbitrage switching has implications when considering it as a topic for expert systems. Most important are the prerequisites that should be fulfilled: First of all we must have available specialized expertise. Then, there must be a reasonably agreed upon procedure that can be codified as rules, and such rules must be mathematically expressed whether in a possibilistic or probabilistic way. Experimentation and optimization require access to an extensive database, with instantaneous update available in regard to prices.

Stock market operations and foreign exchange are areas of highly subjective judgment, where rules become vague and the situation is characterized by uncertainty. But the proper classification and pattern recognition capabilities can be of major help to the trader.

One advantage of solutions based on communications networks, computers, and mathematical models, is to steadily monitor the current portfolio to be sure that all market changes are faced on time, thus avoiding falling behind or losing touch:

- A current portfolio-in-hand analysis should steadily track capital gain/loss upon disposition or maturity of the issue.

- Each time a quotation update is made a history relation must be computed for trend analysis.

- Experimentation also calls for a rate model using Monte Carlo and heuristic techniques.

Such a model should incorporate exogenous variables (inflation rate, gross national product, and the like) to estimate future opportunities. A careful analysis will also evaluate endogenous and exogenous variables and look into associated issues such as trading costs versus the benefits to be derived from a switch or technical reasons: for instance, don't touch "this equity because it is spotty in trading," or "this bond because of takeover risk."

An expert system should filter market input and portfolio status according to established criteria that can be nicely expressed in rule form. One implementation focusing on the prediction of market behavior uses analogical reasoning with graphical visualization as shown in Figure 13.1. Its key components are behavioral analysis, causal explanation, and inference based on expert comments.

USING SIMPLE RULE-BASED MODELS

The basic concepts behind the possible use of mathematical models in market operations have been shown. The notion that there are rules that govern market behavior is not new, and the same is true of the existence of deviations. What is new is that we now use such rules to express the behavior of the market, and we employ the deviations to uncover trading opportunities.

The rules we use and program in a form that computers can comprehend and process do not need to be complex, though we develop sophisticated systems. Nor should the presentation routines be esoteric. They should emulate the way market dealers are accustomed to working, and a graphical presentation like the one in Figure 13.1 is a good example of this.

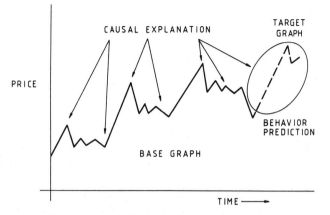

Figure 13.1   Inference based on analogical reasoning.

The evaluation of this and similar graphs within a market setting can give valid indications for needed changes in portfolio structure. A fundamental rule of policy switching is that a change is made as an expression of a view about interest rates. The first rule may be:

- *If* the investor (or broker) has no definite view about the future course of interest rates

- *Then* a policy switch is unadvisable

Once a view regarding interest rates has been formed, for example, that short rates are going to fall a certain amount but long rates by a certain amount less, action may be taken. This will require some mathematical calculations to arrive at an estimate of which holdings may be best sold and which best bought. Mathematical manipulation is an essential aid to switching.

The investor's (broker's or research department's) view of interest rates is taken as input; but it is not said that an operation can be done in all cases. For instance, a second rule may be:

- *If* the investor has no paper that he is free to sell

- *Then* a policy switch is impossible

Typically, the expert system will progress through a number of rules of this form before the possibility of policy switching can be considered. In fact, the idea of *free to sell* can be broken down further, because there are a number of definite reasons why one may or may not be free to sell. The third rule might state:

- *If* a policy switch is possible and timing is favorable
- *Then* a new portfolio pattern should be considered

As seen in this example, three simple rules define a process that permits the expert system to form a view of conditions indicating that a policy switch may be profitable. The next rules should make sure that considerations of timing are right. For instance, they should reflect on the investor's cash flow and tax position.

Still another set of rules will focus on selecting actual investments to switch *out of* and *into* specified market positions. This is what the investor or the broker does anyway. The difference lies in the ability to formulate their sense of the market into logical rules computers can follow and execute.

At the level of bond and stock selection there should be a number of rules expressing relationships and decisions. For instance, "switch so as to slow down (or speed up) your flow of income," if something like that is required or "sell the stock of a given company because its product line decays."

On the anomaly switching side, some of the basic rules are the same, but the principles change. We are no longer concerned with forming a view about interest rates, but with analyzing the past performance of investments: Looking at all possible pairs of bonds X,Y that are fairly similar in both coupon and term, try to detect whether the ratio of their prices or the difference between their yields shows signs of oscillating between reasonably well-defined limits.

This kind of investigation requires a considerable amount of number crunching—a statement valid not only after the rules have been formulated but also, at times, before we are even in a position to name any rules. Supercomputers should be brought into play for very fast number-crunching purposes.

A theoretical background is also essential. In general, bond investments X and Y form an *anomaly pair* if:

- They are similar in term
- They are similar in coupon
- They have been in issue for a reasonably long time
- No special factors affect either price
- Their history seems to show a regular pattern

Although anomaly switching has the reputation of being something that can be done almost mechanically, even simple rules like the one outlined through the five items just listed are packed with imprecise terms: *similar, special,* and *regular.* And there is also fuzzy judgment: *seems.*

This is precisely how and why AI can be of significant assistance. Heuristics help express fuzzy notions, which involve a great deal of subjective judgment and improvisation—something that cannot be done through algorithmic approaches and classical, procedural-type programming.

Once a valid expert system has been written, it can be networked with market data to steadily review portfolios, assess opportunities, and improve the return on assets. This has obvious consequences for arbitrage and switching. Hence, the emphasis is on deciding the *principles* that one will apply for selecting a switch rather than on actually carrying it out, which is the job of a trading module.

Whereas the expert system example we have seen is very simple and it is advisable to start this way, AI constructs get more complex as the problems compound. For instance, we must look at a portfolio *globally,* not only at a single, stock-by-stock level. A modern portfolio has global duration and volatility and a global pattern of cash flow.

There may be constraints on some or all of the trading and portfolio management rules that come into consideration. There is also the need to optimize the return on the portfolio, subject to these constraints. In some ways, this is both a problem in linear programming and in expert systems, and it is advisable to use hybrid systems.

MODELS FOR SOPHISTICATED TRADING

An *index* is a measure of the value of a group of foreign currencies, stocks, debt securities, and the like. Stock indexes are among the most familiar, and they are the only indexes that are currently the subject of options trading. Compiled and published by various sources, including securities markets, indexes may be designed to be representative of:

- The stockmarket as a whole

- Stocks traded in a particular market

- A broad market sector such as industrials

- A particular industry, for instance aviation

An index may be based on stocks traded primarily in U.S. markets, stocks traded primarily in a foreign market, or a combination of stocks whose primary markets are in various countries.

Like a cost-of-living index, a stock index is ordinarily expressed in relation to a *base* established when the index is originated. This base may be adjusted to reflect such events as capitalization changes that affect component stocks or to maintain continuity when stocks are added to (or dropped from) the index group. Adjustments are usually designed to ensure that the index level will change only as a result of price changes during trading.

Being similar to stock options, index options are traded in basically the same manner, but there is a significant difference in the way exercises are settled. When an index option is exercised, the operation is settled by the payment of cash, not by the delivery of stock. The assigned writer is obligated to pay the exercising holder cash in an amount equal to the dollars difference between the exercise settlement value of the underlying index, on the day the exercise notice is tendered, and the exercise price of the option, multiplied by a specified factor.

The multiplier for an index option performs a function similar to the unit of trading for a stock option. It determines the total dollar value of each point of the difference between the exercise price of an option and the current level of the underlying index. Such a multiplier is fixed by the market where the options are traded, at the time when they are first opened for trading.

An *arbitrage* operation *on index options* can be effectively assisted by using fuzzy logic (possibility theory)* to set up streams of different markets, comparing to or coordinating with other financial instruments:

- Monitoring in realtime

- Evaluating alternatives

- Establishing margins and projecting on the risk of the margin closing

Similar approaches, but not the same models, can be used in proposing multicurrency paths in arbitrage operations. Using neural networks, one of the leading financial institutions worked on both currencies and securities arbitrage, developing a multiprocessing capability for swapping a whole portfolio for another and taking into account:

- Exchange rates

- Options and futures

---

*See also D. N. Chorafas, *Knowledge Engineering*, New York: Van Nostrand Reinhold, 1991.

- Investment horizons
- Required margins
- Risk embedded in the portfolio
- Costs associated with swapping

Another financial institution currently is working on fuzzy sets and neural networks to develop a computer-based system for *contrarian trading*, aiming to obtain early indications of clear-cut trends in selected markets and to identify consistent strengths or weaknesses. This approach capitalizes on current experience generated through a model that manipulates past price behavior to predict future market activity.

Known as technical trend follow-up, the approach just mentioned waits until a trend has established some momentum before flashing buy or sell signals. This has also been tried with algorithmic approaches—the trouble, however, is that sometimes such momentum has been fleeting, therefore algorithmic models cannot capture the opportunity at the moment it is about to develop.

From index options to currency futures, we should have more powerful tools in our toolbox than our competitors. Intelligent graphs, for instance, is the way to go, leading to *pattern recognition* and providing significant benefits in human-machine communication.

The solutions we seek should be integrative and should utilize the best that technology can offer at the time. They should be modular, permitting updates to the knowledge bank (KB) of the expert system without upsetting what already has been accomplished.

As an example on the implementation of a highly modular architecture, Figure 13.2 shows a session manager for advisory and trading purposes constructed by means of networking six specialized expert systems. These are specializing on the following issues:

1. The analysis of competitive forces in a global market

2. The elaboration of details reflecting a treasury strategy

3. Evaluation of business opportunity based on the outcome of modules 1 and 2

4. A critical look into currency mix in the portfolio, given the latest economic and political information from First World currencies

5. A similar analysis done for debt and equities in different stock markets

6. Recommendation on buy, hold, or sell concerning securities, currencies, and a combination of both

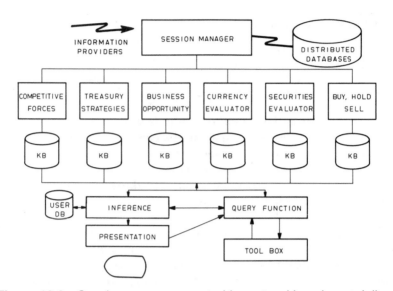

Figure 13.2   Session manager created by networking six specialized expert systems.

A dual solution involving both rules and fuzzy sets has been adopted with the constructs stored in the knowledge bank. The session manager accesses on-line both private and public databases; it also receives a steady news and quotations stream from information providers.

It is a good policy to make available to the more computer-oriented trader a software toolbox permitting the use of shell commands for individualized programming routines. This is both efficient and expedient when the trader requires a greater level of elaboration than that provided by the modules of the available and running expert system.

LIABILITY MANAGEMENT AND SPREAD MANAGEMENT

Spread management is the calculation and monitoring of net interest margins. A net interest margin is the spread between the cost of money to our bank (or to our treasury), and what we earn on it.

In all the major countries of the First World, the financial industry complains that the net interest margin is steadily shrinking. This makes very important its monitoring to provide the right information flow and tools necessary for improving profits. What we closely monitor can generally be revealing of ways for improving our portfolio and can provide indicators on action that should be taken to better the bottom line.

Vigilance is important because the situation faced by banks in the 1990s is considerably different from the one we have known in the decades after World War II. During the 1950s, 1960s, and much of the 1970s, banks were in a position of having more than sufficient flows of deposits; hence management attention focused on how to best employ those deposits as earning assets.

Precisely for this reason the timeframe of the decades I just mentioned was marked by the term *asset management*. Let's also recall that prior to the end of the 1960s over half the clients' deposits were demand deposits. The goal was how to *allocate assets* for the most favorable return. But with the deregulation of the 1970s it became obvious that a bank's greatest single source of funds, *deposits,* could not satisfy the growing requests of borrowers. Traditional deposits were shrinking, siphoned by the money market.

Money market is the open market for lending or borrowing short-term funds and dealing in negotiable instruments (see also Chapter 11). Participants are mainly banks and large companies. Typical money market paper consists of Treasury bills, bankers acceptances, commercial paper, and so on.

Under market impulse in a changing financial environment, since the mid-1970s aggressive bankers have seen the opportunity to improve profits by seeking out new sources of funds to satisfy strong borrowing needs. They also became more aware of the growing money market instrument that previously had no particular attraction because interest rates were regulated (Resolution Q in the United States).

The larger banks actively purchased the excess funds of smaller banks through the Fed funds market. As larger dollar negotiable certificates of deposit became more prevalent, *liability management* was born in contrast to asset management.

Liability management quickly became a tool for expanding assets and meeting a part of a bank's liquidity needs. This has been further underlined with the growth of *debt financing* by corporations and most particularly the action taken by the junk bond market during the 1980s.

But there are prerequisites to be observed in this major switching of equity for debt and a new market emphasis. Liability management implies the control over levels of deposits and borrowings and the matching of liabilities to earning assets. This matching of funds has been a further evolvement of asset and liability management and brought under perspective a process of *spread management*.

Although all funds are homogeneous in terms of the uses to which they can be placed, they are gathered at vastly different costs. Assigning these costs in an equitable and meaningful manner is a challenging task.

Just as important is knowing the margins that exist between the cost of funds and income from their usage.

This is a subject wide open to mathematical analysis, and experimentation is necessary in analyzing the money we are planning to use prior to commitments. Financial literature addressing itself to *Matched funds* and the crucial subject of *gap management* is usually referring to a narrow group of interest-sensitive liabilities and assets. Spread management and matched funds are the basic concepts to be considered when we refer to the purchase of liabilities and matching them to assets, as well as the optimal allocation of these assets.

This is the area where analytical techniques such as the Monte Carlo method and heuristics approaches provide great help to the trader and the investor. Mortgage-backed financing and asset-backed financing are examples of domains where random walks, multiple regression analysis, binomial distribution approaches, and fuzzy engineering have been successfully used.

Bankers with experience in the management of financial resources will recognize the fact that controlled growth is essential to a steady stream of favorable profits. Too rapid growth, whether of liabilities or of risky assets, can bring the bank (and the investor) into a very uncomfortable position. The regulatory authorities are looking hard at capital adequacy, because lending and investment risks can be quite important.

Spread management should therefore center on the ability of our treasury to identify, administer, and optimize the growth of our statement of condition so that it stays in relative balance, thus ensuring a favorable picture. Such balance must look at the growth of *Interest income* and *interest expenses* so that net interest income (margin) will more than adequately offset noninterest expenses, if the market conditions permit it. Market conditions alter the perspectives connected to *interest-related liabilities*, including money market operations, Fed funds purchases, repurchase agreements, and capital notes or debentures.

Also changed are the *interest-related assets*, that is, the bank's earning assets—primarily loans and security investments. With interest-related liabilities and assets in the background, bank management should bring its attention to the foreground: the *net interest income*, that is, the positive difference between the revenues on earning assets and the interest costs of all liabilities.

Mathematical models can be instrumental in the evaluation of assets, liabilities, and net interest income. Interactive computer solutions provide a basis for rapid evaluation before commitments get out of hand. In addition, they allow investment and disinvestment decisions to be reached in a factual and documented manner.

NONINTEREST REVENUES AND POLICY PLANNING

The able management of business opportunities as they develop is the financial industry's competitive arena of the 1990s. From the analysis of any reasonable investment possibility benefiting the clients' account can be derived the best documentation for fee income, which has become a necessary complement to bank profitability as the margins between the cost of money and the lending rate shrank after deregulation.

Traditionally, bank management did not deal too seriously with non-earning assets, nor did it cover in a thorough manner the administration of noninterest revenues and noninterest expenses.

- *Noninterest revenues* are generated from service charges, income from information services, safe deposit rentals, trust free income, auxiliary service fees, and so on.

- *Noninterest expenses* cover all expenses that are not directly an interest cost on bought funds or related to the intake of money.

Yet, both noninterest revenues and noninterest expenses are of growing importance on the balance sheet, whereas nonearning assets can seriously affect the need for increasing the capital base.*

Rush moves can be avoided when strategic goals are reflected in long-range plans and budgets and when all costs are properly analyzed. Such costs include interest and noninterest expenses being investigated through a profit center reporting system. Balance sheets and income statements should be combined interactively into financial decision making, feeding the obtained results into the funding and asset-allocating strategies.

Banks that do not pay due attention to the noninterest domains of their activities and to the proper allocation of assets and liabilities find themselves in serious difficulties when hard times hit. Some try to come out of the squeeze by selling assets, which is precisely what they should not do.

One of the best criteria on which to judge the quality of management prior to investing in a financial institution, is determining the origin of the capital used for dividend purposes. Dividends may not necessarily be coming out of profits as is the logical course. Banks in trouble try to mislead the market into believing that everything is fine, while disposing of their assets and distributing the proceeds to the shareholders.

*See also D. N. Chorafas, *Bank Profitability*, London and Boston: Butterworths, 1989.

In his book, *Breaking the Bank: The Decline of BankAmerica,** Gary Hector cites such a practice. It happened in 1984–1985 and was condemned both by the Federal Reserve Board and the Controller of the Currency. "The two agencies issued a joint policy statement saying they would frown on any banking company that uses the cash from a sale of assets to pay a dividend. Dividends, they argued, should come from a bank's profits, not from the slow liquidation of the company." And in certain circles on Wall Street, this ruling became known as *the BankAmerica decision.*

Another valid criterion for evaluating the quality of management is the strategic moves being *made*—not just those announced to the press or to securities analysts. *Redimensioning* and *refocusing* are examples—both calling for a significant amount of homework.

In the mid-1980s Bank of America reduced its international activities under pressure from huge losses in its loans portfolio, and in 1990 Security Pacific decided to retreat from European markets in an orderly, planned manner. In late February 1990 Security Pacific said that it was restructuring its international operations, and even though it would maintain a presence overseas, its enthusiasm, particularly for Europe, had waned considerably because those operations had failed to provide a favorable return.

High-performance banks are keen on locating top-priority markets and operations and making them part of their overall business-planning process. Their asset/liability management includes funding and allocation; projection on rates and volumes; and *what-if* scenarios in conjunction with fund allocation operations, spread management, and gap analysis studies. Wise policy decisions call for a significant amount of experimentation.

Like the trading in index options, spread management, and the other examples given in this chapter, all financial allocation and investment decisions can be effectively assisted through artificial intelligence. In fact, given that this is a domain where experience is accumulating, research projects should go beyond rule-based expert systems and into the construction of machine learning heuristics.

Figure 13.3 shows two approaches followed by an experimental project in this domain. The upper half describes an ideal situation where action from the real world impacts on a system to produce a correct output. A realistic solution (in implementation terms) is presented in the lower half of the same figure.

- Stimulated through an input, the knowledge bank (KB) gives an output, which is recycled through a *learner.*

*Boston: Little, Brown, 1988.

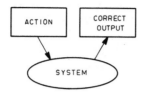

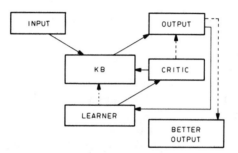

Figure 13.3 Machine learning system: ideal situation and realistic solution.

- The learner impacts on the rules of the knowledge bank by means of a *critic*.

- Learner and critic recycle the output through repetitive loops, until the critic accepts it.

- Upon acceptance, the critic bypasses the knowledge bank, since the system now provides a better response than when the recycling has started.

This approach is fairly generic and could be used in a number of situations where machine learning is important. Although the specific application to which it will be put after development may vary from one financial institution to another, it must be emphasized that the objective is not one of substituting for management but of providing an advanced learning tool.

SOLUTIONS TO GAP ANALYSIS

Gap analysis is a term often used in the financial services industries to refer to the historical trends of the balance sheet as well as a forecast of liabilities (deposits) and assets (loans and investments). There is both a practical and a theoretical background to this approach.

Asset and liability management should not be done without forecasting, but even the best forecast seldom results in an equality of liabilities and assets. The inequality is referred to as *the gap*, and it directly affects the financial margin.

- If the trend shows that liabilities exceed assets, it indicates a potential liquidity problem.

- An excess of assets may well mean unemployed capital or a developing loss of market opportunity.

The most common method of treating an inequality in a balance sheet forecast by the treasury is a set of simultaneous equations that balance the differential as short-term debt or generated cash. This has been traditionally done on a one-country and one-currency basis—an approach that has proved to be increasingly inadequate when operations are multinational and they affect income, expenses, and portfolio composition.

What the treasurer needs is a *multidimensional*, in-depth gap analysis to be done on both a static or dynamic basis, enhanced through AI and enriched with graphics. This graphical presentation should:

- Present an overview of the maturity structure of rate-sensitive assets and liabilities

- Quantify the maturity mismatch that exists within a set of multinational balance sheets

- Show whether the organization is *asset-sensitive* or *liability-sensitive* for each particular maturity category, as well as the cumulative effect of mismatches

A computer-based evaluation should calculate the annual income exposure in different currencies, comment on projected exchange rates, and provide an estimate of how net interest income would be affected if interest rates should change.

Through the visualization of this information, management can project the impact of a change in the interest rate of any currency in the portfolio, as well as estimate the consequence on earnings. This, too, can be done on-line, assisted by expert systems. If the impact is material, the model should assist in determining what strategies to implement in order to offset this interest rate risk.

Currencies left aside, many other variables are involved in an evaluation of the types we are discussing, which are partially controllable by management. Such as:

- Growth rate

- Inventory levels

- Price trends

- Collection policy

But it is *exchange rate* fluctuations that make the financial services balance sheet forecast more complex. Furthermore, because of regulation based on liquidity, financial services cannot simply plug the difference with short-term debt or cash. The gap must be closed by assumptions for strategic moves in product offerings.

All this reinforces the wisdom of a learning mechanism, described in the preceding section. What is needed is a version able to reflect on swings in inflation rates, currency rates, and money rates and able to address itself to relationships between short-term and long-term rates— making feasible a rapid response to change as an essential element of managerial performance.

Such an approach contrasts to that commonly used today, where many financial institutions and manufacturing industries have static gap-management systems. These are typically implemented to enable statistical calculations rather than learning and corrective action. Hence, their usefulness is limited.

Without artificial intelligence constructs, gap analysis approaches are rigid in logic and allow little or no interactive redefinition of rules. Many are processed in batches or on slow computers. As a result, in the time a processing run takes, the situation may have changed several times and opportunities lost.

Static gap reporting procedures use historical data and are typically done with month-end information. By contract, dynamic gap reporting employs simulated data and looks at how a particular *what-if* scenario impacts the maturity mismatch over time.

Different planning periods have to be examined, and experimental steps should allow users to perform simulation as well as optimization on different exchange rate hypotheses. The user should be given the ability to view the results of each scenario on the sceen both in graphical and in tabular form, as desired.

Expert systems must provide the user with the ability to define between one and twelve months for each planning period in order to construct simulation scenarios with various time horizons. The model should also be capable of projecting monthly for two years, one year, quarterly, or any timeframe serving the user.

14

A Financial Advisor
System Project

Through expert systems, foreign exchange trade is handled in a more sophisticated manner than with standard computers. The best implementations are interactive; they are networked workstation to workstation and
workstation to database. If supercomputers are used as number crunchers, response time is a matter of milliseconds.*

Advanced-applications design maps the global market into the machine. It also sees to it that every time a deal is done there is an updated
P + L statement to guide the dealer's hand by currency, corresponding
bank, client firm, day of trade, value date, and so on.

- A *cross-rate* screen gives both raw data and evaluations relating to
  key decision factors.

- An *arbitrage* screen permits the review of different scenarios for
  getting, say, pounds into dollars — including barter agreements if requested.

- The money market implementation has *feature analysis* for comparing what the cash market is doing against the futures market.

A forex system designed along these lines of reasoning evaluates what
the futures price should be, based on spot interest rates and expectations. A knowledge engineering module predicts which position to take
to offset any movement between, say, buying January pounds and selling
July dollars.

*See also D. N. Chorafas, *Using High Technology in Forex and Treasury Operations*, New
York: Wiley, in press.

251

The expert system knows a lot about the business it is operating in—that is, the trader's business. It understands what the corporate policy is, who are the users of the system, what kinds of trade each person is allowed to do, and so on. It also has expertise on the return required on forex projects to be undertaken in order to break even.

The knowledge engineering construct has all of this information because the knowledge engineers taught it. They learned the art of the domain experts, in forex through knowledge acquisition and custom tailored the system to the needs of forex operations, including:

- Business assumptions

- Corporate clients

- Corresponding banks

- Users' privileges

- Users' options

- Terminology

The business assumptions customize the calculations that take place as news and prices come in. This module also identifies traders and managers who have failed to correct their positions. Other features include deliberate options, analysis of the entire day's transactions, canceled deals, and exceeded deals.

These and similar applications are dynamic; their success depends both on the skill of the knowledge engineers and the tools at their disposal. For this reason, the following case study exemplifies the steps followed in an evaluation project that was undertaken to help decide which *expert system shell* should be used.

PROTOTYPING THE EXPERT SYSTEM SOLUTION

Bank ABC decided to develop an expert system prototype, to gain experience in the practical use of the technology. The development of the prototype was done in three different versions, using software shells X, Y, and Z—one of the main objectives being to analyze various shells with respect to:

- Specific aspects of forex operations

- Different techniques of knowledge acquisition

- Flexibility in knowledge representation

- System performance of the applications mapped into these shells

Management wished to learn more about the delivery of a faultless, overall system as well as what is necessary in gaining users' acceptance. Another aspect of the project was to provide a "test-bed" for evaluating the sustainability of the AI construct during further developments.

Management conducted both the *applications tests,* for accuracy of on-line usage, and the *technological tests,* regarding response time and cost-effectiveness. Detailed records were kept regarding performance.

To provide a solid ground for comparison purposes, all three expert system shells were used to prototype the same model, which was purposely kept simple. It basically consisted of a network of formatted solutions aiming at enabling the bank's dealers to respond to bets, capitalizing on inference capabilities.

The model of the artificial intelligence construct shown in Figure 14.1 is composed of five modules arranged along two axes of reference:

- *Stimulus-Inference-Course of Action.* The first application focused on this axis going from stimulus to course of action through the inference module.

- *Knowledge-Inference-Rules of Behavior.* This sequence was defined with the goal of being exploited at a later date as a self-sustaining knowledge repository.

Every one of the three shells X, Y, and Z chosen for the test passed the first evaluation, which focused on new form design. However, a differentiation in performance started becoming apparent when graphics presenta-

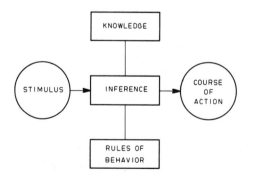

Figure 14.1 An artificial intelligence model: from stimulus to action.

tion was added, and most particularly after the incorporation of decision rules for the evaluation of different exchange rates from the global financial market—hence after the computational aspects were added.

Rather than making an experimental model, the project focused on accomplishing a leap forward in the real production environment, which over a period of 15 years (in the 1970s and 1980s) had gone:

- From nonintelligent terminals on mainframes

- To terminals on dedicated minicomputers

- TO PCs for each trader operating on a local area network (LAN)

- To expert systems support on the PC

- To a supercomputer on the LAN as number cruncher

Let's notice that this five-step evolution has been rapid, with the transition from step to step taking about four years. To understand the challenges, we should look at the historical aspects.

Bank ABC did not care merely about the mechanics of the job to be done. Management was indeed primarily concerned about the cultural change necessary to make this five-step evolution a proposition acceptable by the human capital—and, therefore, to make it a profitable one.

For instance, the passage from the mainframe to the minicomputer applications was labeled a "Forex Front-end System," with forex personnel developing some of their own applications, because the centrally developed ones (by the data processing department) had failed to fulfill requirements. By the late 1970s, this new generation had been adopted by all of the bank's branches abroad—but it was already getting obsolete.

The user involvement had, however, opened new vistas: with the personal computer implementation, the wisdom of using a graphic tablet at the workstation level by the end-users themselves. Part of the culture change came with the LAN solution. This application started in 1980–81 and eventually covered operations in 20 countries. By the mid-1980s all forex and treasury operations were supported by homogeneous systems worldwide.

Electronic messaging went global soon after, and in a short time it became capable of addressing every key function: messages, positions, and deals/transactions.

The next improvement was that of installing a group of dedicated servers to reduce response time. Subsequently, the workstation itself went into redesign. "It dates back to 1983. Hence, it is by now old fashioned," said a senior executive in 1986. The same man made the same statement in 1990 about the system he had designed and implemented in 1986.

It was exactly at that time that the idea of incorporating expert systems and testing different shells prior to a final selection came up. Experimentation was seen as the better approach prior to decision because of the policy that once a choice is made it should be applied throughout the bank's network.

"All of the forex and treasury operations are supported by the same system functionally, no matter where the branch office is," suggested the same executive. But the problems to be faced with expert systems went beyond those encountered in the past, because the management of Bank ABC felt there was a major change being made: the transition from data processing to knowledge engineering.

The following milestones were established for the knowledge engineering project: definition of objectives, feasibility study, development of a prototype, pilot project, practical use of the pilot, and evaluation of the experience. Each shell ran on the same configuration of workstation, supporting the same rules and formats.

In parallel with building knowledge-engineering expertise, the bank developed a currencies database for dollars, pounds, yen, D-marks, Swiss francs, and French francs. This has been supported by the data flow from the quotation system's expert system modules to evaluate trends in money rates, losses, and gains.

Figure 14.2 shows the policy followed in the expert system shell experimentation, from writing the specifications to the feedback for corrective action. After the three prototypes of the first, relatively simple, expert system module were put into productive use, refinements were made both to the rules base and the knowledge bank. Fine-tuning also required some changes in the conceptual design.

The differentiation of the models came by way of *shell performance*. All three had been handling critical questions by providing systematic access to information, however:

- The primitives of shell X were found to be wanting in terms of the *graphics support* they provided, as well as the ability to integrate a graphics package in order to improve their supported features.

- Shell Y was too rudimentary, and, apart form the deficiencies in man–machine interfaces, it was limited in the mapping of the rule base as well.

- Shell Z gave the best results: Some traders said the expert system is "another colleague." However, the problem that was presented has been one of machine power. The i386 chip on the WS was too slow to face the power requirements posed by this shell in order to obtain an acceptable response time.

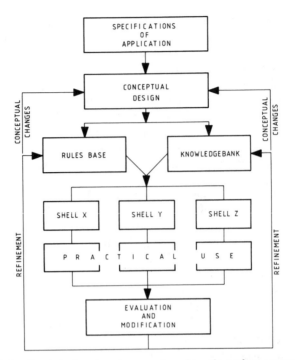

Figure 14.2   System for development and testing of an expert system.

After discarding shell Y and improving the interfaces of shell X, the bank made one more test between shells X and Z. The latter came up as the traders favored solution. Hence the decision was taken to install an accelerator board per WS and design another board whose mission has been to convert into firmware the most frequently used primitives of shell Z.

CAPITALIZING ON THE PARALLELIZATION OF DATA

One of the greatest challenges with new technology is integrating its functionality with the already existing data processing system. Hence it is wise to make new developments very modular in their interfacing with the available environment and to see to it that portability between different installations is ensured.

Any and every major financial organization has ongoing applications that simply cannot be discarded when new, more modern implementations are developed. *Hybrid systems* have to be built, while the able handling of information elements (IE, data sets) remains at the center of large computational problems. Both with artificial intelligence and with super-computers, information elements have still to be selected, combined, and operated on—but the style of processing has radically changed.

Whether through networked workstations or by means of parallel pro-cessing, as in a *hypercube* architecture,* operations can be performed simultaneously on many IE, as far as system structure allows it. The no-tion of parallelism is fundamental in all implementations taking place in the 1990s, and this is a major step beyond the simpler expert system perspectives examined in the case study of Bank ABC.

In foreign exchange operations, data-parallel computing associates one of several processors with each IE—for instance, banks or other entities. The goal is that of exploiting natural computational parallelism inherent in many data-intensive problems. Such an approach significantly decreases execution time and also simplifies programming. *Data-parallel* hardware both looks like and works like an intelligent memory. This is precisely the reason that the *new generation* of computers and AI go hand-in-hand.

A fully distributed information environment has no centralized mem-ory; as a result, information elements are neither stored nor accessed by serial operators. Rather, they move along the edges of the data-flow graph, providing the basis for system synchronization.

Message exchange is the key—precisely the way a forex specialist oper-ates. Messages are the carriers of information elements: text, data, voice, graphics, and image. The system must also handle intermediate values exchanged among network nodes and final results returned to the user or sent to a destination. Data exchange is basic in all foreign operations deals.

Figure 14.3 shows the exchange mechanism that takes place among three layers of reference, with the financial institution interconnecting to the outside world of customers, corresponding banks, and brokers. Communication is ensured by the fact that the nodes of the semantic network exchange messages with one another.

In a hypercube-type computer architecture, the exchange of messages is effectively done in parallel through logical connections corresponding to the edges of the hypercube. Parallelism in execution fits high-risk operations (forex or securities) much better than anything that has taken place in the past.

Most of the numerical programs we have had so far with classical applications in data processing do a lot of calculation on a small amount of data. In more than one aspect this is an antithesis to what forex-type problems require.

---

*See also D. N. Chorafas and H. Steinmann, *Supercomputers*, New York: McGraw-Hill, 1990.

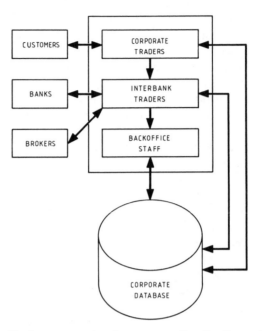

Figure 14.3 Exchange mechanism connecting the financial institution with customers, corresponding banks, and brokers.

- Forex-type implementation is largely based on symbolic, pattern-actuated, knowledge-oriented processing.

- Execution by computer media must sift through large amounts of stored and incoming information.

- A significant number of possible solutions must be evaluated instantaneously, and this evaluation is heuristic rather than algorithmic.

Little work needs to be done at the front-desk level in processing each item. But speed is very important; hence support through current data-processing technology is not always effective and in some cases it is quite inefficient.

THE CONTRIBUTION OF A SEMANTIC NETWORK

Key to the new approach is the *semantic network*, which consists of a connection of nodes interlinked through edges. Each node represents an object, which may be physical or logical, as well as a relationship, event, or chunk of data and commands. Each edge represents a binary relation. The parallel handling of such objects is a different way of expressing their instantaneous processing requirements, which can be effectively mapped into a hypercube architecture.

Semantic networks are a data-parallel style of programming associating one processor with every information element connected to the program. Data-parallel programs can be expressed in terms of the same structures of a serial program. The difference is that individual IE of a composite data structure (such as an array) are spread across parallel processing elements.

As a result of the facilities provided through parallel computer architecture, each information element belonging to corresponding banks, financial centers, and defined currencies has an associated processor dedicated to it. This makes up a powerful tool for forex-type applications where changes regarding the same currencies are handled in different financial places all the time.

The serious reader will appreciate how significant a change there has been since the mid- to late 1980s when (as demonstrated earlier) attention was paid to the selection of the best shell, but not necessarily to the parallelization of the procedures. The foremost banks in the First World have now raised their expectations much higher. In one short decade we have moved:

- From minicomputers and personal computers to workstations networked through LAN.

- From procedural-type programming done through Cobol and Fortran to fourth-generation languages and from there to expert system shells, which are fifth-generation languages.

- From serial processing (on maxis, minis, and workstations) to parallel processing on supercomputers and minisupercomputers.

At the same time, the attention we pay to *detail* is much greater, and we focus on the problem in a more systematic way. This is part and parcel of the emphasis on semantic networks.

Forex-type programs contain many decision points and also many branches. Each branch handles some special case or combination of cases. There exist complicated interactions among the branches. These are typically cases of heuristic search to be executed in an active memory manner with networking being a pivot point of our approach toward a solution.

Such a system could also resemble a *connectionist* model. Connectionism derives its inspiration from neural networks. The aim is that of creating computing engines from complex interconnection of neuron-like elements. Each neural element has a number of inputs and outputs—as well as an internal state. Each node is, in fact, a decision point.

The resulting operation is subtle and is facilitated by parallelism. This is precisely one of the approaches taken by at least two leading financial institutions. The approach depends on neural networks for *pattern recognition* of *exchange rate* and *interest rate* flows.

Another financial institution has implemented AI models on data-parallel hardware in a memory-based reasoning development. This applies massive amounts of parallelism to closely related clauses. The aim is one of:

- Locating relevant information in a large database

- Finding stored descriptions that match a set of inputs (new data or queries)

- Effecting simple inference using such knowledge

Another valid approach to parallel forex-type processing is exemplified through the Hearsay system, which was originally developed for speech understanding. In Hearsay, a problem is broken up into a number of modules. Each module is an expert on some aspect of the problem and is assigned to a separate processor or group of processors.

Provided the proper design is made, communication among modules is kept to a minimum. The small amount of shared information is ensured through a *blackboard*, which pipelines data structures flowing through the problem. Figure 14.4 presents the architecture in a nutshell. The first two practical uses to which this system was put were information selection and interpretation and computer-based training. This approach is particularly important in a forex environment where our real challenge is not an inability to store enough information, but rather to exploit vast amounts of available information in realtime. Such action requires parallel processing to search simultaneously through both data and the defined body of knowledge, identifying information items relevant to the problem at hand and evaluating different paths that could lead to a solution.

UTILIZING THE POWER OF NEW GENERATION COMPUTERS

Tailoring a financial advisory system is a design challenge—but also a power supply issue. If we have enough computing power available, for instance, more than one giga-instruction per second (GIPS), we can instruct the machine to scan at high speed every item in memory, looking for one or more information patterns.

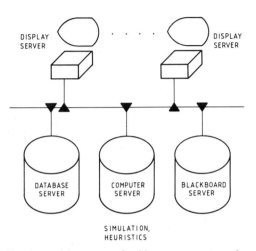

Figure 14.4 Basic architecture of a Hearsay system for artificial intelligence implementation.

Both *pattern recognition* and *exhaustive search* are powerful tools in the trader's arsenal, but they are prohibitive with serial computers because of the time such processes require. Massively parallel machines do not have this constraint. For them, both pattern recognition and exhaustive searches are feasible within acceptable response time.

Therefore, it is in the interest of every forex department to find and exploit high degrees of parallelism, making it also feasible that both symbolic and numerical components of hybrid software systems can be computed in parallel modes.

Parallel processing is of particular importance in forex because, whether we realize it or not, many foreign operations problems are pattern-directed. As a result, the programs handling such problems should be featuring distinct computational modules that represent chunks of knowledge modeled along real-life structures, rather than twisting such structures to fit the serial-processing characteristics of mainframes or other computers.

Just as significant is the fact that such pattern-directed activities do not call each other explicitly but collaborate indirectly through commonly accessed databases and blackboards. Superficially, this process looks complex, but when we know how to approach it, it becomes simple and flexible.

But there are challenges that must be faced in a skillful manner. As modules are processed in parallel, conditions that trigger execution can be satisfied by more than one of them. Hence an added parallelism is derived from the steady evaluation of arguments and the associated unstructured process of invocation. This results in concurrent processing, enabling an agile mapping of real-world situations into the machine.

The obtained degree of flexibility can be further appreciated if we remember that, in a rapidly changing financial environment such as foreign exchange, the information we search is not actually available in an explicit way. It must be computed from a large number of information elements by a process of *classification, identification,* and *inheritance.*

As discussed in the preceding sections, this process of logical inference can take the form of an active semantic network. If so, it consists of nodes and links.

- The nodes representing noun-like concepts (for example, financial centers) or other information elements

- The links connoting relationships between concepts

With this approach, the long-term knowledge in the system is embedded through a pattern of interconnection of the nodes and links in the network. As mentioned, this storing of knowledge as a variable pattern of active connections is known as connectionism and finds one of its applications in the development of a *news grid.*

A massively parallel computer, for example, can be very helpful in foreign exchange applications because it supports programmable grids with many arbitrary dimensions. These are typical of foreign operations involving many financial markets as well as different currencies and commodities.

For instance, the Connection Machine-2 (CM-2) (from Thinking Machines of Cambridge, MA) features such a *News Grid.* Possible grid configurations include 256×256, $63 \times 32 \times 32$, 64×1024, and so on. The process makes it feasible to pass data to a regular rectangular pattern, then manipulate these information elements in a parallel-processing form.

In a two-dimensional grid, each node (processor and memory unit) of the computer receives IE from any one of its neighbors or operates on a routing scheme involving the power of the whole computer. There are complementary activities like *get-from-news* and other operations in which data can be rubbed around, boundary values can be discarded, or decisions be based on the boundaries of the grid.

- In-depth database search is done by heuristics

- Matrix multiplication and vector summation are done through algorithms

- Interprocessor communication is done by the hypercube network

Classical operations such as sorting and merging are enormously simplified through this approach and complex operations are expedited.

On a Connection Machine with 64,536 physical processors, sorting 64,536 32-bit fields takes about 30 milliseconds (ms). This includes ranking the fields as wanted by the user and rearranging them and also presenting the results through the front end—which, incidently, consumes the largest part of the 30 ms elapsed time. That explains why much more complex operations do not require an appreciably longer time.

VIRTUAL PROCESSORS AND TERAOPS POWER

An equally powerful operation is *virtual processor abstraction*, on which most higher-level software depends. For example, if a foreign exchange or securities operation requires the simultaneous processing of a million different information elements, it can request the availability of 2^{20} virtual processors and obtain it from the operating system of the Connection Machine.

What is truly happening with the virtual processor is cycle sharing on the same arithmetic unit by different objects. Such a process in itself is not new; it has been done on mainframes for 20 years. But mainframes have just *one* arithmetic and logical unit (ALU) and cycle-stealing creates long queues of processes waiting to be served. As a massively parallel computer, the Connection Machine has up to 64,536 ALU working in parallel, each with its own memory. And software ensures that each physical processor on CM-2 supports 16 virtual processors.

It is precisely the power of the instrument and what can be done with it that attracts the more progressive users. Dow Jones has two Connection Machines that it employs for text retrieval. Each has 32,268 processors and executes six billion instructions a second, one thousand times faster than any other computer at Dow Jones.*

Because of the power of the dual CM-2, the company's subscribers can search a vast database of magazine and newspaper articles using English-like commands. The system identifies key words in the command and uses them to search the database. Not all of the articles it returns will be appropriate, but a user can pick the best ones and then do a second, more refined search.

This type of application is very important in large databases and even more so in a dynamic interactive environment, as is the case with forex. Many queries in forex, securities, and treasury are ad hoc. They cannot be preestablished and normalized, as is the case with accounting, because they steadily change as the market moves.

*Wall Street Computer Review, November, 1989.

The type of application discussed here lends itself very well to parallel computer architectures:

- The thousands of processors work in unison, each searching a small part of the database in a fine-grain manner.

- A more conventional serial computer would have to examine each page of data one after the other, doing so in a coarse way, while also taking much longer time.

Having evaluated its operating environment in a careful manner, Dow Jones decided that the system had to be able to handle 40 simultaneous sessions, with a delay of one or two seconds as a maximum. As a result of this implementation, all of Dow Jones's subscribers now have access to the system—and this means a five-digit number of on-line users.

Following the success of the first implementation on a parallel computer, Dow Jones now has a second application that it has considered moving from its mainframes to the Connection Machine. The firm markets the *Professional Investor's Report*, which tracks the movements of about 6,000 stocks.

- Any unusual activity in a certain stock is a pointer to Dow Jones's reporting staff that something newsworthy might be afoot.

- Searching for patterns in mountains of data is an application that runs well on a fine-grain parallel computer.

Most artificial-intelligence processes address nondeterministic problems because they are so much closer to the real nature of operations. With many such problems it is impossible to plan in advance the procedure to execute and terminate even using all available information.

Nondeterministic processing calls for adaptable, software-oriented computer solutions. By now, we have enough experience to appreciate that the efficiency of any computer system strongly depends on this knowledge representation as well as the language being used. Valid approaches should be designed around:

- A high-grade knowledge acquisition regarding the problems to be solved

- An agile knowledge representation approach

- The astute choice of the high-level languages to be supported

- A fine grain of parallelism in execution

Another prerequisite is the handling of large knowledge banks. Idea databases answer complex forex problems, and one must always keep in mind that flexibility is most important.

Once the problem of parallelism has been faced in an able manner and working solutions have been provided, these solutions can be portable to more powerful engines as they become available. For instance, although the parallel processors on the Connection Machine currently operate at 10 giga-instructions per second peak power—and that is nearly two orders of magnitude better on mainframes—DARPA's *teraops** projects will provide a significant leap forward in terms of power.

Farmed out to two U.S. parallel-computer manufacturers, Thinking Machines (as Project TERA) and Intel (as Project TOUCHSTONE), DARPA's effort aims at one trillion operations per second, or roughly 1,000 times faster than the swiftest computer ever built. Results are due in 1992 or 1993.

According to the directives of the Defense Advanced Research Projects Agency (DARPA), both contractors will build scaled-up models of massively parallel computers. Results are awaited with great interest as the machine that can do double-digit teraops will unleash computer capabilities that in some ways match the human brain in thinking power.

There is as well the 1990 AT&T announcement of the first *photonics* (optical switching) computer, which also aims at operations 1,000 times faster operations than the most powerful machines available today. Significant power improvements are coming. But is the finance industry ready to use them in a wise manner?

---

*The units of measuring computer power change with time. In the 1950s the early commercially available computers worked at the level of a few thousand instructions per second, but by the mid-1970s the unit of measurement had become a *million instructions per second* (MIPS). Today, Thinking Machines, Intel Scientific, and Cray have supercomputers that work at *giga*-levels—1,000 to 10,000 MIPS. *Tera*-levels are equal to 1,000,000 MIPS or more, identified by the unit *teraops*.

Looking Forward: Treasury Operations in the Year 2000

The company of year 2000 will be rich in professionals, and thin in managers. As Dr. Peter Drucker suggests, it will resemble an orchestra with 200 professionals and one conductor.

An orchestra does not have "subconductors" in the way that an industrial or financial organization does. But it does have a concertmaster, a top professional who is distinguished by being a *virtuoso*. This book addresses itself to the virtuosi of the 1990s, who will be opening up the new era.

Knowledgeable people understand that for growth and survival in the 1990s the financial industry necessitates major *quality* improvements in its products and services. It needs high-grade professionals but also intelligent networks providing the ability to trade anywhere in the world, at any time of the day, in any product a financial institution or manufacturing organization is supporting.

The cutting edge of competitiveness requires approaches that are enriched by knowledge engineering and are able to ensure 24-hour banking through worldwide business transactions along with their monitoring and compliance to regulations. We have to make the existing systems operate more efficiently, and the best way to do so is through imaginative solutions.

Solutions for treasury, forex, and securities must work in realtime. The information and know-how on which our decisions are based are highly perishable and therefore must be current. Decisions taken after the key parameters have changed, with obsolescence sneaking into our concepts or embedded in our equipment, are very dangerous things indeed.

1. An accelerating pace of change in technology and in the business world at large

2. Increasingly more demanding marketplaces

3. Deregulated financial environments that are globally accessible

4. Growing business diversification in many industrial and financial sectors

These are pushing and pulling toward a knowledge-based society, with further progress heavily dependent on improved means through which both information and know-how can be captured, transmitted, stored, retrieved, manipulated, and used around the globe without delay.

Over the years, the breakthroughs achieved by science and technology resulted in communications over long distances. Networks today operate at rates of billions of bits (gigabits) per second. This has created a continuous stream of information that flows among business centers, as well as between these centers and the user organizations.

Although three-quarters of Earth suffers from a lack of adequate communications facilities, in America, Japan, and Western Europe, communications technology has progressed rapidly, as users have set forward ever more demanding goals. Professionals today require high technology, just like high technology is made for the best professionals which exist in banking, the manufacturing industry, engineering and science at large.

This is another way of saying that *quality* in financial services does not come cheap, and the same is true of *cost-effectiveness*. Both demand insight, foresight, and know-how—and, above all, clear goals.

Corporations can achieve improved results in treasury and in forex only if their computers and communications resources are rationally organized and steadily kept up to date. Technology has to be used to advantage for maximizing *business benefits* and gaining leadership in a tough, competitive market. The other vital components of a sound strategy are:

- The employment of first-class *human capital*

- The development and marketing of *innovative* financial products

- The exercise of strict *cost control* coupled with the proper organizational measures

Strategy and structure are interconnected. The structure of efficient organizations is flat; it seldom has more than four or five layers. Dynamic organizations are centered on *names*, not roles. When the treasurer changes, the person who takes up the post rarely if ever executes the treasury functions in the same manner as the predecessor.

Clear-eyed management has understood this fact, even if it runs contrary to what all of us learned in our university studies and textbooks.

The world has changed and those who capitalize on this change develop *profile* analyzers through expert systems to learn the *personality* of the clients and what makes them tick.

Although absolutely necessary, it is not enough to master the mechanics of treasury and foreign exchange operations to which the first six chapters of this book are addressed. Dealing in currencies involves political, social, and demographic dynamics—hence the issues treated in Chapters 7 through 10.

Furthermore, as this decade advances, success in forex, securities, and treasury will increasingly depend on sophisticated financial instruments like commodities, futures, and options. Chapters 11 and 12 have been written with this goal in mind.

Within this same timeframe, technology will be the arbiter between the able and the *very able*. As the last two chapters of this book suggest, technology does not need to be a headache—it can be a grand *business opportunity*.

Index

A

Accountability, 27
AI modules, 231
Alcatel, 143, 158
American Institute of Certified
    Public Accountants, 29
Analytical queries, ad hoc, 42
Apricot, 147
Arbitrage, 83
    switching, 235
Arithmetic and logical unit (ALU),
    263
Artificial intelligence constructs,
    84, 121
    sophisticated, 80
Asset management, 243
Asset swaps, 92
Automation, 84
Aveling, Tony, 143

B

Baker, Howard H., Jr., 187
Bankers Trust, 28, 33, 36, 107
Bank for International Settlements
    (BIS), 9, 92, 93, 97, 99, 107,
    149, 155–157

Banking, internationalization of,
    51, 52
BankInter, 18
Bank of America, 25, 27, 246
Bank of Japan, 38
Bank of New York, 13
Banque Commerciale pour
    l'Europe du Nord, 164
Basket hedging, 100
Beales, Michael, 144
Bellmann, Richard, Dr., 39
Bolton, George, Sir, 164
Boulding, Kenneth, Dr., 171
BP Finance, 63
Brady, Nicholas, 191, 192
Bretton Woods agreement, 88,
    110, 131, 132, 139
British Petroleum, 63
Bundesbank, 105, 133, 137, 144,
    161, 162

C

Canon, 147
Capital flows, 118
Cash commodity, 196
Cash management, 57
CFTC-SEC, 195

Chicago Board of Trade (CBOT),
95, 96, 193, 194, 199, 224,
228
Chicago Mercantile Exchange
(Merc), 82, 193, 228
Chicago Rice and Cotton
Exchange, 193
Citibank, 39, 53, 56, 78, 79, 186
Citicorp, 64
Clause, bilateral, 120
Clause, minimum, 119
Clause, option, 120
Clearing account, 157
CHAPS, 78
CHIPS, 78, 79, 150
Collar, 216
Collateralized mortgage
applications (CMO), 46
Commodities, 191, 197
Commodities and Futures Trading
Commission (CFTC), 191,
194, 197, 209, 219
Commodity Exchange Act (CE
Act), 192, 193, 220
Commodity Exchange (COMEX),
221
Commodity exchanges, 193–195,
207
Computers and communications,
82
Concurrent engineering, 81
Connection Machine-2, 262–265
Consolidation, 12
Contract market, 194
Contracts, aleatory, 132
Contracts, forward, 196, 219
Contracts, spot, 196
Conversion, 217
Cost center, 106
County NatWest, 38
Cross-database access, 41
Cross-hedging, 100, 217

Cross rates, concept of, 57
Currencies portfolio, 90
Currency clauses, composite, 119
Currency exposure, 86
Currency futures contract, 199
Currency hedging, 100
Currency integration, 152
Currency management, 91
active, 89
Currency options, 218, 223
Currency policy, 86
Currency swaps, 95
Currency volatility, 88

D

Dai-Ichi, 42
DARPA, 265
Database mining, 41
Data-driven environment, 84
Data networks, 145
Data-parallel programs, 259
Decision process:
crisp, 45
fuzzy, 45
Delivery, open, 218
Delors, Jacques, 133
Delors plan, 136
Deregulation, 9, 10
Deutsche Bank, 186
Dillon, Read, 191
Diversification, multinational, 51
Dow Jones, 263, 264
Drexel Burnham Lambert, 194
Drucker, Peter, Dr., 76, 171, 266

E

Ecofin, 134
EC-EFTA Treaty, 167

EC Executive, 137
EC membership, 136
Ecopoints, 168
ECU Banking Association (EBA),
    150, 157
ECU sight account, 157
Eisenhower, Dwight, 176
Electronic Funds Transfer
    (EFT), 3
Electronic messaging, 254
EMU, 137, 138
End-user computing, 42
Eurobond, 149
Eurodollars, 164–166, 196
Euromarket, 119, 142
European Bank for Reconstruction
    and Development, 181
European central banks, 148
European Community (EC),
    128–130, 132, 134, 139,
    151, 153, 159, 166, 167,
    169
European Currency Unit (ECU),
    128, 129, 132–144, 147–152,
    154–159, 164
European Free Trade Association
    (EFTA), 166, 167, 169
European Monetary Fund, 144
European Monetary System
    (EMS), 128, 132–136, 142,
    148, 157, 206
European Monetary System's
    Exchange Rate Mechanism,
    100
European Parliament, 137
Exception reporting, 84
Exchange Rate Mechanism
    (ERM), 134, 135, 139, 140,
    142
Exchange rates, flexible, 110
Exchange rate system, flexible,
    116

Expert Swap Trader, 97
Expert systems, 18, 33, 79, 97,
    252
    networked, 44
    second generation of, 45
Expert system shell, 252, 253

F

Factoring system, 119
Federal Reserve Board, 11, 13, 16,
    88, 127, 134, 186, 202, 219,
    246
Fedwire, 79
Fiat, 147
Financial advisory system, 260
Financial engineering, 8, 124
Financial Information Systems
    Center (FISC), 38, 39
Financial intermediary, 152
Financial management, global,
    60
Financial products, 39
First Interstate Bancorporation,
    25
Floating rate assets, 29
Follow-the-sun overdraft, 78
Forecasting, 90, 172, 173
Forecasts, 170
Foreign exchange market, 103
    turnover, 88
Foreign exchange trade, 251
Forex information, 75, 76
Forex operations, 55
Forex portfolio management, 91
Forex room, 84
Forex trading, 76, 79, 81
Forward discount, 122
Forward markets, 123
Forward premium, 123
Forward rates, 122, 123

Forward transactions, 58, 59, 94, 222
Fuji Bank, 41, 42
Fujitsu, 147
Futures, 195
Futures contracts, 196
Futures Trading (FT), 226
Fuzziness, 44
Fuzzy engineering, 47
Fuzzy logic, 240
Fuzzy query system, 84
Fuzzy sets, 44

G

Gap analysis, 248, 249
General Electric, 185
Giannini, Amadeo P., 25
Gibb, Sam, 38
Giga-instruction per second (GIPS), 260
Global custody, 67–70
Globality, 76
Globalization, 10
Global networks, 83
Globex, 82
Goldman Sachs, 206
Goldman Sachs Index, 206
Gonzalez, Felipe, 114
Gorbachev, Mikhail, 114, 134
Graphical representation, 84
Greenspan, Alan, Dr., 127
Group of Seven (G-7), 163

H

Hardware, data-parallel, 257
Harvard University, 186
Hector, Gary, 246
Hedging, 50, 92, 117, 119, 208
Hedging costs, 94

Hedging on interest rates, 95
Hedging strategy, 100
Heuristic models, 101
Heuristics, 43, 239
High technology, 22
High-technology supports, 50
Hitachi, 147
Holmes, Oliver Wendell, 170
Horsham Corp., 179
Hybrid systems, 256
Hypercube architecture, 257
Hypercube-type computer, 85

I

Index, 239
Inflation, 87, 88, 112
Information elements, 256
Intelligent networks, 146
Interactive visualization, 84
Interest rate and currency swaps, integrating of, 121
Interest rates, fluctuation in, 87
Interest rate swaps, 28, 29
International Commodity Clearing House Limited (ICCH), 197
International Forex Association, 78
International Monetary Conference, 186
International Monetary Fund (IMF), 3, 157, 166
International Monetary Market (IMM), 198
International Swap Dealers Association, 93
Investment bank, 14
Irving Trust, 13
ISE, 195

J

J.P. Morgan Global Government Bond Indices, 105
J.P. Morgan Government Bond Index, 161

K

Kansas City Board of Trade, 193
Keynes, John Maynard, 121, 157, 158
Kindleberger, Charles P., Dr., 113, 127
Knowledge bank (KB), 241, 242
Knowledge engineering, 41, 251, 255
Knowledge engineering constructs, 24, 252
Kohl, Helmut, Dr., 130
Kopper, Hilmar, 186

L

Laboratory of International Fuzzy Engineering (LIFE), 38
Latin Monetary Union, 158
Lawrence, Robert, 127
Lazard Brothers, 35, 36
Le Rond d'Alembert, Jean, 124
Leveraged buyouts (LBOs), 15
Liabilities, contingent, 26, 27
Liability management, 243
LIFFE, 198, 199
Liquidity, 14–16
Logical and analytical tools, 101
London Interbank Offered Rates (LIBOR), 201, 203
Long Term Credit Bank of Japan, 40
Long transactions, 94

M

Major, John, 144
Management, good, 86, 87
Management information systems (MIS), 41
Margin, 196
Margin calls, 197
Market volatility, 49
Marshall Plan, 118
Mars network, 52
Marty network, 53
Marx, Karl, 178, 181
Mathematical models, computer-based, 198, 236
McKinnon, Ronald I., 187
Meltzer, Allan, 126, 127
Message exchange, 257
MidAmerica Exchange, 193
Milken, Michael R., 125
Mitsubishi Electric Europe, 147
Mitterrand, François, 114
Model, connectionist, 259
Money center bank, 63, 65
Money management, international, 119
Money market, 243
instruments, 203
Montedison, 175
Morgan Bank, 52, 107
Morgan Guaranty Trust, 29
Morgan Stanley, 115, 205
Morgan Stanley Capital International Europe, Australia, and Far East (EAFE) Index, 104
Mortgage-backed financing, 105
Mortgage portfolio, 104
Mulroney, Brian, 90
Multimedia integration, 84
Munk, Peter, 179

N

National Futures Association,
220
National Mortgage Equity
Corporation, 27
NEC, 147
Netting, 155, 156
Network, semantic, 258, 259
Neural element, 260
Neural networks, 241, 260
News Grid, 262
New York Futures Exchange
(NYFE), 193
New York Mercantile Exchange
(NYMEX), 193, 221
New York Stock Exchange,
78
Nikko Securities, 228, 230,
231
Nishino, Seigo, 147
Nokkia Data, 147
Noninterest assets, 245
Noninterest expenses, 245
Noninterest revenues, 245
North Carolina National Bank
(NCB), 13

O

Off–balance-sheet finance,
26
Olivetti, 147
Optimization, 31
Option, 211, 216
call, 214
put, 215
Options trading system, 224
Options Trading Training
(OTT) expert system, 228,
230
Oryx Energy, 63

P

Parallelism, 257
Parity, uncovered, 101
Pattern recognition, 241, 261
Penn Central, 175
Philadelphia Exchange, 193
Photonics, 14, 146
Planning, 174
far-out, 177
long-range, 171, 177
Planning premise, 170
Plans, strategic, 172
Pöhl, Karl-Otto, Dr., 144
Polak, Fred, Dr., 174, 175
Policies, 180
Precious metal options, 223
Precious metal spot, 218
Precious metal transactions, 222,
224
Price/earnings (P/E) ratio, 12
Processing, parallel, 261
Profit center, 106
Prudential-Bache, 25, 126

Q

Quotron, 81

R

Racketeer-Influenced and
Corrupt Organization Act
(RICO), 27
Real Estate Investment Trust
(REIT), 125
Realspace networks, 121
Realspace solutions, 24
Realtime connection, 69
Reed, John S., 186
Regulation Q, 164

Regulations, 180
Republic Bank of Texas, 13
Return on equity (ROE), 33, 44
Reuters, 79, 81
Revaluation, 219
Risk, 21, 22, 24, 26, 27, 29, 152
Risk-adjusted return on capital
    (RAROC), 21, 33, 34, 44
Risk Assessment, 34
Risk control, 38
Risk evaluation, 22
Risk, hedging, 39
Risk management, 50
Risk premiums, 102
Risk values, acceptable, 23
Rocket scientists, 54
RTZ Corp., 63

S

Sachs, Jeffrey, 186, 187
Salomon Brothers, 27, 115
Sanwa Bank, 41
Sanyo, 147
Search, exhaustive, 261
SEC, 191–194, 220
Securities, 193, 204
    fixed-income, 102
Securitization, 19, 54
Security Pacific, 10, 246
Security Pacific Automation
    Company, 11
Semiconductor Industry
    Association, 146
Settlement function, 155
Siemens, 147
Simulation software, 226
Simulators, 43, 101
Singapore International Monetary
    Exchange (SIMEX), 198, 199
Single European Act (SEA), 129,
    130

Smith, Adam, 178–181
Smithsonian Agreement, 132
Special Drawing Rights (SDR), 3,
    149, 166
Spot contract, 218
Spot rate, 122
Spot transactions, 57
Spread management, 242–244
Spreads, 213
Stagflation, 71
Stanford University, 39, 187
Stock index, 240
Stop loss order, 219
Stop order, 219
Strategy, 172
Sumitomo Bank, 41
Supercomputers, 238
Swap-CAD, 230
Swap costs, 94
Swaps, 92, 93, 96, 99
Swap transaction, 93

T

Tactical Asset Allocation, 54
Telekurs, 81
Telerate, 81
Thatcher, Margaret, 153
Thinking Machines, 262, 265
Tokyo Stock Exchange (TSE),
    48
Trading, 191
    contrarian, 241
    forward, 122
    internationalization of, 82
Transactions:
    forward, 56
    spot, 55
Transamerica Corporation, 25
Transnational company, 56, 57
Treasurers, 30
Treasury bills, 201–203

Treasury functions, 1, 12
Treasury services, 4, 5
Truman, Harry, 164
Tungsram, 185

U

Uncertainty principle, 21

V

Value differentiation, 53
Value matching, dynamic,
    98

Volatility, 46, 50, 89
Volcker, Paul A., Dr., 186

W

Wall Street, 12, 124
Walters, Alan, Sir, 140
Westpac, 143, 144
Wolfensohn, James D., 186
World Bank, 157
Wriston, Walter, 56, 165

Z

Zadeh, Lotfi, Dr., 39